A BALLAD for Baghdad

An Ex-hippie Chick Viet Nam War Protester's Three Years in Iraq

Ali Elizabeth Turner

MORGAN JAMES PUBLISHING • NEW YORK

A BALLAD for Baghdad

ISBN: 978-1-60037-495-1 (Paperback)
ISBN: 978-1-60037-496-8 (Hardcover)

Library of Congress Control Number: 2008934125

Published by:

MORGAN · JAMES
THE ENTREPRENEURIAL PUBLISHER™
www.morganjamespublishing.com

Morgan James Publishing, LLC
1225 Franklin Ave Suite 325
Garden City, NY 11530-1693
Toll Free 800-485-4943
www.MorganJamesPublishing.com

Cover/Interior Design by:
Rachel Lopez
rachel@r2cdesign.com

Habitat
for Humanity®
Peninsula
Building Partner

To my father, Lt. Roy White, Jr., USN Air Corps, (Ret.)
1919-2000
Thank you, Poppo, for my freedom.

And to my adopted brother, CW2 John H. White, U.S. Army, (Ret.)
1949-2007
Yours truly was a just cause.

*"If you say the truth,
there's at least a chance that people will hear it,
and if you don't, and you shy away from it,
the truth never has a chance."*

Contents

FOREWORD   x

PREFACE   xii

ACKNOWLEDGMENTS   xvi

INTRODUCTION   xviii

CHAPTER 1   Subha the Smoke Woman   1

CHAPTER 2   The Early Adventures of Ali Kazammi   3

CHAPTER 3   Heading over the Edge into the Great Sandbox   13

CHAPTER 4   Contractor Camp   21

CHAPTER 5   Losing Lobo   27

CHAPTER 6   Living in a Hair Dryer Stuck on High   33

CHAPTER 7   Journalistic Jihad?   41

CHAPTER 8   Saddam's Evil Eden   57

CHAPTER 9   Life in the Land of Two Rivers   67

CHAPTER 10	Terp Tales	75
CHAPTER 11	Don't Mess with the Babysitter	89
CHAPTER 12	A Tale of Two Hostages	95
CHAPTER 13	Stellar Soldiers	109
CHAPTER 14	The Day Saddam's Air Conditioner Went on the Blink	119
CHAPTER 15	The Unholy Ghraib	125
CHAPTER 16	Bart Simpson Is Sleeping with Your Wife	133
CHAPTER 17	A Hoot of a Hostage Incident	137
CHAPTER 18	Have Yourself a Merry Little…	145
CHAPTER 19	The Dance toward Democracy	151
CHAPTER 20	Stetsons for Terri Schiavo	159
CHAPTER 21	The Iraqi-Coalition Soccer Tournament	177
CHAPTER 22	The Army-Navy Football Game	183
CHAPTER 23	Have Leave, Will Travel	187
CHAPTER 24	Purple Pointers for Freedom	205
CHAPTER 25	R and Z, Our Sunni Twins	209
CHAPTER 26	Salt and Light	221
CHAPTER 27	Unsung Ugandans	231
CHAPTER 28	The Bluez Brothers	237
CHAPTER 29	Every Dog Has His Day	241
CHAPTER 30	Strangely Saddamless	247
CHAPTER 31	Barney Fife, Aunt Bea, and the WMDs	253
CHAPTER 32	Crawling out of the Sandbox	261
CHAPTER 33	Reentry à la Renoir, Road Trip, and Beyond	267
AFTERWORD		281
CHRONOLOGY		285
GLOSSARY		287
RECOMMENDED READING		289
LYRICS TO "A BALLAD FOR BAGHDAD"		293
NOTES		297

Foreword

WHY IS A GUY LIKE ME —who has never been in the military, knows relatively little about the war in Iraq, and spends all my time in America and abroad trying to keep the disabled from being starved and dehydrated to death—writing the foreword to *A Ballad for Baghdad: An Ex-Hippie Chick Viet Nam War Protester's Three Years in Iraq?*

It's because I, along with my family, understand all too well what it is like to be in the middle of a literal life-and-death battle and have to deal with the media misrepresenting it. I am entirely too familiar with the thinking of people—whether they are doctors or dictators, judges or jihadists—who believe that their obligation to society is to kill people who are somehow in the way of them reaching their goals, either personally or ideologically.

My disabled sister, Terri Schindler Schiavo, was brutally starved and dehydrated to death in March 2005 despite the valiant efforts of many to save her. Our family and our nation were subjected to a nightmare that did not end when Terri took her last painful breath. The fact is, we are under siege from the death culture, whether by religious terrorist groups who kill the innocent by detonating a bomb, or by teams of so-called experts who have the audacity to demand that an innocent disabled person demonstrate that she is "competent enough to live."

Because all of my family's energy was involved with the task at hand—trying everything we could to save my sister's life—we had no idea that the shockwaves of our family's as well as our nation's struggle were felt all the way over in Baghdad. We could not have known that Terri's torture had harmed our fighting men and women, as well as the people of Iraq. Ali Turner told me that there were soldiers who would have given their lives to rescue my sister from her literal hostage situation, and who are so good at what they do that they would have no doubt succeeded in their mission. More importantly, they take their obligation to protect life so seriously that they would have given theirs to save hers. I also learned that there were Iraqis who left the Iraqi army and possibly returned to the insurgency, all because they couldn't understand why the most powerful nation on the earth wouldn't save one disabled woman. Ali's account of Terri in chapter 20, "Stetsons for Terri Schiavo," was incredible—extremely sad, but very moving.

That being said, there is much more to *A Ballad for Baghdad* than a unique perspective on Terri's death. It tells the stories of Iraqis, Coalition soldiers, and civilians from around the world that haven't been reported by the mainstream media. They are tales of triumph and defeat, courage and compassion. They are funny, sad, hopeful, honest, and human. Above all, they are the stories of people who will not let anything or anyone stand in the way of life, liberty, and the pursuit of happiness. You deserve to hear them. They know they have lost some battles, but they are winning the war. My family knows we lost a major battle, and we *must and shall* win the war for life.

I believe both the book and the song *A Ballad for Baghdad* will give you strength for your own struggle and inspire you never to give up or give in.

Bobby Schindler,

co-founder of the Terri Schindler Schiavo Foundation

July 2008

Preface

WHY WRITE *A Ballad for Baghdad*? Because I *gave my word*.

I went to Baghdad not knowing what to expect and was wonderfully turned upside down by what I experienced in the three years I was there. It was truly life changing. The proof? I miss the Great Sandbox in all its craziness, and I would go back in a heartbeat.

I promised Iraqis, Americans, Ugandans, Sudanese, Filipinos, Australians, and Nepalese; people from Fiji, India, El Salvador, Puerto Rico, Mexico, the UK, and Europe; and interpreters who hailed from throughout the Middle East and Africa that I would tell their stories. I committed myself to them because they committed themselves to me, and their remarkable presence in my life made me a better person.

Because of all of them, I am so deeply grateful for my freedom, and I also have my own story to tell. Liberty is one of many things I used to take for granted—a reprehensible failure about which I can no longer keep silent and which needs to be rectified. The people who bought and paid for and are still buying and paying for my freedom—those folks, living and dead—deserve to be told "thank you," even if it's late in coming.

For the most part, I chose to use only first names in telling these stories to maintain personal privacy and security. In the cases where only initials are used, the need to protect and keep safe was even greater. Throughout the writing of this book, I consulted with various members of the military to ensure the highest level of Operational Security.

Throughout my three years in Baghdad, I kept a personal journal, which has served as a source for many of these stories. In some cases I have incorporated my original journal entries into the text of this book when they pertain to events of great historical significance to preserve my authentic, initial reflections at the time the events occurred.

Why should you read *A Ballad for Baghdad* or listen to the song? Because it comes from a unique perspective—one that evolved painfully over thirty-plus years.

Once upon a time I was an antiwar protester who, along with fellow students from Oberlin College, tried to shut down Wright-Patterson Air Force Base as well as block the entrance to the Cleveland County Courthouse in Ohio during the Viet Nam War. My antics landed me on the evening news in Cleveland, Ohio, gleefully spouting socialist buzz phrases like a "true believer." Today I am a wife and mom in my midfifties who is in awe of the Constitution. Once I refused to salute the flag; now the sight of it can and does move me to tears. Once America was the location I was deeply ashamed to live in; now it's my country which, in spite of its flaws, I love unashamedly.

I am not a soldier, interrogator, analyst, journalist, or anybody special. I just listened to people's stories and asked a lot of questions while I passed out Ping-Pong paddles, made coffee, and played movies for soldiers and civilians on the bases where I worked. In the three years I worked in Morale, Welfare, and Recreation, I spoke with literally hundreds of people from every imaginable religious, racial, political, educational, and socioeconomic background from over twenty countries.

They became my kids, brothers, sisters, and friends whom I'll carry in my heart for the rest of my life.

So, just how did I, in the amused description of Capt. Sean Michael Flynn, one of my "Baghdad Brothers" and the author of *The Fighting 69ᵗʰ*, go from being a "hippie chick to a soldier supporter"? Come and find out, and in my heart I'll make you some coffee or tea while you do.

Acknowledgments

WHEN A PERSON writes a book whose major theme is gratitude, there can be no more important section than the acknowledgments. I suppose that there can also be no other chapter where it is easier to fail. This is simply due to the sheer force of the tidal wave of support and blessing that has hit my personal beach, altering its coastline forever, and my limitations in describing and acknowledging the impact of all whose lives made up that wonderfully wild wave. Please forgive me for any unintended omissions.

Mary Jo Tate, my editor, book coach, and wondrously skilled "bibli-O.B." — Girl, you saved the book and my sanity more than once. Let's do this again!

David Hancock, Rick Frishman, Margo Toulouse, Cindy Sauer, Rachel Lopez and the entire crew at Morgan James Publications — Thank you for taking a risk with my first-born book. May there be many more.

Woody and Shirley Johnson and Paige Figueroa — For the "producin' and the prayin'" necessary to record the song "A Ballad for Baghdad" as well as the audio version of the book. Thank you for your patience with endless takes until it was just right, your belief in the song and the book, and your generosity.

Mary White, my mother — Thank you for the boxes of tea sent for me and the soldiers. You warmed us more than you know, and I love you more than you know.

Sharon McAuliffe and Kathryn McAuliffe, my sisters — Your passion inspired me to dig deep and ask difficult questions.

Bobby Schindler — Thank you for your unwavering commitment to fight for your sister Terri and others like her, and for your openhearted encouragement of this project and me.

Master Sergeant USAF (Ret.) Bill and Nellie Mae Schueler — Thank you for making Steve and me part of the family and especially for being so "fonda" your li'l ex-hippie chick.

Jean Huber, the librarian at the Athens, Alabama, Public Library — For hugs and gentle wisdom.

Those who sent care packages for the soldiers and me — The many members of Mt. Gilead Church, as well as Houch, Connie, Karen, Saul, Mary Jo and her boys. The packages were always perfect and right on time. I daresay you made it possible for me to have the cutest hooch in camp, and no s'mores have ever been more greatly appreciated by man or beast.

Jean Turner, my mother-in-law and faithful prayer warrior.

Chuck Turner, my brother-in-law, and my "cousin-in-law" Sgt. Major LaVerne Dose — For your service in Operation Iraqi Freedom.

All who wrote innumerable supportive e-mails and cards, and all who prayed — When I needed you the most, you fought for me and us. I owe you a debt of love that can never be repaid. I rest in knowing that God will reward you, as I know I can't.

My beloved blended family: Kim, Stef, Cheri Lynn, Gabe, Jessa, and Barry — You mean more to me than I'll ever be able to say or show.

My husband Steve — You are the love of my life, "small l."

Yeshua — You are the Love of my life, "large L."

All for One, One for all!

Introduction

AS A VIET NAM WAR VETERAN, I found myself cautious about entering the *Ballad for Baghdad*. I knew it would likely stir up some not-so-fond memories this soldier had somewhat successfully repressed over time. It surely did. One recollection was the famous protest refrain we had all heard so often: "Well, it's one, two, three, what are fighting for? Don't ask me, I don't give a damn. Next stop is Viet Nam."[1] But we—and the patriots whose lives we are privileged to share in this journal—did and do give a damn.

Ali Elizabeth Turner relives her own journey from youthful antiwar protester and attempted base-closing activist to combat-zone veteran who, when shaken by IED or incoming explosions, would "look around to see if we were in one piece, then

---

1. "I Feel Like I'm Fixin' To Die Rag," words and music by Joe McDonald, ©1965 renewed 1993 Alkatraz Corner Music Co. Used by permission.

go on." Go on serving, befriending, entertaining, encouraging, and becoming one with those delivering and then protecting what we and the Iraqis are fighting for. Freedom. Freedom for all, freedom forever.

I am jealous that my buddies and I didn't get to have an "Ali" in our midst during our tours, but I found comfort as I read these stories just knowing so many today are blessed with MWR angels among them.

LOREN KRENELKA

INTELLIGENCE ANALYST

541ST M.I.D.

11TH ARMOURED CAVALRY REGIMENT

CHAPTER I

Subha
the Smoke Woman

When Saddam Hussein's mother, Subha Tulfah al-Musallat, would come to an Iraqi village to practice the world's oldest profession, she would start a small fire and set some cheese over it. The pungent smoke would signal interested male patrons in the area that she was, indeed, open for business. She was known as Subha the Smoke Woman.

I once met a man who knew her, and his name was Hassan. I did not inquire as to just how well he knew her; for a woman to do so would have been way out of line, even in post-Saddam Baghdad. However, I think he would have overlooked my gaffe for two reasons. The first was that he claimed Saddam didn't pay him for the thirty years that he spent in the Iraqi army, and he was wildly grateful that the Coalition I was serving was employing him. The second was that my staff of unfailingly

1

tenderhearted Filipinos and I treated him for heat exhaustion on a typical brutally hot Baghdad day in June of 2004.

One would think by Hassan's effusive response that this one act of garden-variety kindness was the first he had ever received in all his life. We laid him down on the marble floor of what had been Saddam Hussein's hunting lodge and put frozen bottles of water under his armpits. I wet down a clean terry cloth towel and moistened his hair, then very carefully lifted his head to give him just a few sips of water while his core body temperature normalized. As I gazed into the face of this little leathery faced, snaggly toothed man, we exchanged smiles. Then I put the damp towel over his forehead and a dry towel under his head for a pillow and let him rest.

Ironically, in Saddam's Baghdad, the building which was now used for a clinic had been used by Saddam, the son of an abandoned-wife-turned-whore, and his home boys as a house of ill repute. We kept an eye on Hassan, ready to radio for help if he needed to be transported to the clinic down the road. For days afterwards, he would point to me then to himself, mime the actions of drinking water out of a bottle, point at me again, grin, and then bow.

It saddens me to think that there are people in the Middle East, as well as in my own country of America, who would think that my husband would be duty-bound to have me stoned for touching this man. But my husband, Steven Mark Turner, is the loving man who gave me the strength to live in a combat zone for three years during one of the most remarkable periods in recorded history, and I can promise you that he would have thought it more appropriate to have me stoned for *not* helping Hassan!

You can imagine how honored I felt to eventually receive brotherly hugs from Iraqis who were grateful to have an infidel "sister" who could only speak a few words of Arabic but whose eyes said she loved them. I spent three years listening to their stories, sometimes through an interpreter, and I promised them and the Coalition soldiers that I would tell their stories to anyone who would listen.

To you, dear reader, I say *Shukrahn* (thank you) for choosing to pull up a log at the campfire of post-Saddam Baghdad, sit a while, and listen to the inspiring tales of the Operation Iraqi Freedom tribe from all over the world.

CHAPTER 2

The Early Adventures of Ali Kazammi

he nickname "Ali Kazammi" became my *nom de plume* while writing from Baghdad. My full name is Alice, and when I was small a friend's father started calling me Ali, which I began to use for everything except official documents about twenty years ago. Over time many variations developed, including Ali Baba, Ali Shazzam, Ali Kazzam, Ali McGraw, and Ali Oop. A dear friend's two-year-old came up with Ali Kazammi, and the name stuck.

My birth in 1953 occurred squarely on the upsurge of the Baby Boom. I was born the same year that Dwight "Ike" Eisenhower was inaugurated as the thirty-fourth president of the United States. My mother tells me that a unique thing about that particular election was that you could get diapers stamped with either the GOP elephant or the Democrat donkey; my parents' political persuasion assigned my tiny self to be cared for by the elephants.

I grew up in Seattle, Washington, on what could have been the set for Beaver Cleaver's neighborhood. There were sixty kids in a square-block radius; most of us went to the same school, church, YMCA, summer camp, and grocery store. We played with complete abandon in the woods, down at the beach, and even in the street. Though our neighborhood couldn't have been considered diverse in the classic PC sense, by the time I was seventeen and left for college, my neighbors had included Jews, Muslims, Jehovah's Witnesses, Christian Scientists, Catholics, all kinds of Protestants, and one black family.

We had all-neighborhood picnics, parades, games of capture the flag, hide and go seek, and king of the hill. We were members of every imaginable club: Girl Scouts, Boy Scouts, Job's Daughters, Camp Fire Girls, Indian Guides, Junior Leaders, Senior Leaders, and others I am sure I am omitting. We took swimming lessons, climbing lessons, all types of music and dancing lessons, gymnastics, and skiing; my older sisters Sharon and Kathy took ballroom dancing lessons. It was an era where girls always wore hats and little white gloves on Easter; and if my grandmother had her way, no lady would think of going downtown in pants.

My father, Roy White, was a retired Lt. Senior Grade in the U.S. Naval Air Corps, and after WWII he got his degree in air transport engineering from Purdue University. My mother, Mary Hersman White, came from a long line of teachers and received her degree in home economics from the University of Illinois. They both worked very hard to provide us with the American Dream, and as I look back I can now perceive blessings that the rage of the sixties hid from my view.

My parents fell in love with the Northwest while Dad was in the Navy, and after he graduated from Purdue they came out to Seattle to settle. Dad took an engineering job with Boeing Aircraft, and Mom was fully occupied working at home. They purchased their first home with a view of Puget Sound for $7,000 on the GI Bill. Their house payments were $49.00 a month. This was the era when nonhomogenized milk in glass bottles was delivered to homes, doors were often left unlocked, and kids could walk to school and not end up on the back of a milk carton. There was very little chance of getting shot or stabbed at school, and it was highly unlikely that a teacher would attempt to have sex with a student.

Not to say that all was perfect. It never is. Some things happened that were dysfunctional or just plain not right, and sometimes they were denied. But honestly, from the bottom of my heart, when I look at the Big Picture I see that I was given a shot at living life to its fullest potential, long before there were self-help seminars costing big bucks to assist in self-actualization. For these things I can now say I am grateful, and I am sorry it took me so long to be able to do so.

Author Jack Canfield of *Chicken Soup for the Soul* fame talks about the necessity of having a high "GQ," or "gratitude quotient." Once upon a time my GQ was less than moronic, and my goal now is to have a GQ that surpasses Einstein's legendary IQ.

The first person to whom I am grateful for my blessings is God. It was my "heart-on collision" with Him during the Jesus People Movement in 1970 that began some deep and ongoing changes that continue to this day.

My second expression of thanks goes to my family, immediate and extended, who sacrificed for me so that I could have a moral base, an excellent education, and a compass to head in the direction of my gifting. Even when they didn't agree with my choices (which has been often), they valued my right as an American to find my own way.

I can now say, without any hesitation, "Thank you" to my country, which I violently hated for about seven years beginning in 1965. During that time I honestly thought America was the worst place on the planet to have to live. Unable to see the "big picture," I projected the historical failures of our nation with specific regard to African-Americans onto every aspect of American life. I could not see America's good, and I refused to see that returning to the biblical principles of the Constitution held within it the foundation for the changes I wanted to see.

I passionately wanted to see America destroyed—through nonviolent means, of course. In my pride I thought I was too nice to support armed revolution. I just wanted my country on its own to choose to be socialistic; sadly, it now appears that I am getting my dysfunctional and ideologically obsolete wish.

The fourth group to whom I am profoundly grateful is all members, men and women, past and present, of our armed forces. These are people whom I intensely despised for about the same amount of time as I did our country, and for the same now-defunct ideological reasons. I only began to actively love and appreciate them when I landed in Baghdad. I do not now, nor will I ever, deserve the love, grace, mercy, forgiveness, support, and freedom from any of those I have previously mentioned. I will never be able to repay all that they have given me. I will, however, never stop trying.

Another thing I am grateful for is my parents' insistence that we always "do the right thing." One of my earliest memories is being on a shopping trip with my mom when I was about three or four and stealing a really ugly pair of sunglasses. I hid them behind my back, thinking I was so clever, and when she saw them she marched me right back to the vendor and made me give them back. I can still remember the unpleasantness of the whole experience, and I am quite sure that if she hadn't confronted me I would have lifted more than the one Tootsie Roll from Mr. Hoff's neighborhood store and erasers from my elementary school supply room.

My dad didn't spank me much, and I probably needed more paddlings than I got. One thing that would just never fly in our house was lying, and I do remember one notable spanking for lying. I had danced through the mud on the way home from church and had really messed up my good shoes. My dad asked me what had happened, and I made up some goofball story about how they got so muddy. My dad then turned me over his knee, swatted me a few times, and then looked at me and said, "Never lie." That was it. Two words. No situational ethics, no latest child development theory, just "It's wrong, so don't do it." Man, am I glad for that.

We grew up under the shadow of the Cold War as well as the Space Race. When Sputnik was launched in 1957, my mom, ever the educator, and my dad, the air transport engineer, found out about its flight path, bundled us up, and took us down to Alki Point beach in Seattle to watch it go by. I remember looking and looking up into the sky, but it was partly cloudy that night (something quite common in Seattle), and Sputnik eluded our gaze.

In 1963 I began to undergo huge changes inside, as did my country. No one from the government on down was prepared for the decade that was to follow, and a riptide of unrest pulled us all out into deep waters. Some of us never returned, either because of drugs or hatred or rebellion or confusion. Our country started to come apart as Camelot, the "kingdom" of JFK, was attacked through his assassination. It seemed that the Hounds of Hell had been released to hunt down our culture and chew it up, and as a child I could only watch and fear.

Just prior to JFK's death, an act of terrorism in Birmingham, Alabama, galvanized my commitment to the Civil Rights movement at the tender age of nine. The Sixteenth Street Church in Birmingham was bombed on a Sunday morning in September of 1963, killing four little girls, some of whom who were my age. I remember being horrified and scared. Who would want to kill kids going to church just because their skin was dark?

The previous month, on 28 August 1963, I had watched and listened with rapt attention while Martin Luther King gave his "I Have a Dream" speech on TV. I felt such hope for our country—such young, idealistic passionate assurance that centuries of injustice were finally going to be addressed. Between 1963 and 1965 several more things occurred that shocked my young sensibilities. Civil Rights leader Medgar Evers was assassinated. Three young college student activists, both black and white, were killed during the summer of 1964, known as Freedom Summer. Dogs, billyclubs, and fire hoses met up with demonstrators in Birmingham, Alabama, and demonstrators were beaten on Pettus bridge in Selma, Alabama. At the age of twelve, I made a deeper commitment to the Civil Rights movement, something that would change me forever.

When my sisters went away to college, I, as the adoring little sister, hung on their every word of disillusionment with America. Protests against the Viet Nam War began; college campuses were hotbeds of activism and violence; and Newark, Detroit, and Watts all had fatal riots. Haight-Ashbury was the "happening place." I wanted to go visit San Francisco and be a part of all of it. I have no doubt I would have ended up either getting killed or taking my own life.

It was the era of "sex, drugs, and rock and roll." Timothy Leary told us to "turn on, tune in, drop out." The Beatles were hanging with the Maharishi, the Black Panther Party sponsored pancake breakfasts at a local sister church, and Eldridge Cleaver was running for president on the Peace and Freedom Party ticket in 1968. My sisters voted for him, my father understandably had a fit, and times were tense in our household. Now that I have kids of my own, I can begin to understand how painful it must have been for my parents to see everything go crazy.

In the summer of 1968, there was a riot at the Chicago Democratic Convention, and I watch transfixed as demonstrators clashed with the police. It was played over and over again, and each time I saw it I hated the police more. The summer of 1969 brought Woodstock acid rocking its way into our cultural consciousness. I was fifteen, and if I had been old enough, I would have hitchhiked to get there. If my parents had let me, I would have gone to Berzerkeley for college. I wanted to be in the middle of it all. I must have been a real handful for my folks.

I was the only white member of the Black Student Union at my high school. While I stayed steadfastly committed to the principles of nonviolence as taught by Dr. King, I had friends who were Black Panthers and who wanted to "off the pig." I would retort, "When you pick up the gun, you become the pig."

I ran for Associated Student Body president on a feminist platform in 1970, narrowly beating the captain of the football team. Ironically, I also seriously considered going out for cheerleading. To say I was a highly conflicted and depressed young lady is an understatement. I refused to salute the flag at school assemblies and organized a "peace concert." I was in the honor society, making good grades, and full of hopelessness about life in general and America in particular. I wanted to get a good education, be wildly in love, marry, and have kids; I also announced at a rally that I "would never be a man's baby machine." Adolescent angst—that was me.

I wanted to make a difference in my world, and I still do. I wanted to see racism eradicated, and I still do. My passion for justice still burns with a hot flame, but since becoming a Christian, my ideas about how to make that come about are radically different.

My home state of Washington was one of the first states to pass a pro-abortion law, and one of my great griefs is that I bought into the idea that it is OK to cut up an innocent preborn baby in the name of "choice." I do know this: if I had known at the time what I know now about fetal development, I would have never bought into the "fetal material" or "products of conception" propaganda that was the psy-ops coup of Planned Parenthood and NARAL. Though I personally never had an abortion, I helped one of my high school students get one—a fact which horrifies me and an action for which I have deeply repented. Some lessons, such as how easily one can be duped and how far reaching is God's forgiveness, are the crucible of both pain and grace—a wild mix, to be sure.

After graduating from high school in 1971, I went away to Oberlin College in Ohio. I was a student in both the college and the Conservatory of Music. Oberlin was only thirty miles away from Kent State, where the previous year four students had been killed by National Guardsmen in a demonstration turned ugly. Oberlin considered itself "Kent State in exile." It was the classic college scene of the seventies: free love, drugs, rebellion, Gloria Steinem speaking in Finney Chapel, and protests of all kinds; if there was nothing to protest on our own campus, we went elsewhere.

My first foray into antiwar protesting occurred in the fall of 1971 when we tried to shut down Wright-Patterson Air Force Base in Dayton, Ohio. I am quite sure that the God of Second Chances laughed as He watched me on that day and said, "Girl, do I have a field trip for *you* in about three decades!" In the spring of 1972, we tried to shut down Cleveland County Courthouse to protest the mining of Hanoi Harbor. That time I ended up on the evening news.

Soldiers were "baby killers"; we were the enlightened ones who would set everyone straight. At that time I could not in any way have imagined myself having the slightest tolerance for someone in the armed forces, let alone coming to the place where I would be willing to spend three years with them in an unpopular war.

During my time at Oberlin College two things happened that would alter the course of my life dramatically. The first was when the Students for a Democratic Society (SDS) took over a protest and wanted to get violent. "Bring the War *home!*"

they shouted. I could not believe what I was hearing, and instant disillusionment set in. The second was that dear childhood friends were attending a theological school in Seattle, and their transformation made me more than curious. After my first year of college, I went home to Seattle. I decided to join my friends and give up my scholarship to Oberlin; I never returned. This was hard on my folks, but I know that if I had returned to Oberlin, I wouldn't have survived, physically or mentally.

I graduated from Pacific School of Theology in 1977. I had married in 1976, and with my then-husband Rance was very active in ministry. We had two precious children, Gabe and Jessa, and then my world and dreams fell apart again when our marriage broke up in 1989. For the next several years, I did the single mom thing. It was a very difficult time, trying to be mom and dad, keep the wolf out the door, homeschool the kids, and go back to school at Southwestern Assemblies of God University in Texas. I was busy—too busy actually—with ministerial activities. I was active in our church choir, sang for ten years with a quartet, wrote and recorded music, was involved with a number of prayer teams, and had many folks in my life who wanted counseling. Without the help of friends, family, and faith, I never would have made it.

My political beliefs had become somewhat more conservative, but for several years I didn't think about anything other than survival. Then in 1995 I met Steve Turner at a prayer meeting, and my life was turned upside down yet again. To say that I was swept off my feet does not do justice to how wildly I fell, and to this day am still, in love with the man. We married in 1995, and not only did I gain a husband, but also two wonderful stepkids, Kim and Cheri.

Our backgrounds were completely opposite. I was a Left Coaster; he was from Minnesota. I was a recovering socialista and feminista; he had been a Boy Scout. I was a musician; he was a cabinet maker, and an artisan at that. I could be a professional student and just keep going to college for the rest of my life; he had a high school education. However, he is also one of the smartest and best educated men I have ever met. After high school he essentially homeschooled himself by being a voracious reader, and he continues to this day to consume mass quantities of print.

I could not have been prepared to have my thinking or philosophical beliefs so thoroughly challenged. Steve was relentless in demonstrating my need to think things through to their logical conclusion—something I did not realize I had never done. For the first time in my life, I often found myself stymied or backed into a corner, and I painfully had to admit that my former "thought grids" were woefully inadequate. It was a slow process, and one for which I'll always be grateful. When we were ordained into the ministry in 1998, I used to joke that he would be "the Right Reverend, and I would be the Left." Those days are certainly over, as I have undergone a personal revolution that I don't think is finished yet.

In 1998 Steve and I sold everything and moved to an orphanage in Mexico after having been to Juarez on a short-term missions trip in 1997. I didn't realize it then, but it got me ready for Iraq. It was in the middle of the desert, in poverty, and in danger from the Juarez cartel. We started a school at the orphanage that is still going to this day. For the two years that we were there, more changes occurred within me, and I would have been content to stay there forever. I found the simplicity of living off-grid most attractive and the pleasure of helping people deeply satisfying.

However, while we were in Mexico, Steve became desperately ill, and we had to return to the States. He nearly died. This is what I have affectionately called the "Bug-on-the-Windshield Era of Our Lives," when everything went "splat." Steve was in bed for almost two years, our finances suffered, our marriage suffered, my father died, some of the kids were having trouble, and it was tough all around. Again friends and family were there to support us as we waded through the alligator swamp, and God had us in a whole new boot camp. Just as things had quickly fallen apart, they were put back together better than before—a process at which I still marvel.

My life is a crazy quilt of second chances, and I count getting the opportunity to see our remarkable soldiers in action as one of the biggest. I just hope that in some way my "quilt" will serve to bring both warmth and color into the rooms of my readers' hearts and minds.

As if my personal history of dramatic contrasts and opinion changes weren't enough, the combined political, religious, emotional, and philosophical viewpoints from all sides of my family couldn't be more diverse.

Some of my family believes in global warming; some do not.

One was asked to be a part of the Clinton administration and declined; one picked up President Bush and Secretary of State Rice at the airport when they came to Baghdad for Thanksgiving in 2003.

One advised Paul Bremer and General Ricardo Sanchez about how to help the Iraqis get back the seven billion dollars stolen by Saddam; one was a consultant to Nelson Mandela.

One took to the road to campaign for John Kerry; one has a bumper sticker that says "The War in Iraq Helps Keep American Families Safe."

One clerked for Supreme Court Justice Thurgood Marshall; one helped to process Syrian and Iraqi terrorist detainee interviews.

One knows former NSA advisor Sandy Berger, who was fined $50,000 for taking documents from the National Archives; one took the bag off Saddam's head after Saddam was captured and transported to BIAP.

One works for a large civil rights law firm; one is a Sgt. Major in the Army.

I could go on, but I think you get my point. Some of my family was proud of me for going to Iraq, and some thought I was evil for doing so.

Bottom line—no matter what position you take politically, at the end of the day it is the soldier who protects your right to take that position. And it is the soldier who far too often is either marginalized or vilified. It is my fondest hope that when you have finished reading *A Ballad for Baghdad*, no matter where you are politically, you'll live the rest of your days in a state of "shock and awe" over how remarkable these men and women of the Coalition and Iraqi forces truly are and how much they deserve to have their stories told.

Who knows? You just might come to the place where you'll actually "sing the Ballad."

CHAPTER 3

Heading over the Edge into the Great Sandbox

22 November 2003 was the fortieth anniversary of JFK's death, and all the networks carried flashback pieces describing that dreadful day in 1963. How well I remember where I was and even what I was wearing. I was home from school, sick with the flu. I had on my green and white checked bathrobe, one of two that my mother had made for my older sisters; like everything else she skillfully sewed, it had been handed down to me. Well worn and snuggly soft, it was comforting as I lay on the couch with a bowl close by.

Betty Winders, our next-door neighbor, came running in and cried, "Our president's been shot!!" Our big old black and white TV with its three knobs was on the blink, and so we went next door to watch the news coverage. Walter Cronkite wiped away tears as he announced the president's death, and I remember feeling sad and scared. The headline of the *Seattle Times* front page was huge that night, announcing the president's assassination. I scrunched myself into the couch, staring out the window into the dark, crying quietly, half believing that it couldn't possibly be true.

While our family was Republican—and at ten years old I was clueless as to what that even meant—I remember that my Mom made a statement years prior to President Kennedy's death that really affected me. She said that even though we had not voted for him, we needed to support him as the president of our country. In the years following, I have struggled at times with that attitude, especially when the sanctity of the office has been sullied with corruption or dishonesty, irrespective of the party affiliation of the occupant. The more recent presidential sexual misconduct and vivid descriptions on the nightly news of DNA stains on a particular intern's dress were, at the least, singularly unedifying. I would have greatly preferred that the parents of our county not have to look into their children's eyes and try to figure out a reasonable reply to "Daddy, what's a DNA stain?"

Walter Cronkite was interviewed for the flashback piece, and he recounted the events of that day forty years ago as though they had just occurred. While I will always remember this day for what happened in Dallas forty years ago, what occurred in my life forty years later, on 22 November 2003, changed it forever. That morning I "happened" to be on the Turner family chat site on the Net, and we had an unexpected family reunion. My brother-in-law Chuck, who was over in Baghdad with the Baker Group as a systems analyst, had come on the chat to let us know that he was OK. The Ministry of Oil had been mortared, but thankfully he had been in another building. Chuck's job was to help get the seven billion dollars that Saddam Hussein stole back to the Iraqis.

My husband Steve, an over-the-road truck driver, was somewhere in the Lower 48. I got him on his cell as the rest of the family was on the chat and read him everyone's chat contributions. Chuck mentioned that jobs would be available, should anyone be interested. What happened next would prove to be one of the most powerful defining moments of my life. As I read Chuck's statement to Steve, I strongly thought, "I need to do this." In the next breath my husband softly said into my ear, "Hon, you need to do this."

We knew it like we knew we were supposed to sell our stuff and move to an orphanage in Mexico. We knew it like we knew we were supposed to get married. We also knew that I would be going and he would be staying at home—a prospect neither one of us was jumping up and down about. Some things you just know in your "knower," and this was one of them. Most things, though, don't have the upfront potential of getting you blown to smithereens, so both of us bathed the next six months in prayer.

I went to the job Web site Chuck mentioned and filled out my preliminary application. Two weeks later I received a call indicating the company's interest in me, and then everything went dead calm. Was I going? Should I inquire? Would I come off as too pushy if I did? What should I say to people who had heard I had been hired but saw that I was still hanging around?

I knew the company was busy with fulfilling their personnel contract requests, and I found out later that they deployed over 38,000 people to either Iraq or Afghanistan in 2003 alone. This was no small task for a private company, one of 15,000 companies deploying around 120,000 employees. Somehow I slipped through the cracks, and months went by with no further word as to when or where I would be going. For a very brief time on the Web there was a jobs hotline, which I called with no response.

I once heard Jeff Olson, a former member of the U.S. Olympic men's ski team, say something that I have tried to apply in my life: "Brick walls are there for you to hit in order to see just how bad you want it and to keep the Other People out." I badly wanted to help out in Iraq, and so I decided to try one last time. I called Steve to see what he thought, and he said, "Try the jobs hotline one more time, and if nothing happens, then we'll assume that the door is closed for right now, and you can look for a job elsewhere. Maybe the door will open later." I did just that, and for reasons that no IT person has ever been able to explain, the jobs hotline number rolled over into the private voice mailboxes of the company poobahs. A miracle? Maybe.

The directory was accessed by the first three letters of a person's last name, so I started at the beginning of the alphabet and got the mail box of a Steve Austin. "Mr.

Austin," I began, "you don't know me, but my name is Ali Turner and I have been hired to work in MWR in Iraq. I haven't heard from anyone in months, and if you would be so kind to just direct me to someone who could tell me whether it's still a go, I would greatly appreciate it." I left my phone number, gulped, and thought, "That was either one of the stupidest, goofiest, most unprofessional things I have ever done, or it was just exactly what the doctor ordered."

Two days later, I received a call from a delightful man named Danny Lambert, who happened to be originally from my town in Alabama. He became my greatly encouraging phone friend, and after more stalls he e-mailed the Vice President of Recruiting and bluntly interceded by saying, "Would you *please* find this woman a job in Iraq?" I suppose it would seem quite odd to the average bear that a middle-aged wife and mother would be begging to go to a place where she could easily die, but I have always figured that it is actually safer to be doing what you are supposed to be doing than to be running from it and trying to protect yourself. No guarantees, though. You can *still* die doing what you are supposed to be doing, but I am totally convinced that giving your life in the process is never a waste.

The first week of May, I received a call from my recruiter, Cheryl, and it was Game On. During our Big Talk, she did her best to scare me out of going, regaling me with descriptions of kidnappings, mortars, IEDs (Improvised Explosive Devices), camel spiders, and the horrors of contracting leishmaniasis, while simultaneously making it clear she really wanted me to go. Yikes—what a job *that* must be! This isn't exactly like interviewing for Wal-Mart, and I can't imagine what it must have been like to be in her shoes.

I got an in-depth description of what my duties would be while working in the Morale, Welfare, and Recreation (MWR) Department, and had to agree to be cremated in country in the event that I was killed by biochemical warfare. I learned about the dress code, which for our department could best be described as "business casual," and where I could purchase the two heavy black plastic trunks that were the best choice for luggage in a place where gravel and sand would beat the snot out of my well-worn and not-so-designer bags. We discussed the required inoculations, and I later scurried out to purchase homeopathic compounds that would protect me from the possible presence of mercury in the malaria shots. That particular procurement was somewhat on the QT, but I knew that my mission was not to take on Big Pharma, much as I would have liked to. I would find that in the nearly three years I spent in Iraq, as in the rest of life, one must choose one's battles.

As my deployment date approached, I divided my time and energies between what seemed like packing for a bizarre vacation (such as trying to figure out if the shade of hot pink in a recently purchased polo shirt was "too much" for a combat zone) and getting my affairs in order in case I died. I lay in my husband's arms and let him know what I wanted for a memorial service in the event that I perished, and I also assured him that I had come away from one prayer time with a strong sense that I would not be coming home in a body bag. He had a sense of peace about my going that some considered downright irresponsible and infuriating, though I drank deeply from it. I did have two episodes when I thought, as my dad used to say, "What in the Billy Blue Sam Hill am I doing?" but they didn't last long. My chin was set, as was my heart. My trunks would follow quickly.

My daughter Jessalyn and her husband Barry drove down from Minnesota to say goodbye. Jessa, who I would like to think inherited her straightforwardness from her mother, asked me a question I shall never ever forget and shall always cherish: "Mom, there is just one thing I need to know. Have you prayed about this? God knows you don't need an adventure fix." (How well my daughter understands my unusual thirst for adventure, most likely because she possesses the same quality.) I assured her I had prayed, which satisfied her, and proceeded to explain something that probably sounds strange to most other folks.

One day while I was praying, I asked the Lord what was my real purpose in going. I knew my soul well enough to know what I could do in my job. I had been a camp counselor, a PE teacher, a ministerial counselor, a school administrator, and a waitress. I had worked in a women's fitness studio, and most importantly, I had valiantly endeavored to be a good mom to my blended family of four children—the jury still being out on the success of that particular effort. I was sure that all of these experiences would be called upon in Iraq, and I ended up being right.

But what was the reason behind the reason? While I would be making about seventeen dollars an hour, working twelve hours a day, seven days a week, that was in no way enough to justify something as crazy as going to Iraq, no matter what anyone says. I simply sensed that I was being called out into the desert to worship, just as my people had thousands of years ago. I was going to the place where anthropologists concur that civilization began—where some of the deepest epic, personal, and corporate battles with destiny and purpose had been fought and their outcomes eloquently recorded in the holy texts of at least three religions. I was being given a chance to say "thank you" from the Top down. Regardless of what was going on politically and militarily, or its outcome, I went to offer myself, as modern-day psalmist Kent Henry says, as a "lean, mean, worship machine."

That premise would sustain me through all that would transpire, both positive and negative. Are there contractors who go over just for the money? Yep, and you can spot them an emotional mile away. Are there soldiers who are serving our country just so they can get a college education free? Yep, and they stick out just as glaringly. Both are a pain to work with and for, and thankfully they are in the undisputed minority. But here's the deal: they still put themselves in harm's way to do something that most folks would shrink back from, and I commend them for it. Regardless of how close I came at times to biting off my own tongue to avoid saying or doing stupid stuff in the face of what I thought was Super Stupid Stuff, we still owe them. Add to that Martin Luther King's wise adage that what doesn't kill you just makes you stronger, and you're set. Ain't nobody that can truly take you down or out but you.

Understanding that was immeasurably helpful in dealing with the swirl of friends' and family's opinions over my admittedly controversial decision to go. I was hailed as a hero and was also told I was a "self-important carpetbagger," possibly even evil. Some family members were furious with Steve for backing me in my decision; one of our kids thought I had lost my mind (an opinion held for quite some time now); and I knew my mother would be facing something she hadn't for nearly sixty years—having a loved one in a combat zone. If I could have, I would have spared her the worry; she no doubt paid a hidden price, for which I hope she is lavishly rewarded in every regard.

The morning of 23 May 2004, my friends Karen and Jerry Snyder prayed for me in their kitchen. Steve had had to go back out on the road the day before, and we parted in a state of unquantifiable and delicious peace that we would see each other again. My darling friend Rita Kaye took me to the airport. Three years later, she would also come and join me in Europe on my way home for the last time, and her love and presence strengthened me. She dropped me off; and I checked in, cleared TSA, and got on the plane for Houston.

As I was making my way down the aisle of the plane toward my seat, I was hit with the second panic attack I have ever had in my life. The first was over going back to college and having to face taking algebra—which seems kind of dumb, now that I think of it. I thought to myself, "What have I done?" and, for a moment, considered the possibility of getting off the plane and bailing on the whole prospect of hopping into the Sandbox—not just then, but for good. However, what happened next is an example of the kind of Providential intervention that has occurred so often in my life that I don't think of it as being unusual anymore.

I looked down on my assigned seat, and on it was a paperback Bible. The sight of it gave me at least a cursory sense that the person to whom it belonged might just be an ally in quelling my fears. Indeed she was. Her name was Cecilia, and as she retrieved The Book so I could sit down, I explained what I was doing on the plane. She smiled and proceeded to tell me that her husband was in Iraq, had temporarily come home to do some additional techno-training, and had just spent the weekend with her before going back. What was wild was that he was stationed at Camp Victory (where I was going). She said, "There is awesome worship going on at North Victory in a tent."

To say that she was powerfully used to defeat my panic attack is an understatement; we jabbered all the way to Houston. I would find her e-mails in ensuing months to be nourishing, and the blessing of knowing that other folks were in the desert to worship gave me what I needed to get over that hump. That hump having been hopped, I landed in Houston that afternoon and prepared for the next part of the adventure, Contractor Camp.

CHAPTER 4

Contractor Camp

*A*fter getting past my "what in the world am I doing" jitters on the flight to Houston (thanks to my instant connection with Cecilia), I landed and began an unforgettable three-week crash course on Sandbox Survival. As I dragged my ninety-pound trunks toward the bus, two guys helped me get them squared away as we were taken to processing. Felipe—to whom chapter 5 is dedicated—was Latino and an ex-Marine, and Thurm is African-American and a Viet Nam vet. I could tell that I was in good hands with these guys—the first of literally hundreds of good guys that I would meet over the next three years.

I didn't have to shave my head like some kind of GI Janie or drop and give a drill sergeant twenty for slouching in line, but Contractor Camp was psychologically challenging in its own way—mostly from dealing with the Great Unknown. For all first-time recruits in any new, strange, and challenging situation, it is the people with whom you "huddle and muddle" that get you through it. Such was the case there.

It was there that I heard every imaginable reason expressed for wanting to go into harm's way. One guy actually wanted to go to Afghanistan because he heard the drugs were "outrageous." Thankfully, he washed out in the psychological testing phase. Many people were ex-mil, had survived Nam, and were going to make sure that our soldiers weren't subjected to the same stuff they had experienced during and especially after their tours of duty. Some from Bosnia, Macedonia, and Kosovo valued freedom and protection from ethnic cleansing like no one I had ever met before.

Contractor camp, which was held in the primitive confines of Houston hotels and a mall meeting room complex, was an unscripted diversity adventure. There were Latinos, whites, blacks, Asians, rednecks, ex-hippies, ex-soldiers, newly divorced people wanting to make a new start, fat and thin people, high school dropouts, highly educated people, Jews, Christians, Muslims, Buddhists, truckers, bankers, teachers, investment brokers, social workers, plumbers, nurses, EMTs, heavy equipment operators, coaches, cabinet makers, massage therapists, construction workers, and the list goes on. All of them believed they could make a difference in the lives of Coalition soldiers and Iraqis.

We went through background checks, passport procurement if necessary, and medical and psychological screening. The one hint our recruiters had been allowed to give us about the psychological test was that "Bungee jumping is something I am planning to do someday" was the *big* no-no, since the company had a real focus on workplace safety. An outstanding parking ticket on our background check could send us packing. Throughout the first week we were frequently given the chance to bail out before signing our contracts if we decided it was all too much.

Our training included workplace safety, IED recognition, cultural sensitivity, insurance benefits, and how to be a civilian on an engaged FOB (how to live in the middle of a war with the Joes, Janes, and Brass). We learned about what to do if we got arrested in Dubai, how not to be an idiot in Dubai, finance and tax laws, dealing with the media, travel safety, sexual harassment, NBC (Nuclear, Biological, and Chemical) warfare, basic self-defense, and life in the Sandbox. We were also fitted for our Kevlar, body armor, and chemical warfare gear.

Our trainers showed us pictures of gigantic camel spiders and dispelled the Internet myth that camel spiders could "numb your leg so you couldn't feel it while they ate it off in your sleep." (Camel spiders were my son Gabe's chief concern about my going to Iraq, and I was glad to dispel that fear at least.) We saw pictures of cobras, several types of vipers, scorpions, and tarantulas and were assured that Vector Control would do its best to protect us from the beasties. The day of NBC warfare training was when I came closest to saying "I'm outta here." After a "cheery" lecture on what would happen to us if were exposed to NBC warfare, we were more than motivated to learn how to use our masks and suits in a hurry. The masks had all kinds of vent gizmos and filters, and we had to be able to check them for holes, clear or seal off various vents, make sure we had a tight seal around our faces—all while holding our breath. For la pièce de résistance, we had to put a seal of duct tape between the hood of the NBC suit and the edge of the mask. We also had to seal off any space between sleeves and gloves, as well as between pants and boots. I managed to get a good chunk of my hair in the mix, and I don't want to talk about how much it hurt to remove the duct tape. If I had been able to keep my NBC suit as a souvenir, I would have converted it into a mobile steam cabinet and used it to sweat off pounds for the prom. I am more than glad that I never had to use my NBC gear and that for the whole three years it lived under my bed gathering dust.

Tommy Hamill, the truck driver who had escaped his insurgent captors just three weeks earlier, addressed our group and got a standing O, along with those in our group who had signed up to be truck drivers and were on their way into the eye of the storm. They were statistically the most likely to be killed, were not weapons authorized, had to rely solely on the military for protection, and were willing to be targets seven days a week. No amount of money is worth that kind of risk, despite some folks' claim that contractors are just carpetbaggers. In talking with the truckers at meals, I saw that like our soldiers, the road warriors had signed on out of a commitment to the mission.

One day a film crew from a Japanese TV station came to Contractor Camp, and a few of us were selected for them to interview. They were incredulous that we were volunteering to go, and they kept asking us if we were afraid. Everyone said "no" and indicated that if they did die, they would have no regrets. I was selected for the last interview, but at the last moment I had a strong feeling that I should let a Viet Nam vet named Melvin take my slot. He launched into an eloquent discussion of wanting to be there for the troops in a way that had not been the case when he was serving us back in my Fonda days. Melvin thanked me for letting him have the chance to deliver his soul, and as this man had actually been called a baby killer thirty-five years earlier, I was glad to do it.

Getting my military ID was nothing short of a comedy. It was another day of "hurry up and wait," so I was punchy already. When it was my turn to get my fingerprint digitally encoded, for some reason the machine would not read the print of my right index finger. After several tries, the technician looked at me and with a completely serious face said, "Mrs. Turner, you are going to have to use your communication finger." She meant the middle one used for the universal salute that is typically not meant as a compliment. I looked at her in disbelief, burst out laughing, and complied. It worked. Our ID cards even contained some of our DNA in order to identify us if we ever got blown to bits; they were just about the most important thing we would possess in Iraq, even more than our passports.

Mealtimes were my favorite, not because the food was so great (it wasn't), but because that was when we got to know just who we were going to be in the desert with. I remember one night when a whole group of Christians ended up at the same table. We shared our dreams about how to help people with what we would earn and our conviction of being called to go over there. By the end of the meal we were a close-knit tribe.

One morning I had breakfast with a tall, blond, lovely young woman named Tania who was from the Balkans. At first I was incredulous that she would want to go back into harm's way when she had grown up in a war zone. She explained simply, but with passion: "One day when I was a young teenager, I was at my cousin's apartment. Muslim extremists tossed a grenade into the apartment, even though it was well known that there were just civilians living there. We were just kids, you know. The grenade went off, and the next thing I knew, I was holding my cousin's brain in my hand. I want to do anything I can to stop them." It is not widely known that Al-Qaeda was active in the Balkans during the Bosnian war and was engaged in its own brand of ethnic cleansing that never made the press. Five of the mujahideen who fought in the Bosnian Muslim Army crashed into the World Trade Center on 9/11.

I was stunned but somehow managed to keep my breakfast down as we moved to lighter topics. It would be my experience that "Bozzys"—the affectionate and inaccurate term for anyone from the Balkans—were incredibly tough, especially the women. They had been kids in a hell I could only imagine. In retrospect, I realized that this "breakfast briefing" marked the beginning of a new life of complete extremes. I learned to move from discussing ethnic cleansing to karaoke lyrics, from having my friend Julie paint charming flowers on my trunks and filling them with going-away treasures to being able to recognize IEDs hidden in soda cans.

One day on the bus to the training center I met my first friend from Alabama. Angie Blackmon was a single mom and a social worker who specialized in training foster parents. Coincidentally, I had just been to an introductory seminar on becoming a foster parent before I received the call to come to Houston, and the chances would have been good that at some point I would have met Angie in Alabama if we hadn't gone to Iraq. It is indeed a small and wonderfully strange world. She had been in Houston a week longer than I had, and she became my instant "big sister," even though she was significantly younger than I. Her mom Earline "adopted" me sight unseen and spoiled me with care packages until she had to face her own battle with cancer as well as deal with losing her husband in a tragic accident. Angie also had a dynamite singing voice, and we would do karaoke together. She could crank out a pretty convincing rendition of Aretha Franklin's "Respect," and I sang backup, but we couldn't get through the song all that well because we were laughing too hard.

I spent my last weekend in Houston with my brother-in-law Chuck and his family. Chuck had worked in Iraq for four months in 2003, and he was the one whose example inspired me to apply to work as a contractor. I knew he had mixed feelings about my going. He was excited, told me cool stories, and made it clear that he missed Iraq, but at the same time he was worried.

He did his best to orient me to what lay ahead and gave me treasures to take with me. They included a Sunni as well as Shia headdress, a radio, tiny TV, ID holder, mosquito netting, face mask for the sandstorms, and other treats. Then it was time to say goodbye, maybe for the last time, although we didn't go there. Man, was that hard. How I wished that both he and Steve were going with me, and how glad I was that I had several Turners back home who were so solidly in my corner.

The last thing I did before boarding the plane was answer e-mails from family members who were livid over my decision to go to Iraq and felt it bordered on being evil. How could I assure them that I had no intention of "destroying an ancient and time-honored culture"? I knew that there really wasn't anything that I *could* say that would make a difference. I just wanted them to know that though we didn't see eye to eye, I loved them more than they knew.

I was given my passport, a packet with my travel orders, 500 bucks to last till payday, my medical records, and military ID, and prepared to fly to Dubai via London on 13 June. For the first time in my life I actually fell asleep during takeoff, and I awoke a few hours later to begin the next phase of my adventure. It would indeed prove to be Alice in a blistering hot Wonderland, and the heat would soon produce more than one Mad Hatter contractor.

CHAPTER 5

Losing Lobo

Felipe Lugo was a big, tall ex-marine. He adopted me from the moment I got off the bus struggling with my two newly stenciled trunks that refused to stay lashed to my newly purchased, exorbitantly priced two-wheeled luggage cart. It really was not the fault of the trunks or the cart. I simply had not gotten the hang of making the bungee cords fit in such a way that the trunks didn't go sliding when I hustled around the corner trying to keep up with the crowd. I don't know if he wondered how long I'd last in Iraq and felt sorry for me or if he was just doing what Marines do—help those who are weaker, but he became my friend the moment I arrived in Houston for training and processing.

He didn't talk too much about what had happened with his marriage, but he had recently gotten custody of his fourteen-year-old daughter, and he was going to Iraq for a year as a labor foreman to rebuild their life and be able to provide for her. At the time of our deployment his daughter was living with a relative he trusted. In retrospect I can see him becoming the kind of team leader for whom TCNs (Third

Country Nationals) would take a bullet. He strongly believed in the mission of Operation Iraqi Freedom, and if there was someone I would want to be in a foxhole with, it was Lobo, as was his nickname.

Lobo means wolf in Spanish, and I wondered at first if that moniker was an omen of behavior I didn't want to contend with but have encountered from time to time, both in the States and abroad. It was the shock of my life to get "hit on" by guys who were young enough to be my kids! I am pleased to say that with me Lobo was the perfect gentleman, and knowing he was nearby on the way into danger helped me forge ahead. While in Contractor Camp we would often share meals, our conversation flowing back and forth between English and Spanish, and I told him about Steve's and my adventures while living at the orphanage in Mexico.

As would be the case with so many, Lobo was fascinated by my change of heart regarding the military and really wanted to understand what in the world I "had been smoking" when I tried to shut down the Air Force base years earlier. I did a fairly reasonable job of explaining the delusional thinking necessary to attempt such a task, and he just chuckled.

I think he was interested in as well as conflicted over our lives as missionaries. I don't know if he had enough of organized religion, as is understandably the case with so many, but he really wanted to know about my faith, so I told him. One night after a long talk at dinner he said, "Keep it up; you just might save me." I laughed and let him know that saving was God's business, but it was apparent that something was going on inside him, and I was humbled that he sensed something genuine about the results of my head-on collision with Yeshua in 1970.

After three weeks, the day finally came when we got on the plane to head out to God alone knew what. We flew American Airlines to London/Gatwick, and then experienced the Emirates Airlines version of *Planes, Trains, and Automobiles*, with harried clerks fending off the verbal attacks of passengers whose flights had been cancelled. "Madam, I simply cannot pull a flight out of my hat!" a young acne-ridden agent would say as he backed up from the pointer finger emphatically jabbed at him by an irate customer in a sari.

We all huddled together for around twelve hours waiting for the next flight to Dubai, and I have found that inconvenience and boredom often forge the best friendships. I think back with such fondness on those tiptoe times of wondering what was next. We got on the Emirates flight and were promptly bowled over by how cushy Emirates was just in coach. The seats were brocaded and actually had footrests—something that someone as short as I am finds invaluable in surviving a fourteen-hour transcontinental flight as a sardine disguised as a newbie international traveler.

All of us were quite amazed that in coach we had actual printed menus with a choice of entrees; the food rivaled anything in a fine dining situation. Lobo's delight with the food was contagious; I'll never forget his "Wow, could you believe that we were in *coach*?" He looked like a kid whose birthday cake had just arrived, and it was one of many times in my three years in Iraq that I would see dear vestiges of young boys in grown men's bodies that they probably had no intention of letting slip out.

Once we got to BIAP (Baghdad International Airport), we sat outside in the Dante-level heat at a picnic table waiting for our assignments, and that was the last time I ever saw him. I had hoped that we would be assigned to the same camp, but he was going to convoy into the Green Zone. I hoped at least that since our deployment dates were the same, our R and R dates would coincide and we could experience Emirates afresh on our way home to R and R in four months. We all exchanged e-mail addresses, and I still have the torn slip of paper on which he wrote his.

E-mail is, of course, a luxury that until recently no one had experienced in a combat zone, and my department did its best to make sure that soldiers and civilians had access to it on a daily basis. However, there were always kinks to be ironed out, and the server would go up and down, sometimes for days at a time. Lobo and I would fire off "hey, how's it goin" type messages from time to time, but after a while I didn't get any answers from him. I had been transferred to another camp that had huge problems with the Morale computer system, and so I didn't think much of the silence. R and Rs came and went, and of course I looked for him as well as anyone else with whom I had survived Contractor Camp, but I never saw him.

Almost two years went by, and Thurm and I happened to be headed out on R and R at the same time. We had dinner one night in the Dfac and began to get caught up. He was so used to the sound of cannon fire both from serving in Viet Nam as well as where he had been working as chief of services at a camp in the Red Zone that he didn't even wince as the controlled detonations shook the ground on our way to and from chow.

"Have you heard anything from Lobo?" I asked as we sat across from each other. He looked at me and shook his head slightly. "I guess you didn't hear." Something in me scrambled valiantly to deflect what I sensed was coming, and I said, "I have e-mailed him and e-mailed him, but he doesn't answer. Did he de-mob?" ("De-mob" is pronounced "DEE-mobe" and is Armyspeak for "demobilize.") "Lobo was killed about a year ago," Thurm replied. "He had just pulled up in his Mule [kinda like a golf cart], and he was cut in two by mortar. He died instantly."

As I write this, my tears are starting to flow again as they did that evening at the dinner table. Thankfully, Lobo was the only contractor I knew personally who lost his life while I was there. Sometimes the whole camp would join together to commemorate the fallen, and camps were sometimes renamed in honor of them. At the time I left, our company had lost about eighty people, and throughout Iraq about eight hundred contractors had died as of 2007.

So what happens when a contractor dies? Not much. *Stars and Stripes* ran a piece decrying the fact that basically UPS delivers their personal effects to their families, and of course there is no flag-draped casket or twenty-one-gun salute. It is not that I feel that contractors should in any way be given something that is reserved for military members who have fallen; I just wish there were a systemized way of honoring those who make up the Second Army. Thankfully, because Lobo was an ex-Marine, he was entitled to a burial with full honors. I wish I could have been there to help lay him to rest.

I have no idea how his daughter is doing, but if she happens to pick up this book, I hope she will know that her daddy was my friend, her daddy watched my back, and her daddy was a wolf only to those who would try to harm the flock.

Rest in peace, my friend. I hope I see you soon in a place where the Banquet will so outdo Emirates that by comparison the glorious food in coach will look like an MRE. Vaya con Dios, hermano.

CHAPTER 6

Living in a Hair Dryer Stuck on High

*L*anding in London, we limped through the inconvenience of missing our connection due to the storm back in the States. As mentioned in the previous chapter, the bonds we had forged back at Contractor Camp were strengthened and new ones made. We tried to get comfy in airport chairs, slept some, and managed to laugh a lot. We landed in Dubai, but due to the flight mess-up, no one was there to meet us. After several hours they even brought the hotel manager to expedite our settling in to the transit hotel.

Besides Lobo, there were two other "ex-mils" (veterans) in our group: Charles Michael Smith and Heather. Both would become dear to me, and I briefly roomed with Heather while we were in a holding pattern in Dubai. She and I became instant pals, and she taught me the first Arabic I ever learned: *shukrahn*, the word for "thank you." The Army teaches its soldiers just how important it is to learn even a tiny bit of the local language wherever they are, and I noticed at our first meal in Dubai that Heather thanked the waiter in Arabic and he smiled.

She had just gotten out of the Army and was heading back to the camp where her husband was stationed with First Cavalry out of Fort Hood, Texas. This would prove to be both wonderful and difficult for her, as the rules prohibited any contractor from being in a soldier's hooch. Delicately stated, there was to be "no fraternization" between contractors and soldiers. She also had to deal with being so close to her husband while he was in constant danger and yet not being able to do anything about it. The upside was that what she did for a living directly affected the well-being of her husband and that she would at least be able to see him—something that thousands of wives back in the States wished they could do.

In Dubai Heather and I stayed up all night "fixing the world" by discussing our solutions to innumerable societal ills. We weren't even aware of how late it was until the morning call to prayer was broadcast from the mosque across the street at about 0430 hours. Oh, how I loved the way her mind and heart worked. How dear as well to be allowed to see her soft side, illustrated by her love for her cats and her skill with quilting. A tough and tenderhearted crack shot and smart soldier-girl—that was Heather.

Charles Michael Smith was a veteran and a medic who had practiced combat medicine in some wild places and even wilder situations. He has one of the best senses of humor I have ever encountered, and through the years in Iraq he would regale me with e-mail tales recounting his escapades that left me slumping across the keyboard, my shoulders shaking in silent laughter.

His free spirit had often gotten him into trouble, but it also made him a boon to our ragtag little group of travelers. He had already been in Afghanistan and had auctioned his desert boots on eBay. Billed as "the actual boots of world-famous world traveler Michael Smith," they sold for the tidy sum of thirty-nine dollars. Only in America would someone pay close to forty bucks for someone else's stinky, tired boots!

When the time finally came for our flight to Baghdad, we piled onto a commercial charter flight manned by a crew from the former Soviet Union. Back in Houston we had been warned about the angle and sudden steep dive that would be used to land the plane, and it made me miss my dad. I know he would have had a blast literally "comin' in on a wing and a prayer."

Like Dubai, Baghdad was "hotter than the hinges of Hades," as my dad used to say, but while Dubai was humid, the Baghdad climate felt like I was blasting my whole body with a hair dryer stuck on high. The airport was still in the custody of the Coalition, so getting through customs was not as dicey as it would become on subsequent trips. On the bus ride to Camp Victory, our driver, John, told us some unsettling facts about the kinds of things that had occurred in the buildings we drove past. For example, in driving by what was known as the "Perfumed Palace," we learned that sex slaves as young as twelve had been kept there until they were freed as a result of the invasion. The Hussein "playground" is described in more detail in chapter 8, "Saddam's Evil Eden." Driver John certainly had my attention and my admiration for his passion toward the mission, as well as his grasp of recent local history.

We had our noon meal at Bob Hope Dfac, and for the first time in my life I sat in a room with hundreds of soldiers. I was sleep-deprived, hungry, excited, scared, curious, and probably somewhat in shock. I was now officially in the middle of Operation Iraqi Freedom with the folks who were going to make sure Iraq was permanently free from Saddam Hussein or literally die trying.

When we got to Camp Victory North, it was time for more orientation: a crash course on the threat levels, camp communications, where to muster for a mass casualty event, a graduate-level course on how to fill out a time sheet, and more shots. We also began the process of adjusting to the sound of explosions from incoming as well as controlled detonations, or our guys firing out for the purpose of reminding "Baghdad Bob" that we were still here. After a while we could tell the difference between the two by the concussion and timing of the blast.

I met my regional boss, Johnny, and then was taken to Camp Victory South, where I met my immediate boss, Jorgia. She took me to Billeting to get my tent assignment, we stowed my stuff under my cot, and off we went to explore my new digs. First stop was the MWR building, which will also be described in chapter

8. It was there that I met Marty McIntyre, "The Pool Guy," who maintained the swimming pools. Marty looked out for me even when I was at other camps, and he remains my dear friend to this day. He is most definitely on my permanent "Good Guy list," and I know Steve was relieved to know that there was a guy in Iraq who had my best interests and safety at heart. Most guys did, with a few exceptions, who shall remain nameless and storyless.

When I first moved into my tent, there were just a few of us in there: one terp, a few female NCOs, and six contractors. All but one was quick to make me feel welcome, and I started to get my sea legs on the desert sands. One tentmate snored so loudly that I was sure she would cause the tent to collapse by inhaling the walls right out of their pegs. However, working seven days a week from 0600 to 1800 hours made me so tired that I soon just slept through most noise.

My first challenge was getting used to using porta-potties that had been baking in the desert sun. Even more challenging was getting up in the wee hours to make the nightly run and somehow always managing to time it so that it coincided with the arrival of the local "host country" (Iraqi) cleaning crew. This was not exactly the way I would have preferred to meet my new neighbors. My adrenaline level after these encounters would make it tough to get back to sleep, though not as tough as when there were incoming mortar blasts. One night, John, a guy who lived down the row, was having a smoke outside around 0300 hours and observed two hyenas following me as I went from the head back to the tent. There is no doubt that if they had attacked me they would have lived less than ten seconds, given the surrounding fire power of the Army's Three Corps (the division in charge of Camp Victory), but despite their common nickname, hyenas are no laughing matter.

About ten days after my arrival, my world was radically changed when Jorgia decided to quit and go home, and I was temporarily put in charge of the MWR facility. It was a personal stretcher for sure, but it allowed me to explore some possibilities of new things to do for the soldiers. As a result of my new role, I met the chaplains and was so touched by their heart for both the soldiers and the Iraqis. Over the years the chaplains would prove to be a tremendous source of strength for me as profoundly difficult workplace challenges attempted to steal my joy.

Being somewhat of a history buff and knowing that I was in the midst of a historical site that was tantamount to being in post-WWII Germany, I came up with the idea of putting together a historical tour of the grounds. The powers that be gave me permission to organize it, but for some reason later decided to cancel it. However, for several weeks I was able to dig in and find out more about what had occurred in Saddam's Evil Eden. This gave me a chance to meet the Army historians, the intel officers who had to approve everything that our MWR crew was proposing, and the Public Affairs officers who had been burned by the media. I also got to go inside the palace for meetings and see firsthand the opulence in which Saddam had lived while his people suffered.

Back at the ranch, or more properly, the tent, there was continual proof that life was fragile and ours could be over at any time. There were times when we slept in our Kevlar, the plated body armor weighing about forty-five pounds. I got so that I could kind of sleep at about a forty-five-degree angle so the front plate didn't completely squish me.

Our tent, which was designed to house twelve, was the only female tent designated for troops in transit, and at times our occupancy would swell to twenty-two. It was during one of these times, when our tent with its wall-to-wall cots resembled the inside of a full sardine can, that I met Lt. Col. Karen Fair, a JAG officer made of steel. A back injury kept her in constant pain, yet she managed to pass her PTs (Physical Training tests), including the push-ups, every time. She had been in the Pentagon on 9/11, lost fellow soldiers, and nearly lost her own life as well.

She has been conflicted ever since that day that she obeyed orders and got out of the building when her heart wanted to stay and help. She became my friend and saw me through some really hard emotional times; I have the most profound respect for her. Recently she was promoted from Lt. Col. to "full bird" Colonel, and I would have loved to see her get her promotion. The ceremony was held in the very building where her friends were killed. Gutsy woman, Col. Fair. She made me wish I were ten years younger so I could still join the Army and maybe become a JAG officer. She told me I'd be good at it.

The day came when I was able to move from a tent into the back of a storage room in a small building that had been part of Saddam's lair. There was nothing glamorous about it, but a hard building was safer than a tent. Our door was located right next to a porta-potty. It was summer in Iraq, so the night air was more than fragrant. However, I was thankful that I no longer needed to worry about the hyenas and could almost always make my nightly visit before the cleaning crew arrived. I had a cot and a freestanding steel armoire—a step up from living out of trunks. My Bosnian roommate, Bebe, who had grown up during the Balkan War, had the misfortune of having the same last name as Slobodan Milosevic, the infamous convicted war criminal who practiced ethnic cleansing in Bosnia. I think she said they were very distantly related, poor dear.

She also had a personal quirk that I found quite endearing: she was deathly afraid of geckos, which were abundant in Baghdad. I found it fascinating that she had grown up in a combat zone and was now living in a combat zone, yet was afraid of these dear little green guys who are so famous for being friendly that in America we now have one with an Aussie accent selling car insurance on TV. Her solution was to leave the light on all night. Not just a little unobtrusive night light, mind you; this was a fluorescent tube as big as a baseball bat, covered in wire mesh—truly industrial-strength lighting. I felt like I was trying to sleep in the middle of Yankee Stadium. Fortunately, Emirates Airlines had given me a sleep mask which was big enough to block out the stadium light, and it covered most of my face. I looked like a munchkin trying to imitate the Lone Ranger, but in the end it was a true win-win situation. She felt protected from the geckos, and I didn't lose sleep over anything other than mortar and RPGs. We remained neighbors on good terms when we got to move from our glorified closet to trailers. Things were definitely looking up!

It took about a month to recover from jet lag, settle in, and get used to the fact that some of my neighbors over the wall wanted to store my head in a refrigerator. During that time of personal adjustment, Iraq was turned back over to the Iraqis and Saddam went by in a surreal parade on his way to the location discussed in chapter 7, "Journalistic Jihad," where he threw his first official tantrum in court.

Several times a week I was able to call Steve after work and tell him about my adventures. The phone booths were outdoor plywood boxes, and they did double duty as saunas. It was never long before I was dripping in sweat while doing nothing more vigorous than flapping my lips at an aerobically efficient rate. How kind of the U.S. Army and the Iraqi sun to provide us with such spa-like luxury free!

The heat was so draining that it was not at all strange for me to want to hit the sack by 2000 hours. Many times I had to cut conversations short due to incoming and the need to get to a safer place. In spite of it all, I felt like the most blessed woman on the planet. I had a man who loved me and a God who loved me more, and I was surrounded by some of the most remarkable people I had ever known. Therefore, what was not to love about life in this giant hair dryer? It would not take long to find out.

CHAPTER 7

Journalistic Jihad?

"If our intended goal in this age is the establishment of a caliphate in the manner of the Prophet and if we expect to establish its state predominantly . . . I say to you: that we are in a battle and that more than half of this battle is taking place in the battlefield of the media."

LETTER FROM AYMAN AL-ZAWAHIRI TO ABU MUSAB AL-ZARQAWI[1]

"Mutti," I said for the zillionth time. (I had been calling my mother "Mutti" [pronounced MOO-tee]—a German term of endearment for mothers—since I was a teenager.) "If I hadn't been over here to see it for myself, I never would have believed it." I really didn't want to use up the precious minutes I had for a phone call with my mom to bemoan the treatment of our soldiers in the press, on the news, and on the

41

House or Senate floor, but I could tell that it was challenging for her to believe that mainstream media's reports on Operation Iraqi Freedom could actually be so far from the truth.

She was understandably worried about me being in the middle of a war, and an unpopular one at that. Her concern was exacerbated by her memories of being a brand-new bride while my dad served in the Naval Air Corps in WWII and wondering if he'd come home alive, let alone in one piece. She had given birth to my oldest sister Sharon while my dad was still in harm's way in the Pacific, and he didn't see his firstborn baby until she was six months old.

My mom is my other WWII hero, as in her own way she fought for my freedom along with my dad. Especially in her day, holding down the home front was as real as it was honorable. Without fanfare, our whole nation saved aluminum foil, grew Victory gardens, and rationed gas; women even donated nylon stockings, all for the war effort. With the help and shelter of my grandparents and her community's support and companionship, my mom—like thousands of other women—made her own very real and unsung sacrifices. There aren't any medals for wives of soldiers, but there need to be. My mother deserves one.

Now it was sixty years later, and her unpredictable youngest daughter had apparently gone off the deep end, along with 120,000 other civilians. Her baby was in the middle of what was being portrayed by various print and broadcast media as the "quagmire in Iraq." The *New York Times* and the *Washington Post* began using the quagmire analogy when the war in Iraq was only eight days old, according to a FOX news article[2] written in response to Senator Ted Kennedy's liberal use of the "Q word" on 24 June while he was verbally jousting with Donald Rumsfeld during a Senate Armed Services Committee hearing. Politicians like Senator Kennedy who have never been to Iraq are typically entrenched in defeatism, while the ones who actually go over to Iraq come back with a "can do" take (even a cautious one) on what needs to be finished up. My friend Chuck Dunne told me that country singer Charlie Daniels, who has gone over several times to entertain the soldiers, got a chuckle out of the soldiers at his 2006 concert when he said, "I have told Ted

Kennedy that he has a standing invitation to come over here to see for himself what y'all have accomplished, but he never takes me up on it. I've told him I'll even pay his way!"

When Mom was living through WWII, there was no doubt in anyone's mind that Hitler, Mussolini, and Tōjō needed to be summarily stopped; supporting the war was a no-brainer. However, now she had to wonder if her daughter was unknowingly in the middle of something that was evil from the get-go, as was being alleged nightly.

I wanted to tell her "Just turn off the TV and don't believe a word you are hearing," but I knew that wouldn't give her any comfort. I desperately wanted to assure her that while it is true there is real danger in a combat zone, statistically I was safer than if I lived in any major American city.

If she had been computer savvy, I would have encouraged her to go to the soldier blogs to get her news from downrange. These blogs are the refreshingly unassuming cyber-journals of soldiers that are posted nearly in real time, when the memory of situations is still fresh. Never before in the history of man and war has there been a situation where soldiers could serve as both warriors *for* and reporters *to* the general population to such a large degree. In addition, with the invention of e-mail, Web cams, MySpace, Facebook, YouTube, instant messaging, and all the other telecommunication marvels we have access to, amateur soldier and civilian reporters in the field are rivaling the work of the pros with a product whose quality no one could have anticipated.

Chris Anderson discusses the effect of cyber-communications technology on all of global life and economics in his brilliant, groundbreaking book, *The Long Tail.* His model can be well applied to my point that the soldiers' use of the Internet has afforded us a virtually instant, widespread, personal and collective history of Operation Iraqi Freedom that should make the media "doom and gloom" crew quake in their boots.

Honestly, I don't know what we would do without the soldier blogs. There they are, in harm's way, fully able to howl with outrage over the war with complete anonymity, if they wished. For the most part, however, their posts are filled with far more angst over being lied about and marginalized than the fact that they are in a controversial war. Are all their posts sweetness and light, dutifully written after they have symbolically turned right in their Bradleys off of Brainwash Boulevard onto Lockstep Lane? Of course not! These soldiers are not at all afraid to express their frustrations with everyone from Congress to their peers or superiors, as well as their passionate desire to see the mission accomplished and the fledgling Iraqi democracy secure.

The soldier blogs not only complain about what is and is not being said at home, in print or on the news, but they also relentlessly report the good stuff. I also have a feeling that if the soldier blogs were not so consistently different from the mainstream news, it would be possible for the media to do what was done to me in my "Fonda" days: cause people to buy into the idea that soldiers are a lower life form. In my youth from the midsixties to the midseventies, soldiers were portrayed as knowing how to do two things: kill and blindly follow orders. There were three main contributors to this perception. The first was the incomplete and therefore distorted media coverage of the My Lai incident during the war in Viet Nam. The second was Arlo Guthrie's wildly popular talking blues album entitled *Alice's Restaurant*. The third was what most vets feel was the treasonous testimony of then-Lt. John Kerry before the Senate Foreign Relations Committee on 22 April 1971, wherein he described the soldiers as behaving routinely like Genghis Khan.

The soldier blogs are the historical records of a remarkable time. They are written by both soldiers and civilians, many of whom keep volunteering to go back because they have the inarguable proof of what good they are doing and how much the Iraqis want them to be there. Oh, by the way, the "re-up" (reenlistment) rate amongst soldiers is at approximately 130% of the desired quota in the era of a volunteer force. Go figure. And these are the same soldiers who are insisting that their stories not be lost on the cutting-room floor of our cultural consciousness.

Of literally thousands of Web sites and blogs, I have three favorites. One is www.IraqsInconvenientTruth.com, an obvious word play on Al Gore's film, with considerably more accuracy. Its subtitle is "The Truth of Iraq, and How America and Iraq Are Winning the War." What is particularly endearing about this site is the use of photojournals to portray how the soldiers and the children love each other. If you can look at these pics without being touched, I wonder if you have a Jarvik for a heart.

Another fave is www.VetsForFreedom.org, created by Capt. Pete Hegseth along with former S. Sgt. David Bellavia, the author of *House to House,* a remarkable tale of the 2004 Fallujah campaign. Bellavia is a Medal of Honor nominee, Silver Star recipient, and Bronze Star recipient. On 11 December 2007, Capt. Hegseth participated in a UK debate about the war and its failures which the BBC aired to seventy-six million viewers. His outstanding rebuttal of the claims of journalist detractors who have never walked the streets of Fallujah is well worth the eight minutes it takes to watch it on the Vets For Freedom Web site. I don't think the debate's sponsors particularly appreciated the positive response of the audience.

The third is www.Blackfive.net, which has a number of thoughtfully written articles, including Lt. Col. Tim Ryan's article "Aiding and Abetting the Enemy: The Media in Iraq" about this very topic of journalistic assault on the American soldier as well as the American people. Ryan's article documents every point I want to make in this chapter and then some, and he does it from the perspective of firsthand observation from outside the wire, an advantage I never had. He concludes with the following expression of deserved frustration with the media: "Much too much is ignored or omitted. I am confident that history will prove our cause right in this war, but by the time that happens, the world might be so steeped in the gloom of ignorance we won't recognize victory when we achieve it." [3]

I believe that the sheer volume of the soldiers' positive stories that appear on the blogs (in contrast to what the American people are told of their feats) more than justifies the use of the term "Journalistic Jihad" for the title of this chapter. I have two reasons for thinking this. First, to so consistently and systematically deprive both the soldiers and the American people of the truth about what is being accomplished in Iraq is immoral and criminal, as is jihad. Lt. Col. Buzz Patterson has a better term for it, which is the main title of his excellently researched book: *War Crimes: The Left's Campaign to Destroy Our Military and Lose the War on Terror.* This book has had a powerful impact on my life, as it not only addresses the present problems with the media in our era but also exposes a number of willfully concocted lies about the Viet Nam War—lies which I once gladly swallowed because they fit my political agenda. Second, my own life was more than once endangered by the international media in Iraq. In at least one of the situations, everyone I asked said *the reporter knew better, but did it anyway.* I will discuss the specifics later in this chapter.

Being personally endangered, however, is not my focus here. Rather, my main concern is that day after day—in articles, newscasts, blogs and op-ed pieces—soldiers are vilified, dismissed, misrepresented, lied about, and ignored. Their victories are marginalized or outright passed over, their failures exaggerated and distorted. In addition, some articles have included information that could have gotten soldiers, Iraqis, and the rest of us killed. Since death is the usual goal of jihad, I make no apology for the title of this chapter.

Now for the mandatory disclaimer: I realize that there are some amazing journalists who have repeatedly risked and even lost their lives to bring us objective stories that are "up close and personal." They have produced brilliant reports that are tough, compassionate, and fair; Jill Carroll's piece entitled "Hostage" discussed in chapter 12 is one of them. The soldiers' obvious affection for Jill after she had been an embedded reporter, or "embed," with their unit and their desire to find her were no doubt enhanced by her respect for them and their mission. Make no mistake: they would have given their lives to find her even if she had been a pill, but I doubt they would have carried her picture in their wallets.

My own cousin, Dale Russell, an award-winning chief investigative reporter for the FOX station in Atlanta, has jumped into the Sandbox and been in harm's way more than once. I like the stuff he has done on Iraq not just because he is my cousin but because of how he treated and talked about the soldiers.

The journalists who are, in my view, dangerous are the ones who seem to care only about making a name for themselves by having the coolest story. They will sneak pictures and leak sensitive information, apparently without concern for the consequences. This kind of "journalism" blows missions, lowers morale, emboldens the enemy, and gets people killed. After hearing stories from the soldiers themselves about how reporters have betrayed them, it is a wonder to me that the military allows *any* reporters to embed with the soldiers.

Just like military personnel, journalists should be aware of and committed to OpSec (Operational Security), a system of understanding how certain bits of information or seemingly innocent photographs can get people killed. A commitment to the soldiers, and therefore to OpSec, requires that all proposed communication be dealt with from the standpoint of the heart as well as the head. A responsible reporter or photographer must first ask, "Might my report/photo as I want to present it somehow compromise the mission or someone's safety? Is it more important to me to get the scoop and maybe win a Pulitzer, or should I be purposely vague and not have the piece be as sexy or seemingly noteworthy?"

A journalist committed to OpSec from the heart would *cheerfully* volunteer to check a piece with someone who knows its nuances to avoid endangering our troops. On the other hand, reporters who are all about themselves seem to resent the very existence of OpSec and the need to follow it. Their sense of entitlement made us feel like all they cared about was their stories, and our safety could go to a very hot place in a hand basket.

The soldiers and I found ourselves in dangerous situations due to the actions of irresponsible journalists, which I'll discuss from the standpoints of security, journalistic accuracy, and entitlement.

The Coalition turned Iraq back over to the Iraqis on 28 June 2004, two days ahead of schedule, in the early morning for security considerations. Sure, a big ceremony with commentary by all the world's newscasters would have been a much better photo op, but it wouldn't have been "safe"—a rather amusing security classification in a combat zone. We were told by a reliable source that over sixty daisy-chain bombs pointed at the CPA Palace were found, ready to go off and blow everyone to Kingdom Come. Considering how much incoming activity stepped up during that time, I don't have any reason to doubt it.

This is a classic example of a situation that will tick off the media no matter what. If they had been invited to the party and had gotten blown up, there would have been outrage over "poor security" in the "supposed Green Zone." If they were not invited, then whoever made that decision was surely keeping them from the Big Story, and there'd be paybacks on that score.

We were told early in the morning that the transfer had transpired without a hitch, a leak, or a boom. As we stood in line for breakfast, and for the next couple of days, we actually heard broadcasters complain, "We were not informed" or "We were not invited." Honestly, it sounded like a child whining about missing a friend's birthday party. It's true that they were now short on material and had to do a serious chunk of improv, but why not fill the airspace with *thanking* someone for keeping them safe rather than pouting? It would have been great to hear a broadcaster say something along the lines of "You know, I would have loved to be there to see a defining moment in history firsthand, but I'm thankful someone was looking out for us."

Three days later, on 1 July 2004, Saddam pitched his first of many fits in court at his arraignment at Camp Victory. Marty McIntyre, a retired Army NCO (noncommissioned officer) turned contractor who had served in Desert Storm, came into the camp dispatch office and announced, "You are not going to believe this. There is an article out on the Net that talks about the fact that the arraignment was in an octagonal building, next to a mosque, in the location that housed his palace."

Shelly, the dispatch operator, immediately understood what this meant, but as the newbie I needed to be educated. Marty explained that anyone who knew what he was doing would have been able to triangulate or use a mathematical process to calculate the location of a target by using landmarks. "Man!" Shelly exclaimed. "Why not just paint a bull's-eye on our chest while they are at it?"

I don't know if the reporters understood what they had done. They also said the building where the arraignment was held was next to a blue-domed mosque, which was not the case. It was actually next to a very distinctive mosque that was purported to be Saddam's own for private use. Perhaps describing it as the blue one (which does exist at another camp) was an attempt to prevent accurate triangulation; I'd like to believe so. Or perhaps it was proof that the reporter wasn't really there, didn't know what he was talking about, had to file a report to make a deadline, and had to come up with something that *seemed* credible that he heard from someone else. This is either journalistic license or outright sloppiness. What's even more frustrating is that because the news agencies quote each other, misinformation is easily and rapidly multiplied.

All I know is that there were many people who wanted Saddam dead, some who wanted to spring him, and a whole lot of folks who wanted us dead. Anyone watching from the muj Web sites could have filed these infobits away for future use. After that as well as the Great Pout about the transfer ceremony, I knew that I needed to think a new way regarding our supposed "right" to information emerging from the middle of a combat zone.

We had been taught in Contractor Camp about the necessity of not having "loose lips," and I thought I understood it then. However, now I comprehended on a much deeper level my responsibility to be extremely careful about anything that I said over the phone or e-mailed home in a newsletter. Before saying anything I was unsure of from an OpSec perspective, I made a point of asking someone knowledgeable to advise me what was safe to say and what wasn't. I know more than one Public Affairs Officer who would do back flips if they had the assurance that a professional reporter would consider doing likewise.

The second time my life was endangered seemed more willful on the part of the reporter. While I was working nights on the closed base where the Iraqi Special Forces were being trained, some frustrated U.S. soldiers came in from patrol for just a moment to e-mail home and let their families know that they were alright. Why? Because of a reporter's irresponsibility.

The first thing that had gone wrong, according to the hasty report of the frustrated soldiers, was that the photographer who was with the reporter had taken certain pictures which compromised their safety by showing their names and, if someone knew how to read it, their unit or specialty. Sometimes this is OK, and you often see interviews with soldiers that plainly show names. On the other hand, there are times when showing soldiers' names or badges paints the aforementioned bull's-eye on the soldier or the unit because of the nature or timing of that specific mission. The PAO as well as the soldiers explain this over and over to reporters, who typically ignore them. Journalists seize the responsibility of deciding what is and is not OK and why, rather than deferring to the judgment of the ones who not only are risking their lives for the mission, but also for the reporter.

Some soldiers have suggested that reporters who embed with a unit in harm's way should be required to be ex-mil to reduce the chance of being dead weight. That may sound harsh, but the presence of embeds requires that someone be assigned to protect them. At least if reporters were ex-mil they could draw upon what they had learned in basic training to keep their heads on straight. I am sure that idea would be unpopular, but I know that "my" guys who had to hurry to e-mail their families would have never been put in that position if the reporter had had some military experience, let alone integrity.

The second thing that happened that night was that the reporter not only mentioned by name a unit that had some KIAs (thus making it possible for the families to find out about their loss from the media rather than the military), but she also got the unit name wrong. So, here is the net result of the reporter's disregard for policy.

First of all, the soldiers' stress levels were kicked up and they were distracted by having to worry about their families' alarm over their possible deaths. Getting their focus off the mission could have gotten them killed. Their families back home were freaking out because they were wondering if they had just lost their loved ones and why no one from the Bereavement Team had contacted them. The families' understandable stress put more stress on the soldiers—a vicious cycle. Lastly, the rest of us on base were endangered by the soldiers coming off perimeter patrol to fix the damage caused by the reporter. This entire incident is described in depth in Capt. Sean Michael Flynn's outstanding book, *The Fighting 69th*.

I wish I could say that this kind of thing is an isolated incident, but it's not, and I have heard more horror stories about rascally reporters from many other sources. When I was first in-country working on putting together the soldiers' historical tour, as described in chapter 8, I had to get clearance from the Public Affairs Office for all that we were doing. At first I was puzzled by their standoffishness until they explained what they had suffered at the pens of reporters.

I realize that there will be those that will interpret my call for some "reporting restraint" as a violation of our constitutionally protected freedom of the press. Oh well—think away. Your freedom to think what you like is what the soldiers guarantee you can do even while you endanger them. I would hope you would rather sleep well at night, knowing that your discretion perhaps made sure a soldier got to come back home, and not in a flag-draped box.

Sometimes the media assault on the soldiers and Iraqis is accomplished by what is *not* said. For example, in the summer of 2005 there was a specific focus on the part of Al-Qaeda to prevent the Iraqi police/security force from being built. There were several attacks on police stations, resulting in potential recruits being blown up by all manner of bombs—suicide and others. On one occasion, sixty-seven people were killed, and of course, the media spun this as yet more "proof" that "Bush-lied-people-died,-it's-all-about-the-oil."

What was not mentioned was that the next day, *after* the attack, over three hundred people stood in line to sign up to be a part of the police force! The *real* news was that the Iraqis were so determined to have a country that worked that Al-Qaeda's worst had inspired them to sacrifice and put themselves in harm's way. The series of attacks thus *proved* their desire for freedom, rather than showing how badly things were going. This is quite a different take on the situation from the perpetual hand-wringing of Cranky News Network, and it is the honest-to-God truth.

In November 2004, a chemical weapons cache and a huge conventional weapons cache were found in Fallujah. I have seen the pictures of the chemical cache taken while the Chemical Response Team was examining the building's contents. They found the ubiquitous black ski masks, components that could produce poisonous gases, and instructions for producing anthrax. But remember, these things don't exist in Iraq, right? The conventional weapons cache was found in, look out, a mosque! It was *huge*. Both finds deserved nearly Second Coming size type, but the media treated it as essentially a nonevent, telling us instead that the weapons were in the mosque in the first place because of the presence of the soldiers.

In contrast to the media's assertion that soldiers are the problem, not the solution, Capt. Pete Hegseth told millions of BBC listeners on 11 December 2007 that after the Coalition crushed Al-Qaeda in Fallujah, the people were so glad to see them that there was nearly a spontaneous street fair! An Iraqi man who invited Hegseth in for tea asked, "Where have you been?" In other words, "What took you so long?" This is a far cry from how soldiers and Iraqis are portrayed in the 2007 movie *Redacted*, which thankfully flopped at the box office.

People have no idea what it is like for soldiers to be in harm's way, hear clueless politicians thousands of miles away saying things like "the war is lost," and know the media will repeat such nonsense over and over ad nauseum. Hey, who needs Al-Jazeera when the American rags and legislators will do their work for them? I know it gets to the soldiers sometimes, but the fact that they largely take it in stride and see it as their duty to protect other people's right to be ignorant is just another indicator of how remarkable they are.

I think the most compelling proof that indeed something is "rotten in Denmark" regarding less-than-honorable journalists is that it is their own colleagues who are blowing the whistle. Salama Nimat, an outspoken Jordanian journalist, says that most of Saddam's bribing of journalists "was done out in the open." He adds, "Western media has been playing the game, too, including Americans."[4] Stephen Hayes, whose article quotes Nimat, says that the practice of bribing journalists went on clear up to the time of the overthrow of Saddam. "If they are not bought and paid for, they are at least rented."[5] Hayes also says that a top national security official mentioned that there was information to implicate journalists throughout the Arab world and Europe.

The front page of the online 17 December 2003 edition of *Editor and Publisher* was devoted to an interview with *New York Times* writer John Burns, author of *Embedded: The Media at War in Iraq.* Burns took a lot of heat for contending that "American journalists in Iraq often ignored the terror of Saddam Hussein's regime to avoid losing their visas, and plied his ministers with expensive gifts and hundreds of thousands of dollars in bribes to stay on their good side."[6] He also said that there would have been many ways to get out the truth about what was going on in Iraq during Saddam's day without compromising journalistic integrity.[7] There were underground news pipelines of all kinds. There were Iraqis who had escaped to Jordan and other countries. Maybe it would have been the biggest showing of good faith not to even have a bureau in the country at all rather than risk being on the dole or even being perceived as such. I don't think it is unreasonable to ask what CNN, Reuters, BBC, and the AP were doing comfortably ensconced in the Ministry of Information building during the Hussein era.

OK, so that was during Saddam's reign. What about since then? Again, the bloggers or "citizen journalists" are coming to our rescue. Ask them—the soldiers as well as the Iraqis—who have the reports and pictures of what has actually occurred in contrast to what has been reported. A blog called www.IraqTheModel.com, which is overseen by two guys who wisely identify themselves only as Omar and Mohammed, was voted "Best Middle East or Africa Blog of 2005" and won the Weblog Awards of 2005. Their 24 June 2005 post, "More Disgusting Bias from the Media," refutes an article which had appeared in *The Guardian* the previous day arguing that insurgents had won against the Iraqi Police in a firefight, when the opposite was actually true. Omar comments, "This article by *The Guardian* is another striking evidence to the bias of the media whenever it comes to Iraq." To demonstrate the true attitude of Iraqi citizens toward terrorists, he points out, "During the battle, people from the mixed Sunni and She'at neighborhood called 55 times and provided tips to the IP [Iraqi Police] about the movements of the terrorists. . . . But still, the Guardian wants us to believe that the insurgents are winning! How disgusting!"[8]

There are myriad other sites dealing with media bias in reports, photos, and op-ed pieces. I hope you'll have the courage to read and believe the stories of the ones who are there in harm's way and are still positive about what they and the Iraqis are accomplishing through their bravery and compassion.

I have wondered what makes the media so consistently negative, not just about Iraq and Afghanistan, but seemingly everything. It would be too simplistic just to call them self-serving, agenda-driven, or straight-up liars. But here's a possibility which might shed some light on their negativity, without excusing it.

Research in psychoneuroimmunology—how the brain affects the body's immune system by the chemicals it produces—has shown that negativity, depression, and stress are highly physically addicting. I wonder if the media's MO that "if it bleeds, it leads" might stem from such an actual physical addiction to negative news. Do they and Congress have to make sure they get their "depression fix" by mainlining bad news from OIF (Operation Iraqi Freedom) to the exclusion of the overwhelming good news? And what's worse, are they trying to draw us into their addiction? "Misery loves company," as the saying goes, and I for one am belly-full of their blues being barfed on us at the soldiers' expense.

To further illustrate my assertion that some members of the media refuse to see or report anything positive, I need to tell about an experience the soldiers and I had while watching television together. On 13 September 2006, we were watching *The O'Reilly Factor* while Bill O'Reilly and Arianna Huffington were discussing the Kurds. Oh, and if you think the soldiers just read censored, patriotic stuff in *Stars and Stripes,* you'll be pleased to know that every Thursday, Ms. Huffington's op-ed piece took up the entire left-hand column of the op-ed page, and Ann Coulter's fiercely feisty weekly column was on the right. (Nice symbolic visual touch!) Hey, we even showed Michael Moore's *Fahrenheit 9/11* with the Army's blessing! Now *there's* an example of a fair and balanced "documentary."

Anyway, the Kurds had just produced some lovely ad spots thanking America for their freedom[9], and Mr. O'Reilly was showing them to Ms. Huffington. In fact, things are so good with the Kurds (despite the recent rebel activity) that the Kurds are starting a *tourist* industry. Betcha didn't know that, did ya? They describe Kurdistan as "the other Iraq," and Americans are nearly worshipped there. After Mr. O'Reilly showed the clips to Ms. Huffington, he asked his trademark question, "What say you?" Ms. Huffington replied, "*The Kurds were already free.*" The soldiers groaned and rolled their eyes, and the unemotional Mrs. Turner shrieked and pounded the plywood walls of the MWR tent. Aargh!!! If they were "already free," then what in the world were they doing spending big bucks thanking us for their freedom? My friend Mr. Aram, a Kurdish interpreter you'll read about in chapter 10, escaped being gassed only because he was already on the run from Saddam and was up in the mountains. Try and convince *him* that "the Kurds were already free."

It is one thing to refuse to acknowledge the sentiments of the thankful Kurds. It is an entirely different matter to launch a personal attack against someone who has chosen to be in danger in order to lead and protect soldiers so they can keep us free. Such was MoveOn.org's shameless treatment of Gen. David Petraeus. On 7 August 2007, Gen. Petraeus gave incontrovertible proof to Congress that the surge was working, and those left of center had to just take it, despite the "General Betrayus" hit pieces. After independent confirmation that violence was down and cooperation between Sunnis and Shias was up, the good news actually managed to land *in* the papers! It would have been poor-but-tempting form for the doomsayers to completely dismiss what had been proven. So, on 8 November 2007, the *New York Times* and the *Washington Post* grudgingly wrote two reports. The *Times* report was entitled "Sunni/ Shia Fatwa against Violence," and the *Washington Post* piece was entitled "46 Thousand Return to Baghdad.*"* You'd expect such good news to land on the front page, right? Maybe page 2? Not a chance. They appeared on pages A 19 and A 20, respectively. In the newspaper business this is called "burying," and it's what journalists do when they are duty-bound to report something but they don't like it. With all the effort that Iraqi and Coalition soldiers had put into the surge, they should have been congratulated on turning around an admittedly tough situation . . . but perhaps that would not be considered "objective" journalism. At least reporters could have acknowledged the historical significance of what had just occurred.

I can guarantee you that if this dismissive brand of journalism had been pawned off as professional during WWII, while my mom was worrying about my dad, there would have been a hue and cry throughout the country. Now we are so used to it that if we didn't have the bloggers to inspire us to think outside the box, I am afraid that we would just take it like a laboratory dog that has been shocked into learned helplessness.

And that, dear readers, brings me to the crux of this chapter. We are indeed at the cultural Great Divide of perception in our nation. If you want to be addicted to depression, then you'll never be satisfied, even if there is never another drop of American or Iraqi blood spilled in the Sandbox. But if you *want* to know, if you *want* to see, if you *want* to change, and if you can even remotely consider the possibility that there are people who have a vested interest in your believing the worst, then I am living proof that you'll have your "Eureka moment." If you refuse to let them kill your hope with their dirge of depression and frighten you with their journalistic jihadist tactics, you'll see the good and rejoice with the progress, no matter what the topic or where it is occurring.

You will be changed. I was.

CHAPTER 8

Saddam's Evil Eden

Geneal Wesley Clark once described Saddam Hussein as "unpleasant." Unpleasant! I hope from the bottom of my heart he meant that as a joke, or at least an expression of irony. Sadly, I think the general was dead serious. My idea of "unpleasant" is a rude waiter or impatient store clerk. I would love to take General Clark on a tour of the 55,000-acre evil paradise Saddam built with UN Oil for Food money at the height of his glory, but I don't think he would want me to tell him what happened there. It might rock him and force him to come up with a stronger description of Mr. Hussein's behavior, as well as that of Saddam's sons.

I am glad that by reading this chapter, you are coming with me on my verbal tour of an incredibly beautiful place whose elegant Italian marble foundations and edifices were laid on human anguish and whose sculpted canals and designed lakes at times have been the final resting place of murdered humans. I have no desire to be gratuitously gory with my description of the human sacrifices that occurred here in the name of sport, sports, or sex. But honestly, I fear that it will take much less time for people to forget what happened in Iraq prior to 2003 than it did for the Holocaust to become contested as historical fact by Mahmoud the Rude Ahmedinejad. If I can in any way help to keep that from happening, then it will have been worth every moment I spent away from my family for three years and every effort it has taken to be a faithful scribe in penning this book.

The area surrounding Baghdad International Airport was once the lascivious lair of Saddam Hussein, his boys Uday and Qusay, and their Baathist cronies. It was a system of palaces, villas, hotels, artificial lakes, and canals, with fields, vineyards, gardens, a zoo, stables, a game reserve, and swimming pools. It had hunting lodges and fishing lodges with marble dressing counters and hooks upon which to hang their trophies, skillfully bagged from artificially stocked waters or fields.

The entire compound is surrounded by a wall, and there is a system of gates and bunkers throughout. Saddam had a sixth sense about when a coup was being planned. The complex was designed so that if someone tried to overthrow him, he could hunker down behind any of the "gated communities" and defend himself. Legend also has it that supper was supposed to be prepared for Uncle Saddam (as he was referred to by the children) and be ready at 5:00 p.m. in *all* of the palaces. The servants would not know until the last moment if he was going to arrive in their particular domain, but there would be hell to pay if they were caught unprepared.

Beni, my Baghdad-born interpreter friend, says that when Saddam was in the process of acquiring and building all of this, no one in Baghdad knew what was going on. They thought that it was just being made into one huge farm for the Uncle.

It was said that people knew better than to get near the wall, as they could easily get shot. On the perimeter road, it was way better to drive on the rim of a flat tire than to risk getting out to change it. One man told me that Uday and his guards got bored while out for a walk one day, so they got up in the towers that line the place and watched for people to pick off with a single shot. Three men came walking down the road. "See that one?" Uday said to his guard. "Shoot him." He did. Dead. "No, the other one." The scene was repeated. "Give me that," Uday said, grabbing the bodyguard's weapon and shooting the third passerby. This is only a morsel of what I mean by evil for sport.

Once when I was in the Red Zone, I spoke with a man who told me what it was like as Uday hauled out his whole family, set them in a row, and told the man's father to shoot his other son for desertion from the Iraqi army. The father quietly refused. It would have been completely normal in a situation like this for Uday to have whacked the entire family, starting with the father, but he was satisfied with taking his gun out of the father's hand and shooting the deserter himself, in front of small girls and their mother.

Evil Eden sported theaters, an aviary, garages for Uday's thousand cars, toilets and sinks with gold fixtures, a chandelier nearly three stories high, rugs worth a fortune, garish French Provincial furniture, and china rimmed in twenty-four-carat gold—all purchased with UN Oil for Food money while the people of Baghdad starved. This is one of the reasons I typically don't like sanctions very well. There is always a way around them, and the innocent are the ones who suffer.

I saw these buildings, worked in them, sang and danced in them, and climbed around in them. The memory of the things that used to happen there would haunt me at times. I would sometimes put my hands on elaborate doorknobs attached to carved doors and shudder, thinking about the evil hands that had opened them.

When I arrived in Baghdad, our American bus driver, whose name was John, told us a brief history of the buildings as he took us to our in-processing center. I will describe only a few of them.

PERFUMED PALACE

When the Coalition took Baghdad in April of 2003, they came upon a subtly pink marbled palace with a somewhat swirled top, slightly reminiscent of the Kremlin onion-top buildings in Moscow. When they took this Perfumed Palace, as it was known, they found 167 women being held there as sex slaves, the youngest of whom was twelve. Legend has it that Uday was such a sexual predator that when people heard he was in the neighborhood, they physically hid their daughters.

I saw a video interview of a man forced to be Uday's bodyguard and double; he even had to undergo plastic surgery so he would be more convincing in the role. One day in a park in Baghdad, this man watched in horror as Uday had his guys drag a bride who had just been married the previous day to a hotel room so he could rape her. She either jumped or was pushed to her death after he was finished with her. Her husband cursed Uday and was executed for "defamation of the president."

VICTORY PALACE

Victory Palace was built after Desert Storm to commemorate what Uncle Saddam called the "Victory over America." It was never finished, and old construction cranes are nearly rusted in their poised positions outside the palace walls. I find it ironic that Saddam never completed either the palace or his "victory" over America before he was executed. The scaffolding and rusty cranes give a strange tribute to that fact. I passed that palace whenever I "went into town," which meant the large adjacent camp.

AL FAW PALACE

Al Faw Palace, or the Birthday Palace, is the most spectacular of the BIAP palaces. It sits out in the middle of the lake and had a dungeon, a gold medallion above the huge door, an enormous ballroom, and a chandelier second in size only to one in England. This huge palace, built to commemorate a battle victory over Iran, was where Saddam had his lavish birthday celebrations. Its overstuffed throne was the site of many photo ops, and I piled onto it with some female Ugandan officers and a female Korean-American captain while we squished together and grinned for the camera. I hope nothing rubbed off on us.

It had a small, private elevator that would fit about three people, presumably Saddam and two bodyguards. Next to the private elevator is a ladder leading to the roof; from the top you can see across to the center of Baghdad. We had camp-wide church services at Al Faw, as the ballroom was big enough to hold hundreds. Oh, the privilege of making music that speaks of freedom, love, and worship in a place where a madman worshipped only himself and demanded that others follow suit!

The most fascinating aspect of the birthday palace is what is written in elaborate plaster on the walls and ceilings. When we were working on putting together the historical tour that got 86'd, we filmed the inside of the palace. The Army hoped we would produce a DVD as part of the tour. Kahloud, the female terp who helped us, translated the musings of Mr. Hussein, who fancied himself a gifted poet.

Saddam's initials are everywhere in the buildings—carved into the tops of pillars, painted in gold as a kind of chair rail around the middle of a dining room, painted on ceiling tiles. Illustrative of Saddam's megalomania and insecurity was a railing decorated with stylized open hearts with his initials in the middle. I guess the guy was afraid that someone would forget him, let alone not find him lovable. I hope that one hundred years from now his evil is remembered as a warning and his effect is no longer felt anywhere.

A great deal of the decorative plasterwork in Al Faw is devoted to Saddam's self-descriptions: "Saddam the Warrior," "Saddam the Engineer," "Saddam the One Who Gets Things Done No Matter What," "Saddam the Brave," "Saddam the Jealous." (Kahloud explained that jealousy in the Arab culture is seen as a positive attribute, as it inspires one to reach goals.) In the bedroom wing, however is the most interesting stuff. I don't know if the guy ever had any regrets about his butchery or whether he was so mentally fragmented that he thought he was the embodiment of maturity, integrity, and justice; I think it was probably the latter. The prose captured here as part of the decorating scheme, loosely translated, indicates that a man's actions, whether good or evil, will come to light. Another inscription explains that you can look into the eyes of a man and know whether he is good or evil.

Now this is the guy, who, according to a mistress, used to look at himself in the mirror and say, "I am Saddam. Heil Hitler." She also says that the assassination attempt on Uday's life that was allegedly orchestrated by Saddam was "for his [Uday's] own good," according to his father. I wonder if, as Saddam was heading for his final meeting with his Maker, he ever thought back to when Uday and Qusay were just toddlers who would probably run to the door when he came home from "work" and want to wrestle with their daddy. I wonder if Saddam ever mulled over the possibility that he had created monsters or if he ever realized that he himself was a monster. Truly he did a spectacular job of hosting The Monster Ball.

The system of lakes and canals, whose abundant water is a proof of wealth in the desert, was dug within about six weeks, according to a marble sign that names the engineers and describes the project. When it came time to fill them with water, Saddam just turned off the water to the rest of Baghdad! In the middle of the artificial lakes were tiny artificial islands. More than one soldier, one of whom was an eyewitness, said that both women and men were taken out to the islands to be used for target practice. Another manifestation of evil for sport.

SADDAM'S HUNTING LODGE

The first building I worked in was formerly Saddam's hunting lodge. It was beautiful, with a raised dome, and a band of stained glass nuggets just under the dome whose prism light would grace our walls and floors as the sun made its journey through the day. Of course it had a chandelier (all hunting lodges need a chandelier to complete the ambience, you know) and carved doors and ceilings, as well as the ever-present elegant ceiling plasterwork with Saddam's initials.

Most of the buildings had a disproportionate number of bathrooms for buildings their size; sometimes there were rows of them. The buildings were almost always used for prostitution, and bathing right after having sex is a necessity in the Muslim world due to being unclean. The hunting lodge, which was comparatively small, originally had four bathrooms.

In Iraq I saw many things that I have no desire to discuss. However, failing to bring this stuff out into the light would be, for me, tantamount to keeping the horrors of Dachau and Auschwitz from the American people after the camps were liberated and the evil exposed. In Dachau there are signs in several languages that say "Never again."

I tell you about these horrors to give you an opportunity to say in your own heart "Never again" rather than "the war is lost" or, even worse, that our soldiers are "Nazis." These are the opinions of senators who owe their right to be so slanderous to the very soldiers that they slander on the Senate floor, emboldening our enemies.

When I first arrived in country, there was still water in an alligator pit across the street from the hunting lodge. There had been a suspension system across the pit, and Saddam's goons used to suspend people from it for the gators to snack on. They would also take pictures, which were hung in the building right across from me. The pictures were down by the time I got there, but I know people who have seen them. I have two bricks from the alligator pit on my living room bookcase, and on one brick is a stone which I found loose in a barb-wired wall in Dachau. On the other brick is a menorah, the Jewish candlestick. The bricks and rocks are grim keepsakes, to be sure, but they serve as my own personal "Never again" signs.

I spoke at length with a guy who had been on the Delta team that took the area during the assault phase. When they were on the run from the Republican Guard on the way to their rendezvous point, they let out the gators to put some distance between them and their pursuers and quickly tried to see if they could clear the hunting lodge on their way to the waiting helicopter. He would not tell me all the things that he saw in the hunting lodge, except for this one vile scene, which apparently wasn't the worst of it. They found a dead woman tied to a bed; she had bled out because her nipples had been cut off. The room where she was found now houses the Morale computer center, a place where folks can e-mail home and tell their families that they love them. Sometimes I would stand in there when no one was there and just try to imagine what life was like for these people, especially the women.

UDAY'S HUNTING LODGE
AND THE PALACE OF DEATH

The creepiest place of all was at the restricted base, which had largely been Uday's hangout. It housed what was known by the locals as the Palace of Death and unofficially as the Mistress Palace. It's not clear which of Saddam's mistresses it might have been named for, as there were several. According to the locals, when people were summoned to this palace, there was no way they were coming out alive or maybe even at all. The area's reputation was so chilling to the locals that it had an almost voodoo-esque effect upon them. At first no Iraqis wanted to work there because they so feared its past. It would be almost like trying to hire Jews to work at Treblinka after the Soviets liberated it.

I worked in the hunting lodge there, another lovely building with green marble interior walls and suspended across a canal. There were doves everywhere, and I used to enjoy their coos while dancing by myself up on the rooftop at sunrise. Just up the stream from the hunting lodge was what was known as the Rape House, which was also suspended across the stream. We were told that willing sexual partners got to be done in in style in the Palace, and unwilling sexual partners were taken to the Rape House. Either way, depending on Uday's mood, afterward they could be taken to the nearby lion cages and fed to the cats while Uday and/or his buddies watched. Talk about a reality snuff series. Twenty-seven women were known to have been forced into prostitution there, and they just vanished. Their bodies were not among the 105 bodies found in the stream down from our building when Coalition forces took the area.

Uday also hunted humans there. So-called offenders could possibly be freed on one condition. They were given a head start, and then the game of "hide-and-seek-for-keeps" would begin. If they avoided being Uday's prey, they would be let go. Maybe. You never knew with that guy.

Uday was just twenty-one when he became the maniacal director of the Iraqi Olympic teams. When the Coalition took Baghdad, cages were found under the stadium where soccer players had been kept chained for days at a time and tortured. Cuts were made in their skin and human feces smeared into the cuts to cause infection. Sometimes they were dragged around on pavement with their bare backs, then forced to roll in the sand. Sometimes spikes were closed on them so they would be punctured. They were forced to kick a concrete "ball" around the yard and were whipped with steel cables for losing a game or even for winning but not playing as well as Uday thought they should. One never knew what would kindle his wrath. One Olympian escaped to Hungary and blew the whistle to the International Olympic Committee. He blistered the IOC for a full thirty minutes in a formal meeting for turning a blind eye and failing to act on the behalf of Iraqi Olympians.

Another Iraqi Olympian was in the U.S. for the 1996 games in Atlanta. The sight of President Clinton applauding all of the teams inspired him to defect. It seems odd that people would want to risk coming to America if it is indeed the source of all the world's ills, as some of our citizens and politicians, as well as our international enemies, seem to think. Why not go to North Korea, for example, where they could be taken care of handsomely by the Dear Leader?

We were told that a loop of rebar on the ceiling indicated that the room had been used for torture, as some of the "best" torture requires the presence of suspended bodies. Such rooms were found throughout all of BIAP, but there were no torture devices in the elegant ones. We wouldn't want to risk staining the bordello furniture, would we?

Some people were dismayed that TV showed the bodies of al-Zarqawi, Saddam, Uday, and Qusay after they died. While we might find the sight unnecessary, if we had been forced to have our faces surgically changed to look like evil incarnate, wouldn't we want absolute proof of death? The Iraqi people were so afraid that it was the doubles who had been killed and not the real guys that it was decided by the Coalition to show their corpses on the Arabic and western networks. Even after Saddam's hanging, many Iraqis were terrified that it was a double who had gotten the noose and that America would leave and Saddam would re-emerge. However, I think Saddam's verbal spewage down to his last seconds served to convince most of those who had suffered under him and his sons that this part of the nightmare was over forever.

SADDAM'S FISHING LODGE

The thing that made "Evil Eden" truly beautiful again was knowing that the buildings were now being used for redemptive purposes, including clinics, stores, and college classrooms. To try to end your tour on a positive note, I have to comment on the fishing lodge, which the assault phase chaplain chose to be the chapel. I hope you can appreciate the irony of discussing Yeshua's instructing his disciples to become "fishers of men" in the same building where Saddam used to hire someone to put fish in his bathtub so he could catch them for a trophy. Everyone worshipped there—Catholics, Protestants, Jews, Muslims—according to the dictates of their own consciences.

Hands down, my happiest times with the soldiers and other contractors were here. It was the scene of such joy and breakthrough. It was here that a Sunni terp got up and thanked the U.S. for invading his country. It was here that I saw people who had been running away from God's love decide to surrender to it. It was here that I forged bonds with people I will love literally forever.

The fishing lodge is located near where the Iraqi Central Command is headquartered. Sometimes the Iraqi officers would stand on the bridge so they could hear the music from the various choirs and praise bands. I hope it comforted them and gave them strength to keep pressing ahead to make Iraq free for all, forever.

This concludes our tour, ladies and gentlemen, and we thank you for your kind attention. You may use either exit, and as you do, please put your trash labeled "it's all about oil" in the appropriate receptacle. Thank you, and please come back and visit us again real soon.

CHAPTER 9

Life in the Land of Two Rivers

C harles Dickens began his famous novel *A Tale of Two Cities* with the classic line, "It was the best of times, it was the worst of times." This describes my nearly three years in Iraq, except that the "best of times" consistently outweighed anything else. I wish I could just get the hard stuff out of the way and go on to the fun, but that is not how life is anywhere. The best and the worst flow like the two ancient rivers that define Iraq—the Tigris and the Euphrates. Any attempt to eliminate one in favor of the other distorts the geography of my personal landscape, and my desire is to tell the truth as I observed and experienced it.

Everything in a combat zone is more intense: the good is "gooder," and the bad is "badder." Human nobility and selfishness are magnified, particularly in the realm of leadership and its effect on those in one's sphere. The soldiers, Iraqis, and contractors all experienced some of the finest and some of the worst leadership imaginable, and we celebrated one and grieved over the other.

When people ask me, "What was the hardest part about being there?" I have to say it was my own naiveté. I had expected that the wartime camaraderie that had been my father's portion as a WWII Naval Air Corps officer would *automatically* occur in Iraq. I simply assumed that because we were all in a combat zone together, we would really be watching each other's backs. I could not have been more mistaken. I was ill-prepared for the amount and intensity of the backstabbing, lying, gossip, politics, bullying, and manipulation that seemed to negatively energize a few civilian coworkers, some in positions of leadership. Conversely, I am delighted to report that I did get to feast on a level of fellowship, support, friendship, protection, and adventure that proved to me over and over that the negative stuff could not do its wicked work unless I let it. All of it made me stronger.

Besides the determination to faithfully tell the Stories of the Sandbox, my greatest takeaway from my time in Iraq was recognizing the need to improve my own leadership skills. I had always valued leadership, but it wasn't until I saw just how much difference a good leader could make, especially in a dangerous situation, that I saw the need to raise the bar in my own life. One man who was temporarily the camp manager turned the place around in about two days. It went from being a miserable place for everyone to a place where people sang on the walkie-talkie-style camp radio and constantly helped each other out. I want to be like this guy when I grow up.

As I look back, I marvel at how many times when I had "had it" and wanted to go straight to the airport to head home, there would be an e-mail, some snail mail, or a lunchtime conversation that would be exactly what I needed to get back in the ring. I am forever grateful to all who spoke into my life during those times. Pursuing joy in the midst of other people's power trips was rewarding, and I realized that I could only lose if I chose to give in to unforgiveness or bitterness.

Even so, I sometimes felt like I was going to have to permanently bury my teeth in my tongue to keep from saying something ill-advised, and the porta-potties became my tiny "cities of refuge" to which I would flee if I felt tears threatening to emerge. Desperate times called for desperate measures, and I learned to be deeply grateful for those odorous confession cells. Our Human Resource Department officially determined that I was in more than one "hostile workplace environment" and liberated me by sending me to facilities which were run by truly wonderful bosses. For this I was eternally thankful as well.

What made me ache even more was seeing the soldiers go through the same thing—that is, being in a combat zone and wondering if your true enemies were the ones you ate with. It's one thing to deal with people's petty, insecure dishonest nonsense in a combat zone behind the relative safety of T walls—the tall, portable, protective barrier units that create an instant fortress—but it's another thing entirely when you are outside the wire and your very life depends on the same guy who has been verbally dogging you and seemingly doing everything possible to make your life miserable. Now *that's* stress.

The other thing that made me ache was when fellow contractors as well as soldiers had trouble at home. It was so difficult to see someone get off the computer or phone, be able to tell that things were a mess, and know that they had to go straight outside the wire into harm's way. If only people at home could understand how they were endangering their loved ones with their tantrums, selfishness, or infidelity, maybe they'd back up and change direction.

There are some spouses to whom I would like to say, "Honey, I hope you can live with the fact that from nine thousand miles away you compromised the safety of hundreds of people by thoroughly beating up your husband/wife emotionally so he/she couldn't completely focus on the mission." I know a chaplain who would like to see a way for spouses to cool their mouths in jail for that kind of behavior, and I understand why he feels that way.

I saw guys deal with being dumped for another man or their wife being pregnant with some other guy's child, super tough things going on with their kids that they could do nothing about from Iraq, women getting dumped for someone else, and spouses completely cleaning them out financially and splitting. One guy's wife unknowingly took up with some creep who was wanted for murder, and this good guy had to go home to rescue his daughters.

I also got to see communications technology work its magic: beaming faces after Instant Message sessions that required typing at the speed of light, laughs that could not be stifled, the announcement of a pregnancy, good news with the kids at home. Life in the States was flying through cyberspace at warp speed and touching all of us. One guy found a way to broadcast live the high school graduation of several soldiers' kids, and we held "graduation" in our MWR tent. One of my favorite moments was letting a soldier use my Segovia satellite phone account so he could coach his wife while she was giving birth . . . while Saddam was being held a few hundred feet away from him—a truly wild and wonderful situation.

Soldiers helped contractors get through their challenges, and contractors helped soldiers get through theirs. This occasionally became a problem if someone decided that "crossing the aisle" between soldier and civilian was not politically expedient. However, by and large, folks who cared about each other didn't pay much attention to who was in civvy clothing and who was in camos, especially at church. If someone was grieving, we all grieved, and if someone was rejoicing, we all rejoiced.

The passion of the MWR contractors was giving the soldiers a chance to get a break, and there was something for everyone. So many of the good times resulted from folks finding creative ways to have fun. For example, on Fridays we used to have an event called "Closest to the Pin" which was started at our camp by my MWR supervisor, Prince McJunkins, and spread to other camps. The event was open to everyone, and it was one of the times when civilians and soldiers came together to play. The object was to see how closely players could hit a golf ball which had been set on a tee just outside of Uday Hussein's former hotel to a flagged pin in a field; winners got the pizza of their choice. Never before in the history of warfare has it been possible to fly a truck through a mini Red Zone, put in an order at a mobile Pizza Hut, and zip back to deliver it to the winner before it got cold.

We had every imaginable type of tournament: chess, pool, Ping-Pong, arm wrestling (until someone's arm got broken), football, baseball, basketball, and soccer. There were weight lifting contests, boxing matches, and country, swing, salsa, and hip hop dances. Some contractors spent hundreds of dollars purchasing awards out of their own pockets, even though technically they weren't supposed to. It was just too important to make sure that life in the Sandbox was as close to home as possible for the ones who were so far away from home and who were making our lives as safe as possible.

We timed races and made award certificates, flyers, and calendars. Some of my coworkers were truly gifted as graphic artists, and they turned out amazing desktop graphics at a moment's notice. Their artwork really jazzed up the décor. What a difference the addition of color makes when all of life is sandy!

When the weather turned cold, we wanted to provide coffee for the soldiers at the Rec Center, but not all the necessary supplies came with permission to make it happen, so we became "procurement specialists." The practical application of this job description was stuffing enough coffee cups and creamer into our jackets while in line at the Dfac to stock the MWR coffee station until someone with authority could figure out which fund MWR coffee was supposed to come from. Until we got cups, our subcontractors—workers from India, Nepal, Sri Lanka, or the Philippines—used the bottoms of clean, empty water bottles to make do. "Adapt and overcome; it's the Army way" never had a better application. Working for MWR could also require sharpening our lobbying skills. Once I went to the mayor's cell (the Army's version of a camp Town Hall), presented the case for the need for cups in which to actually serve the coffee, and got a letter that essentially said, "Back off and let MWR take what they need. They're doing their job." This was a small and pleasurable victory.

One soldier was going to be a daddy for the first time and was scheduled to arrive back in Germany on his wife's due date. Coaching birth is one of my all-time favorite things to do, so I bought books and a video to practice with the soldier so he could help her as she delivered. He arrived in Germany when her contractions were about two minutes apart, and they went straight to the hospital and had the baby. Definitely not in my job description, but how incredibly satisfying to give really important support to a new family!

There were other supremely satisfying moments: driving an ambulance to a nearby hospital so the EMT could be in back with the patient, helping someone write a newspaper article that was published throughout the theater, being part of a military/civilian food fight that was so subtle no one could tell what was going on, and making music for church services. It was worth going through all the hassle of requesting permission, having permission denied, and finally having a Colonel convince the Assistant Project Manager that "serving the Client" (aka the Army) justifiably included the military using my musical skills on demand. Making music was my chief joy. A close second was giving and receiving hugs.

It was also rewarding to see the American people express their gratitude to the soldiers. Grand Ole Opry concerts that were part of the "America Supports You" campaign were broadcast on Armed Forces Network (AFN), and country music stars such as Toby Keith and Charlie Daniels made numerous trips to Iraq to sing for the soldiers. Sherry Pezzaniti, a woman from my town in Alabama, made "Honor Bags," tiny handmade denim beanbags tied with yellow ribbons, stamped with an expression of thanks, and individually numbered. She wanted to get one to each person serving in Iraq and Afghanistan, and I passed out hundreds in my camp. Her project started when she had a dream where she saw a homeless Viet Nam vet and told him that if she had anything to do with it, the tragic disregard for the soldiers of that era would never happen again.

The gifts generously sent over for the holidays are described in chapter 18, "Have Yourself a Merry Little . . . ," and the sheer amount of donations was staggering. But I think that the soldiers appreciated it just as much when for no special reason, other than they cared, people sent things as simple as toothbrushes and toenail clippers. Letters from children got the soldiers howling with laughter or made them misty-eyed, and we would post these literary treasures on the walls for all to enjoy.

What really got me was when soldiers would share their stuff with contractors or subcontractors. It's true that we supported them and they needed us, but they were the ones who were risking their lives for us. It was a completely different scene than when as a protester I tried to shut down Wright-Patterson Air Force Base! I am so grateful for being given a second chance, and words seem inadequate to convey what a great time I had in Iraq and what a privilege it was to live among such amazing people.

I have come to truly bless the hard times, as they exposed my weaknesses and selfishness and made me take a probing look at myself. I had to decide to change if I was going to end up differently than so many of my generation. What amazing grace has been poured on me to have a chance to do just that. I have never been treated so well or so poorly. I have never experienced such verbal cruelty or greater appreciation. I also have never been given a greater chance to grow more quickly, and by that same grace I'll keep on growing.

I will always treasure the good times as well. The laughter, the affection, and the "can do/will do" spirit of civilians, contractors, Iraqis, and soldiers alike are things that I will never forget; they are safely tucked away in my spiritual rucksack for when I need them. One day I'll be able to tell my grandbabies, "Once upon a time, long ago, your very own Gramali got to be a part of something truly grand in the midst of an ancient desert so hot that the door handles literally burned our hands. . . ."

While writing this chapter I talked to Karen Koenders, founder of Moms on a Mission, one of several organizations founded by regular folks who so sacrificially supported us, the soldiers and contractors. Karen and her husband have literally spent thousands out of their own pocket to support our soldiers. She asked me point-blank if I would ever go back to Iraq. I exploded, "In a heartbeat!!!" and she knew I meant it. I told her that if I had the slightest inkling that it was what I was supposed to do, I'd get on a plane tomorrow. She said she wished she could do the same.

At this writing I have been home for almost a year, and my longing to be a part of all that was grand about Operation Iraqi Freedom has not in any way abated. *I miss Iraq, and I hope I never get to the place that I don't.*

CHAPTER 10

Terp Tales

nterpeters, or "terps" as they are affectionately referred to in Armyspeak, are the unsung heroes of the entire campaign. They are contractors, male and female, from all over world. They are Christian, Muslim, or nothing, or backslidden from either faith. They risk their lives every day with the soldiers outside the wire, spend hours trying to untie the tangled knots of detainee alibis, and help determine whether someone is lying and whether or not a detainee was just in the wrong place at the wrong time and needs to be released.

Although they are paid well, no amount of money could recompense them for the job they do and the risks they take. Their stories are as varied as the countries they come from. Some were tortured under Saddam's regime. Some could see what was coming and got out just before Saddam's rule was absolute. One has spent thousands getting the rest of his family out ever since and couldn't let his remaining brother and sister know he was in Baghdad—too dangerous.

One narrowly escaped the gassing at Halabja in 1988. Some had escaped genocide in the Sudan. Some had been born and raised in America and were the children of privilege, their parents having been educated in the West. Some were born and raised in Baghdad, and until 2003 they had known only the gospel according to Mr. Hussein. They were tall, short, shy, confident, thin, chunky, parents, married, single, divorced, athletic, idealistic, wary. They all wanted to help. Unless they had a passionate belief in the future of Iraq, it was way past dumb to be a terp.

I loved them from the get-go, and these are their stories, which I promised I would tell.

IMAN

When I first arrived and was living in a tent, I noticed a lovely, quiet woman who lived with us, her cot located on the other end of the tent from mine. Our tent was built for twelve, but at times as many as twenty-two of us were jammed together, thus causing us to involuntarily perform our best imitation of sardines. The population would reduce as troops rotated out, and we would go back to the normal level, which was about half contractor, half soldier. It was during the time when we had a bit more breathing room that we finally met.

"Hi, I'm Ali, and I just wanted to introduce myself."

"Hi, I'm Iman, and I have been watching you. You are sweet and kind."

"Oh, man," I thought as I thanked her. Sweet and kind is truly all I want to be, but boy, do I fall short.

Her assessment had come from observing me dealing with some difficult tentmates, both of whom ended up getting sent home for things that had nothing to do with me. If there is one thing I learned while I was in Iraq, it was that civility spoke powerful volumes. I came home with a deepened desire to keep a civil tongue in my head, as the saying from a bygone era goes.

One morning Iman and I met in the MWR center, and she told me her story. She had grown up in a Muslim family in Baghdad, the middle child of six or seven kids.

When she was eight, she had a dream about Jesus. He appeared to her and told her He loved her. She didn't tell anyone, but this went on for years. She would have dreams or visions of Him, and she talked to Him as though He were her best friend. When she came to America, she had the opportunity to worship and grow in her faith that no longer needed to remain a secret. She married, had one child, and divorced. She didn't talk much about the divorce, but it was clear that her son, Joseph, was her life. She was paying for Joseph's college while in Iraq, and she missed him terribly.

I lost track of her while working at another camp for sixteen months, but when I returned to Camp Victory I spotted her near the bus stop. After many hugs and Arabic kisses on the cheek, we quickly got caught up and agreed to meet soon. A few days later she came to visit me at work, and we had tea. At my request, my mother sent me boxes of tea, and I often made pots of tea for the soldiers, telling them it was from my mom. I saved my favorite Market Spice Tea from the Public Market in Seattle for special occasions like this reunion with Iman. As it was wintertime and cold, the spicy, fragrant tea tasted especially good and seemed to warm more than just our innards.

Iman raved about the tea, ached about how outwardly tough she had to seem to those she was interrogating, and told me her latest secret: she was engaged! Sometimes she would get scared about the prospect of marrying again. I could relate, having been through a divorce myself. Finally she took the plunge, wildly happy that she did so. Her groom was an American soldier, and as the odd state of affairs in the twenty-first century would decree, not long after their honeymoon, he returned to the States, awaiting his bride, and she stayed on the front lines. In about another year she went home to her man and her son, and if I know her, she struggles as do I with being so happy at home yet still wanting to help Iraq in person.

KAHLOUD

Kahloud, like Iman, was beautiful and divorced, but with no children. She was originally from Jordan and had gone to the States as a teenager. She was quiet and had lively, piercing eyes. She couldn't talk about her job much, as she had a super-high security clearance and worked in the palace. However, she volunteered to help film the inside of the palace with us and translate the poetry written on the ceilings and walls for and by Saddam.

Kahloud, my MWR co-worker and friend Matt Bullington, and I were working on a historical tour as an MWR activity; a major by the name of David May made it possible for Kahloud to assist us. She, more than anyone, helped me to understand Saddam Hussein, if such a thing is actually possible. She always seemed lonely, and I wanted to make the ache that seemed to be buried deep beneath her graciousness to go away. She wasn't much interested in remarrying, and I wondered how bad it had been. I must admit, I want for Kahloud the same happy ending Iman and I had—a marvelous second chance at marital happiness. After all she has done for us, she deserves it.

BENI

Beni was a true Abu, or father, and was a favorite of the Special Forces guys with whom he worked. He was taller than the average Iraqi and had a shock of gray hair, dry sense of humor, and twinkling eyes. He had been raised a Christian, as is the case with many terps. He had left Baghdad when he was only seventeen, just before Saddam took total power. At the time he urged his family to get out, but for a while they just ignored him. However, as Saddam's madness settled in, they began to see that Beni's predictions regarding "Uncle Saddam" were accurate.

Beni was a mechanic in the States, and while mechanics in our country are not usually thought of as wealthy, he scrimped and saved and paid over fifty thousand dollars to get his family out to safety. Most of them had settled in Sweden, but he still had one brother and one sister left in Baghdad. It was so dangerous for him to come back to Iraq that at first he couldn't even let his siblings know he was anywhere in the area.

He had fascinating stories about growing up in Baghdad. His dad had been a freedom fighter in the fifties and had been a friend of recently elected Iraqi President Talibani. His mother was a midwife of such excellent reputation that Muslims from all over Baghdad would come to her to deliver their children. Her "clinic" was in a spare room in their home, and Beni would sometimes come home from school to the distinctive sounds of labor and delivery. She was a fanatic about cleanliness, he told me, and she really knew her stuff. She delivered literally thousands of babies. Sometimes she would go to other peoples' homes to deliver, but she really preferred her own place so that things could be clean to her satisfaction.

Beni once took me exploring some disused buildings that had been in Uday's stomping grounds. A stream had once run through the middle of one; another had had gorgeous woven patterns of raffia rope in the ceilings; several had beautiful tile mosaics; all had the ubiquitous Italian marble. We would wonder out loud what kinds of things had gone on here. While we were out on our "field trip," what sounded like an IED went off in the distance, and it was particularly loud. As always was the case when explosions occurred, we looked around to make sure we were still in one piece and then went on. There simply was no other way of dealing with it.

Over time, Beni had an opportunity to interact more with Iraqis outside the wire, and finally he made contact with his remaining family, whom he had not seen since the early seventies, though it was still terribly dangerous for him to do so. He met a young woman who decided that he was going to marry her and was not about to take no for an answer. She called his cell phone dozens of times a day; while on the one hand it was amusing, on the other it underscored how desperate women are to be treated kindly throughout the Middle East. There was never a time that I went through Dubai that I wasn't approached by workers from the Philippines or India begging me to get them out of there. How I wanted to!

I asked Beni if he saw any future with this woman, and he said no. He still wanted to help her, but the trick was to somehow convey the fact that kindness didn't mean romantic interest. Ever the tenderhearted one, he longed to be able to take the leftover food that the soldiers didn't eat and give it away. We all wanted to, but the problem was that if some food had gone bad and someone got sick, we could be accused of trying to poison them. Once Beni sent out an e-mail discussing the plight of a single mom, asking for folks in the States to send whatever they could in the form of money, clothing, and toys. I know Beni would be just the type of Abu that would make sure they got every penny, and then some.

SAL

When I first met Sal, he was twenty-seven years old. He was short, powerfully built—especially for an Iraqi, and soft-spoken, with kind green eyes. He was an Olympic-quality soccer player and as a kid had played on two of Uday's teams. When Uday was in charge of the Olympics, he was maniacal about Iraq's status in the world of soccer, and he invested heavily in what would be the equivalent of Little League teams for soccer. It was from this pool that Uday would draw to build his dream team, and recruits had no choice about participating. (See chapter 8.)

Sal was gentle and polite nearly to a fault, and he was the one who told me about the things that had happened to the Iraqi Olympians on Uday's watch. I could tell he didn't want to sully me with the details of Uday's barbarism, but cleaning up after Uday was a part of why he had come. As a Baptist of deep faith, he was glad to see his former country set free from the Butcher and his Boyz.

When Sal was seventeen, he was hot in the world of Baghdad soccer, and by the age of eighteen he would have been conscripted into the Olympic team. It was well known that if the Iraq team lost, the players would be tortured, regardless of how well they had played. Sal's parents knew that they had to get him out of Iraq. After his junior year in high school, he moved with his family to California. He knew no English—a fact I found amazing while listening to him only ten years later. Not only did he become the captain of his high school soccer team, but they won a championship and he was drafted to play professionally in Canada.

Sal had desperately wanted to coach the Iraqis when MWR sponsored the Iraqi-Coalition soccer tournament you'll read about in chapter 21, but he was going to be home arranging for his marriage. I know that he would have loved the chance to play the game that was his passion for the first time in a context where former enemies were treating each other as brothers. It's probably a good thing that he *didn't* coach the Iraqis, or the final score would have been a worse spanking for the Coalition than it was.

ALEX

Alex was the son of an aerospace engineer and had lived in Europe, the Middle East and the U.S. He was about the same age as Sal and had been in the States for about the same amount of time. Home for him, as for many other terps, was Dearborn, Michigan. He was Muslim, and we had some fascinating conversations regarding "the religion of peace."

Alex helped me practice my pitiful Arabic and gave me a treasure that I doubt he would value himself. One day I asked him to write on a 3x5 card the phrase "fear not," one of my favorites of Yeshua's sayings. I wanted to have it to look at and remind myself of my personal goal of defeating fear in my life—all unhealthy fear, that is. I am not planning on bungee jumping any time soon.

PETER

Peter was from the Sudan and exuded the unmistakable graciousness of Africans. He spoke many languages besides English and Arabic and embodied benevolent mystery. He was fascinated and warmed by my personal love for Mozambique, developed while visiting there on R and R. I had stayed with a friend at an orphanage in Maputo, and, as is the case with Iraq, I would go back to Africa in a heartbeat. I regaled Peter with stories of watching the animals in Kruger National Park in South Africa, and he smiled as he said, "Ah, Africa, the place where man and animals live in the same place *almost* the way God intended them to." He wanted to start an orphanage of his own someday, and I was so glad to be able to help him network with people who could help him get started.

What was happening in the Sudan, of course, was wrenching to the Africans in Iraq. As a Christian, Peter was sad that no one had paid much attention to the slaughter of Christians that had gone on for years before the Hollywood A-list made Darfur a household word for the slaughter of Muslims. How warmed I was by his plan to return to his country someday and shelter the children who were orphaned by the bloodletting.

TONY

Originally from Egypt, Tony was probably the oldest of the terps—I would guess in his late sixties—and was the doting father of two grown children. I met him while I was working on the base where Saddam was being held. While we were both Christians, we were from very different traditions, his being Orthodox and mine not being a part of a system at all. We disagreed on most things except the important ones—who Jesus was and what He did. I am sure I rattled his cage at times, and he frustrated me with his traditions that, to me, put God in a box. We agreed to disagree and remained friends.

What I loved the most about Tony was that he came out of retirement, faced health issues, and came over because he wanted to help. When I think of him, I smile.

ZACH

Zach was from Atlanta. He was born in Iraq and had come to the States as a small boy. He drove his mother crazy with his "modern" viewpoints, and sometimes he would take them out for a spin with me, I think just to see my reaction. He would show me pictures from outside the wire or back in Atlanta and wait for me to say, "I am sure your mom loves that one," rolling my eyes at him as is a mother's hard-earned right. "Oh, Al," he'd say, then elbow me, "you're as bad as she is." Zach came back over to Iraq because he saw that in the early days of the war, people were getting hurt or killed because they couldn't understand each other. He realized that since he was completely bicultural and bilingual, he could help. Zach had one of the most dangerous jobs of all the terps I knew who went outside the wire, and I hope he doesn't tell his mom about 95 percent of the things he experienced.

KAL

Kal had one of the more dramatic life stories prior to returning to Iraq. A married Muslim with two children, he had tried to overthrow Saddam right after the Gulf War. Considering the ferocity with which Saddam crushed the rebellion, it is a miracle Kal escaped. He wandered around the desert for three days and had no idea where he was. He was finally picked up by some guys that he thought just might kill him. Mercifully, however, they took him to a Saudi refugee camp, where he lived for three and a half years under dreadful conditions. He never gave up on his dream of coming to America, and through a series of events that would take up a book of their own, he made it to Dearborn, Michigan. He said he came over because he wanted to give back to the nation that had given him his freedom and wanted Iraq to finally have hers.

LAZAR

By the time I met Lazar, he had interviewed twenty-eight *thousand* detainees. He was a master at giving them a vision for the future of Iraq, and his specialty was showing them how stupid it was to fight each other when deep down they all wanted the same thing: freedom. He would give them a going-away speech that rivaled that of any coach, and he had the personal satisfaction of knowing he had turned around several kids who had just gotten caught up in the pathos but didn't know many of the facts. He was unwavering in his passion to see Iraq make it.

BASSAM

Bassam was an ex-officer from the Air Force of Jordan, my favorite Middle Eastern country of my travels. He lived in El Paso, coincidentally near some friends with whom we had worked at the orphanage. Bassam was even familiar with the location of the orphanage where Steve and I had lived. Sometimes the "small world" factor I encountered in Iraq was uncanny.

Bassam embodied kindness and had a quirky sense of humor. He was Muslim, married to a Christian, and greatly embarrassed by terrorism. We were also both embarrassed by Anna Nicole Smith, whose death so dominated the news that Iraqis were wondering who in the world she was and why she was so important. We were wondering the same thing, but it fell to Bassam to try to explain to Iraqis the American obsession with the woman. We were both sorry that she chosen to live such a broken life, had died such a sad death, and had left behind an innocent baby who became a custody football. But to have her be such an iconic, distorted representation of our culture was frustrating to both of us.

Bassam left a good job back in the States to come help, and his kindness to me was a great strength. I hope our paths cross again, which is what I would like for all the terps who came into my life, except one. Everyone wondered if one terp from the Sudan was a sympathizer/collaborator. Interrogators hated working with this one and did everything they could to avoid it. Let's just say that entitlement exuded from every pore, and my hackles would go up on the inside as I dealt with one powerful bad vibe. I hope that this terp got sent home, as the rest did not deserve to have their safety compromised.

MIKE

Mike was from Egypt and was married to an American woman. He adored his kids and couldn't wait to get back to them, but as was the case with all of the terps, he had to feel like he had completed his part of the mission before he went back. He helped me understand the Middle East better than anyone else I met while in Iraq.

He was an expert in Islamofascism, and I got the feeling he was assigned to deal with some of the tougher guys. There was nothing imposing about his size or appearance, but he had an iron will, a quick wit, and an insatiable desire for truth. He told me things about terrorist groups that made my hair stand on end.

He also explained the passive as well as active aspects of jihad and the dovetailing strategies of both. Briefly stated, there are two strategies in jihad. When jihadists are in the minority in a culture, then Islam is portrayed as the "religion of peace," and it becomes a psy-ops operation to indoctrinate those around them for as long as it takes. When jihadists are in the majority position in a culture, then the more familiar strong-arm terror techniques are used to intimidate infidels into submission. Sometimes both strategies are used simultaneously in order to destabilize a culture or region. Mike also greatly increased my understanding of some jihadists' in-your-face goal of global domination and their desire to replace common law with sharia law. Sobering stuff, this.

As of June 2008, Mike's brother, a policeman working in Egypt, was being held in prison on false charges. This caused Mike great concern, and he asked that we pray for both his brother's safety and his release from prison.

DENNIS

I have saved the two terps with the most remarkable stories for last, as their stories are like the fine wine saved for last at the wedding feast. Neither man should be alive, let alone want to set foot in Iraq ever again. The fact that they would risk their lives after what they had been through is one of the many reasons that I am so inspired by the terps.

I once read a book by Dr. Paul Pearsall, a psychologist who studied survivors of Nazi extermination camps, and I was fascinated to find that there were survivors who lived a life of such joy that their families honestly thought they were nuts. One family was considering having their joyful mother committed. These "super-joyeurs," with numbers tattooed on their arms, were brimming with joy and purpose, having lived through hell itself. Pearsall was one of the first people to take the idea of a mind-body connection out of the category of "way out there" and bring it into the mainstream.

A terp named Dennis was my personal example of such triumphant joy, and when I am tempted to complain, I think of him and the impact he had on me. One day this jolly little man came into our building to use the computer. He was short, a bit rotund, nearly bald with a fringe of snow-white hair, bespectacled, and beaming. "Good day!" he said with a smile, and already my day was better from his greeting. Quite a few days later I asked him to tell me a little about himself, but I was quite unprepared for what I was about to hear.

Without a bit of drama or self-pity, he told me of being tortured by Saddam's sadists. Somehow Saddam had gotten it into his head that Dennis was working for the CIA and decided to torture him until he confessed to whatever Saddam thought he was up to. Dennis was nothing more than a business man who traveled internationally, but if Saddam got it in his mind that someone was a spy, his means of interrogating were often lethal.

Dennis was spun from a ceiling fan for eleven days running. I don't know how his system endured that and why he didn't die just from dizziness. From time to time his tormentors would skewer him, and then for grins they poured salt water on him. After eleven days of trying to get something out of him, they decided to let him go.

Terps are subjected to psychological screening before they come to Iraq, as there can't be any revenge in their motives for volunteering. The screening wasn't perfect, but it was necessary. Especially on this particular base, where the detainees were considered "high value" and many had been sent in by Al-Qaeda and Hezbollah from other countries, there could be no mess-ups with a terp "going off" on a detainee.

Dennis passed the test and came to serve in the very place that tried to break him. He was what I imagine Santa Claus would be like if he were Arabic. In all my dealings with him, I never saw him be anything other than a beam of joyous light, and his life changed mine.

MR. ARAM

Mr. Aram was different from all the other terps: he was a Kurd. It was interesting to me that under Saddam, Kurds in Iraq were as lowly as Jews, and it was Mr. Aram who was the terp for the fledgling Iraqi Security Forces in the early days of their training. He would wave to me at the gate and came into our center almost daily to use the computer.

Once when I left for R and R, I came "home" to Iraq to find out that an inside job had gotten twelve trainees kidnapped. Eleven had been killed, but the murderers had allowed the mole to escape. They sent the head of one victim to the widow in a box, and Coalition forces found the heads of others in a freezer. I panicked when I realized that I hadn't seen Mr. Aram anywhere, and I was relieved to learn that he was OK. It is hard to describe what it is like to be in a situation where former strangers who have become so dear can vanish from life and sight in a moment at a coward's behest and likewise difficult to express the depth of relief upon learning that someone was spared such treachery.

Mr. Aram is another whose story would take a whole book to do it justice. He was trained as a mechanical engineer and graduated from Baghdad University in 1982. He never got a chance to practice his trade until he escaped to the U.S. after many years fleeing from Saddam to avoid the draft. He didn't want to have anything to do with Saddam's butchery and was willing to risk his life to avoid being a part of his system.

The only reason Mr. Aram didn't die in the Halabja gassing of 1988 was that he was hiding in the hills. Without warning Saddam struck, just before Newroz, the Kurdish New Year. People were in their homes cooking, decorating, and preparing for the celebration. Then the gassing started, and five thousand died. The peshmerga, armed Kurdistan fighters, were the ones who told Mr. Aram what had happened, and they along with Mr. Aram listened all night to the radio to hear the reports. Of all the European news outlets, the only ones who reported it, interestingly, were the Germans.

He told me the hardest part of that day was coming back into town and seeing all the dead bodies, especially those of the children. Some of their eyes were bulging, and some had been burned by the gas. He said the residual gas had a strange apple-like smell. He lost several relatives, including children, that day.

Mr. Aram had to stay in hiding until 1990, moving back and forth between Sulamaniyah and the mountains. Unable to work, he was supported by his family, who could have lost their lives as accomplices to his "crime." In 1991 he worked with an unnamed organization to rebuild the four thousand villages destroyed by Saddam in Kurdistan. France, Germany, Sweden, and the U.S. all helped. Mr. Aram was married in 1993, and then in 1996 Saddam attacked again. This time Mr. Aram and his wife were evacuated by the U.S. and began their long journey to the States by way of Turkey, Dubai, Sri Lanka, Guam, San Francisco, and New York City, finally settling in Buffalo.

His wife, whose name means "dew," had four miscarriages. In 2001, she was in her eighth month of a high-risk pregnancy and developed complications. On the way to delivery, Mr. Aram promised God that if He would help them and the child lived, they would serve the country that helped *him* live. His baby boy Arriz did live, and his name means "spring after the melt." What a fitting name for a man and a woman who had endured the icy winters of an evil king!

In January 2004, Mr. Aram got a phone call asking if he wanted to volunteer to go to Iraq as an interpreter. His immediate answer was yes. The person doing the interview asked the question that clinches it for all prospective terps: "Why?" "Because of Arriz," he replied. He was willing to leave his little boy in the care of his treasured woman in order to fulfill his promise to God. Would that we all possessed that kind of mettle.

CHAPTER 11

Don't Mess
With the Babysitter

A 1987 movie entitled *Adventures in Babysitting* is a seemingly cotton-candy little flick about a babysitter named Chris who, in the process of taking care of her charges, gets in and out of a bunch of scrapes à la the Cat in the Hat. Like the Cat, Chris manages to get it all back together just before the parents get home, but it's close. She thinks it will take just a quick trip to the bus station to rescue a stranded friend, but everything that could go wrong does. The movie is not something I would have picked out (I'll blame it on my youngest); there is language I don't like; and if my babysitter had risked my kids' lives like this while I was out, I would have gone nuts!

However, the movie has one redeeming factor that explains why I use it as a backdrop to describe how my heart came to leap for joy whenever I see a soldier— any soldier, any branch, either gender. This has been especially the case since I have

89

been home from Iraq, and as there are fewer of them running around town in camo, they really stick out.

As babysitter Chris is madly trying to get to her friend, she has a flat on the freeway but has no spare tire. She and the kids end up on a city train in the turf of a street gang. The gang leader starts to harass and threaten first the kids, then Chris. The guy throws a knife and is so good with blades that it goes right between the toes of one of the boys and nails his sneaker to the floor of the train. He is unhurt, but the terror quotient for all the kids has just gone through the ceiling.

Elizabeth Shue plays Chris, an adorable cheerleader type; please don't get mad at me if, as a graying brunette, I mention that she is blond. What she does next as she assesses the situation with the pinned shoe is what endears her to me. True, she is in way over her head in a situation that she never should have been in in the first place, but this is where she redeems herself. The gang member, after successfully scaring the bazotts out of the kid who can't move his shoe, gets in Chris's face and says, "Don't _ _ _ _ with the Lords of Hell!!!!"

Chris—who is unarmed, unafraid, uninhibited, determined to protect the kids, and flat crazy to try—stands up, gets nose to nose with him and says, "Don't _ _ _ _ with the babysitter!!!!"

The gang leader, duly intimidated, backs off, and the kids are safe.

My dear friends Marcus and Chrissie co-opted the phrase by changing it to "don't *mess* with the babysitter" to illustrate the protective passion of a mother bear when her cubs are being threatened. And that, my friends, is the best way I can describe what happened to me while in Iraq. Take a quintessential Jewish mother and a mother bear, put it all in a 5'2" middle-aged package, and you have me. In one fell swoop I went from whatever leftovers I may have had from my "all-soldiers-are-baby-killers" days to the "you-mess-with-them-and-you-mess-with-me" attitude that now beats fiercely and unceasingly in my heart.

I know full well that the soldiers are perfectly capable of defending themselves and they don't need me to get through life in one piece. But if you want to get me steamed, start calling them Nazis and rapists in front of me. Start dissing them or the amazing things they have accomplished. Or just make sure that their victories and valor stay out of the news. Start saying that "the war is lost."

Start saying, Senator Kennedy, just days before they are going to put their lives on the line so that the Iraqi people can vote, that "the U.S. military presence has become part of the problem, not part of the solution."[10] Or call the man "General Betrayus" who, after being wounded and hospitalized, dropped and gave the nurse twenty to prove that he was well enough to be discharged against her wishes so he could get back to his guys because he knew they needed him. Most of all, if you choose to bronze your brain in willful ignorance and put it on your dresser to hold your change, then please, please just get out of the way and hush so they can do their job!

Want to know how I got this way? It's all their fault. They treated me with unprecedented respect. They were polite to a fault. They were affectionate, funny, brave, tough, tender, hard-nosed, and softhearted. They would just about fall all over themselves to open a door or carry a package. They would miss me. They would e-mail me or tell me that my e-mails really blessed them. They would laugh at my jokes. They would come visit me at work on their time off, sit and eat with me in the Dfac, sing with me at church, and dry my tears.

They would go outside the wire to deliver supplies to the first-ever Iraqi women's shelter for battered women or take soccer balls to adoring kids. They would go online to show me the wedding dress they were going to wear when they got back to the States. They would weep with concern and compassion for Iraqis, especially the children. One single female NCO was willing to adopt an Iraqi teenager who was a major handful.

They would crack up at my goofy attempt to get them to be as good to each other as they were to me. If they were squabbling over whether or not a Ping-Pong ball was "net," I would say, "Alright you two, don't make me pull this car over, and don't think I can't do it!" This was especially effective if they were officers who were about nine feet tall.

I'll never forget one guy I met the first summer. We would chat about all kinds of things as I signed him up for computers or checked out games to him. Before going home to the States for good, he walked all across Camp Victory in the blazing heat in his body armor to tell me goodbye. Dripping in sweat, he said, "You have been almost like a mom to me, and I just wanted to come and say thank you and goodbye." Man, talk about a wipeout. There I was—the one who used to judge them, despise them, call them names, and think their function was at best unnecessary and at worst evil. I am the one who once thought they were stupid and just joined the military because they couldn't think for themselves or couldn't get a job.

They did two things that won me over forever. They showed me they were different, and they freely forgave me! Out of the approximately 130,000 soldiers in Iraq prior to the surge, there were probably a few who fit my old category. But that's not what I experienced. Out of the three years I was playing with them in the Great Sandbox, I only remember two times when someone was either rude or really out of line with me, and one of those was a guy who was drunk. Other than that, I was the Queen of the May, and I got so spoiled that I often wondered how I was going to fit back into life Stateside.

Once two female soldiers who had just gotten in-country came into the MWR center. I would always ask newbies to the camp if they would like a tour of the building, as it was once Saddam's hunting lodge and was fascinating. They said yes, and off we went. When I was finished, I welcomed them to Iraq and thanked them for their service. They said, "Wow, you almost made us forget where we were. Thank you." I have said it before, and it bears repeating: I have never been in a place where the simplest of kindnesses or just bare-bones civility have been more appreciated.

I hate wearing shoes—always have—and get out of them just as soon as I get inside the door. Many times in Iraq I slipped out of my clogs and my feet were shod with just my brightly colored socks. ("When I am old, I shall wear purple.") Sometimes I would walk across the building this way, and soldiers would even thank me for that, as it made them feel at home.

When I would tell them of the old days and my capers as an anti-Viet Nam War protester, they would laugh affectionately, forgive me afresh, or both. Often they would just say "Wow." They often asked me why I came over. When I told them that there were a lot of reasons—a big one being to say thanks to my dad—they would say, "That's so cool, ma'am." "We appreciate you being here, ma'am, more than you know." I heard that over and over. I always replied that it was my pleasure and my honor to be among them, because it was.

I just wish we, as a culture, would be willing to sacrifice for them the way they are willing to sacrifice for us without hesitation. I wish everyone could have experienced what I did. The best way I can give back at the moment is making sure folks know their stories, but lemee tell ya, that's not where it stops.

Be advised, oh "Lords of Hell," don't touch. You're messin' with the babysitter.

CHAPTER 12

A Tale of Two Hostages

J don't think I'll ever be able to fathom or understand the evil that manifested itself here. Trying to describe the good going on all around, all the time seems likewise impossible. There are times when I want to give up even trying, and I can only hope that the attempt, however paltry, does at least a bit of the job.

I have concluded that a situation like living in a combat zone intensifies everything. The blackness of evil takes on a quivering shimmer, and the sweetness of good is a purely disarming and refreshing breath, as we'll see in the stories of two women, Margaret Hassan and Jill Carroll, who were both kidnapped and held as hostages. Sadly, Margaret did not survive.

Sometimes we contractors would talk about what we would do if we were taken hostage and it looked like we were going to be killed. (The chances of being kidnapped were extremely remote in my case, since I was rarely outside the wire.) One guy said that once he was sure they were going to kill him, he'd see who he could take out before they got him. Another said he'd hope that there would be a smile on his face while they beheaded him so that his frozen grin would be shown on Al-Jazeera and the militant Web sites. If I were about to be executed as a hostage, I would want to glow like the first-century Christian martyr Stephen while he was being stoned. I would also like to sing before I was silenced. Who knows, it might just prove to be a tad unnerving to the muj.

All contractors, both male and female, were required to be trained in hostage survival. We learned techniques to "humanize" ourselves to our captors, communicate by codes and other secret ways, build morale among fellow captives, and endure interrogation. There was some (though not enough, in my view) training about Stockholm Syndrome, the psychological breaking process that causes captives to bond with, identify with, support, and protect their captors. At the time we took our training, during the peak of the kidnappings of foreign civilians, there was about an 85 percent live retrieval rate.

While we were taught how to overcome coercion, we weren't trained at all about how to endure physical torture. That is something for the Big Dogs, and as it involves a hands-on learning experience, I don't think it's a gig most contractors—or anybody, for that matter—would rush right out to sign up for.

In December of 2006 while on R and R, I stood in front of the ovens in Dachau and shuddered to my core as I read a plaque dedicated to four female members of the anti-Nazi French Resistance who died there in 1944: Noor Inyat Kahn, Yolanda Beekman, Elaine Plewman, and Madeleine Damerment. The plaque says, in part, "They died as gallantly as they served the Resistance in France during the common struggle for freedom from tyranny." Freedom from tyranny! The things humans will endure to go after what has been put in their DNA, and how indebted we are to all who have given their lives for it throughout the centuries!

Noor Khan's last word before she was shot in the back of the head was "Liberté." Thirteenth-century Scottish leader William Wallace's allegedly was "Freeeeeeeedommm!" I don't know if Margaret made a peep, as the thought of watching the video of her execution makes me want to puke. The idea that this kind of stuff gets sent around the Internet and that people laugh at it wigs me out. She was led, as Isaiah says, as a "lamb to the slaughter," and I pray that the angel that had been with her since childhood held her tight as a bullet ripped through her skull.

MARGARET HASSAN

On 17 November 2004, the night Margaret's death was reported, I wrote the following:

There are only Polish guys in the MWR tonight. Spirited games of pool and Ping-Pong have been going on for much of the evening. Guys who have been out on patrol and have brought in soldiers who are only going to be here for the night came in for water. They needed about thirty 1.5-liter bottles. How glad I was to have cold water for them. Ever polite and respectful, these men never fail to express their thanks and gratitude to us.

Earlier in the evening, American soldiers came in sporting shirts that the father of one of their comrades had made for them. On the front was written in Latin, "O Praeclarum Custodem Ovium Lupum—De Oppresso Liber!"

My knowledge of Latin is sketchy at best, so I went online to find out what it meant. "O praeclarum custodem ovium lupum!" is attributed to Cicero and means "O excellent protector of sheep, the wolf!" "De Oppresso Liber" is the motto of the United States Army Special Forces, and tradition indicates that it means "To Liberate the Oppressed."

On the back was a quote which is attributed to George Orwell. "We sleep safe in our beds because rough men stand ready in the night to visit violence on those who might do us harm." How I wish these men could have saved Margaret Hassan. I know they would have done it in a heartbeat if they had been given a chance.

Margaret Hassan was an Irish and British woman who was an Iraqi citizen married to an Iraqi engineer for over thirty years. She was the Baghdad director of CARE International (based out of Australia) and was kidnapped on 19 October 2004, during the early days of this year's Ramadan celebration.

Margaret worked in Baghdad for over twenty-five years helping the Iraqi people and was regarded locally as a Mother Teresa of sorts. Wherever she went, children would cling to her and call her "Madam Margaret."

Sadly, those who use kidnappings to win support for their cause chose to ignore the good she did for her country, shot her in the head, and then released a video of her execution. Thankfully she was not beheaded. Her husband pleads that they would let him know where her body is, so he can bury her. Her family in the UK says they are "broken-hearted."

The outrage of the residents of Baghdad is fierce, as is that of Islamic people from all over the world. Even al-Zarqawi called for her release. One man by the name of Abu said, "The people who did this are not in any way related to Islam, because Islam respects women. Everyone has to work together to fight these terrorists."[11] Another named Nasarul Islam wrote, "I hope they find these scum and treat them accordingly. She was innocent and a friend of the Arab world. You know this is so wrong when Zarqawi says she should be released."[12] Another said, "Iraq has lost a torch-bearer of faith in its future."[13] One resident of Baghdad says, "We must have a ceremony every year to remember her"[14] and believes a statue should be erected in her honor. "Aid workers would be flowing into Falluja right now if they didn't fear decapitation,"[15] commented Yusuf Ali.

What causes someone to get to the place where they will allow their own people to suffer rather than accept the presence of someone who simply wants to help? How do people get to such a place? Humans are capable of such good and such evil, and it seems that war intensifies the proclivities of both. Margaret, may someone else pick up your torch, and thank you.

I hit "send" and launched my dismay and appreciation for Mrs. Hassan into cyberspace.

Over the next few days, preposterous speculations appeared in the blogosphere to try to make sense of what had happened. Theories as to who was responsible swirled for the next few months, followed by arrests, and then a trial in June of 2006. Mustafa al-Jiburi, the man who was found guilty and sentenced to life for her kidnapping but not her murder, claims that a sheik from a mosque gave him her bag of personal belongings to keep and then disappeared. He also claims that he didn't open the plastic bag for two months, and it was then that he discovered the owner's name by looking at Margaret's passport.

Margaret's devastated family has made it very clear that they feel that her case was botched from start to finish. They decry the strategies used to try to reason with her kidnappers and to secure her release. They were shocked that al-Jiburi was not convicted of murder, and they understandably still want to know the whereabouts of Margaret's body. I am sure that if something like this happened to a member of my family, I'd be beside myself. In the heat of my grief, chances are that I would want someone to blame, even the people who were trying to save her.

The strategy was that when the kidnappers contacted Margaret's husband Tahseen, he should emphasize her "Iraqi-ness" and the good she did for Iraq and minimize the fact that she still retained her British citizenship. He needed to point out that she was indeed a faithful Iraqi citizen, and I have no doubt that her captors knew this. From the training we contractors received about surviving a hostage situation, it seemed like a good plan to me.

But can anyone—from professional negotiators to local police to intel or even an involved family member—ever be able to consistently and successfully negotiate with the illogical unpredictability of organized darkness?

Thankfully, sometimes they can, but sadly, not always.

Some people, ideologies, or situations are just so beyond the pale that they won't fit into a profile or respond to reason. Whether such darkness has a label or not, it must depend upon brandishing fear in a wide swathe in order to survive. Such evil will never be satisfied, even after its victims have been duly subdued by terror. It's only a matter of time before it needs a new scapegoat. While Jill Carroll was still being held captive, she watched incredulously as, for a season, the goal of exploding oneself for the glory of Allah shifted in one smooth motion from targeting infidel Coalition soldiers to Shias, all with the same bizarre intensity. It defies even the most academic attempts to understand it, let alone the reasoning of the heart.

Ironically, money was never demanded in Margaret's case. They just wanted her to denounce Britain's presence in Iraq, or they would kill her. They wanted to see her terrified, and in that they succeeded, then took her life, even though Iraqis demonstrated at their own peril in the streets for her release, and Zarqawi, who himself had no problem with personally beheading the innocent, told her captors to let her go. I will discuss his possible motives for doing so further on.

In her own loving, remarkable, way, Margaret spent herself for Iraq, and she died for it, too. She had been warned that she might be a target, yet she chose to keep going anyway. She never had any children of her own, and her special fight was for sick children to get medical care during the time of the UN sanctions. It seems incomprehensible that Margaret would be a target, since she was actually opposed to the war and Britain's involvement in it! She had spent twenty-five years trying to take care of Iraqis who suffered while Saddam got fat off of the sanctions, and she felt the Iraqis had had enough. Still, they shot her in the back of the head. Why?

While I do understand her thinking about the war, I must respectfully disagree, although in keeping with my dad's words, by November of 2005, I would have fought like hell for her right to disagree passionately with anyone she chose. So would any Coalition soldier. Sadly, if she had lived two more months, she would have seen that it was the presence of the British, Yanks, and the rest of the Coalition that made it possible for people to vote. They made it possible for the long journey toward building that very Iraq for which Margaret had fought for twenty-five years to officially begin. Margaret probably would have taken issue with the young Sunni terp who got up in church sixteen months after she died and thanked the U.S. for invading his country. I wish she could have lived to disagree with him, face to face, Iraqi to Iraqi, if she still chose to.

Why did they kill her? No reason was ever given. When she was so revered by the Iraqis, why did they do it? She *made* the statements they wanted her to regarding British withdrawal and the release of Iraqi female prisoners—the standard coercion-extracted statements of the day. Similar ones were uttered by more than one hostage under horrific duress, including Jill Carroll.

I puzzled over this, as it certainly was a different scenario than the usual. The simple answer is that they were wicked, and that is certainly true. However, I came across a theory that I think bears considering.

Mark Dooley, who is Irish, blames the premise of trying to negotiate in the first place. He says, "The truth is that Margaret Hassan would never have been kidnapped had the Irish government not appealed to Abu Musab Al-Zarqawi on behalf of Ken Bigley. [Ken Bigley was an Irish contractor who was beheaded not long before Margaret was killed. In one of the videos put out by her murderers, she understandably cried out for help and said that she did not want to 'die like Ken Bigley.'] By trying to negotiate with the Baghdad beheaders, the Government made Hassan a prime target. And now the folly of their actions has become tragically obvious. Whereas we are content to do business with despots, the Americans understand that negotiation with fanatics is impossible. For all they want is our blood. Accommodation or compromise with the 'infidel West' is not on the programme. That is why the Fallujah campaign was politically and morally necessary."[16]

The young terp I mentioned, whose fiancee took an IED in Fallujah, would concur. These are admittedly tough words, and I have no desire to pour gasoline on a blame-fest that is already ignited. However, it needs to be understood that dealing with terrorists of this ilk is in a completely different league than sending negotiators to deal with someone who has taken tellers and customers captive in a bank heist. Stolen money will never be as sweet to evil as is innocent blood. The shedding of innocent blood is an addiction loosely disguised as an ideological or theological mandate, and it must have its fix.

As for the now-deceased al-Zarqawi's command to her captors to let her go, there are several theories that could explain his rare video plea on her behalf. Even though the theories totally conflict with each other, any of them is possible. In the Arab world, mothers are nearly worshipped by their sons, even though concurrently wives are frighteningly subjugated. Something in al-Zarqawi's fragmented, maniacal soul may have actually pulled up to his heart the common knowledge that Margaret was a mother to the nation and that she deserved to live.

His plea also could have been a complete ruse designed to portray jihadists as reasonable people. Al-Zarqawi was from Jordan, and he didn't grow up seeing the evidence of Margaret's quiet kindness. He could have just as easily wanted to see her die because, even though she helped the country he himself temporarily hijacked, she was still Catholic and technically an infidel. Infidels are to be invited to convert, and if they don't, it is completely consistent with Koranic principles to kill them. Obviously not everyone in the Islamic world feels this way, but that command is right there many times in the book; you can read it for yourself in Sura 2:191, Sura 9:123, Sura 9:5, and Sura 9:73, amongst others..

One possible reason why Margaret was killed in spite of the questionable pleas of al-Zarqawi is that there is such rivalry amongst the mujahideen that Mr. al-Jiburi and his crew may have gotten the rush of a lifetime in defying the Abu himself and establishing themselves as the baddest in Baghdad. It could have been like a gang initiation where a woman's Achilles tendon is cut while she is getting into her car. Even to thugs she really doesn't have any culpability other than being in the wrong place at the wrong time, but her screams of pain bring validity to the perpetrator's reputation on the street. Terrorism is terrorism, wherever and however it shows up.

Whatever the motivation, for the present and on the surface, it appears that evil won. Certainly, Margaret is gone, her family is crushed, and her captors appear to have been dealt with too leniently. I am sure the anguish of those professionals who tried to use proven strategies that usually work but didn't in this case is unbearable. But this I know: good will ultimately triumph. It always does. It may not be soon, but it is inevitable because love is stronger than even death, and Margaret's love will be proven unstoppable.

May her example of selflessness infect her mourners to shine themselves. Now that the surge has been proven successful, perhaps that annual celebration of her loving life and work as a lifelong Catholic in an Islamic nation won't be too far off. More importantly, maybe more Iraqi Margarets are waiting to pick up her flame, and this time they won't have to die.

Jill Carroll

Jill Carroll's incredible tale provides me with hope—something that I could sure use a good dose of after trying to sort through the senselessness of Margaret's murder.

If there were one piece of journalism that I would strongly encourage Americans to read/view/listen to regarding Iraq, it is Jill Carroll's multimedia interview entitled "Hostage: The Jill Carroll Story." It can be found at www.cnn.com/2006/WORLD/ meast/08/14/carroll/index.html

On 7 January 2006, Jill was kidnapped by the mujahideen (muj for short). For the eighty-two days until her release, the surreality of knowing that she was somewhere literally only a few miles away hidden in Baghdad but hearing about her plight from Stateside news made the situation even stranger for me. I must admit that after Margaret's death, the prospect of a journalist emerging in one piece seemed remote, and I didn't know what to think. All we could do was pray and hope, which we and countless others worldwide did for months.

Because of the protectiveness I felt toward the soldiers because of the way they had proven themselves to me, I also was concerned that if Jill emerged alive she would come after them with a poison pen, so I was a bit on my guard. Of course I wanted her to be rescued; I just didn't want her to hurt "my kidz" with the kind of nonsense I had seen before from other journalists or politicians.

Jill reminds me in ways of my stepdaughter, Cheri, and my daughter, Jessa. The way she rolls her eyes, the faces she makes, her precious irreverence, her razor-sharp wit, and her irrepressible bounce-back spirit are the things I so enjoy about my own girls. Jill is utterly delightful, and though I have never met her, I would love to someday. The interview made me feel like I know her and like she is a part of my family.

The outpouring of support toward Jill and her family was as phenomenal as it was global—something that she is humbled by and still finds overwhelming. She is probably not aware, though, that while soldiers were carrying around pictures of her in their wallets and looking for her high and low, they were also fasting in addition to praying for her. That's right: some of our soldiers, for whom food is one of the few pleasures downrange, chose to fast for Jill's safe return. When the last deadline that her captors had issued was approaching, Col. Dixey Behnken, a chaplain with a true father's heart, invited people to fast on Jill's behalf.

Of course he said that this was completely voluntary—a private thing between us and God. The extent of our fast, if we chose to fast at all, was nobody's business but our own.

Some fasted one or two meals a day, and some went without any food for several days; while they didn't toot their own horn in any way, the fact that they walked right past the chow line spoke for itself. This went on for about two to three weeks.

As I sit here typing, remembering the colonel's resonant voice booming out in prayer for Jill, the tears of gratitude which are always just below the surface are dripping down my cheeks and onto my shirt. How blessed I was to be in the company of men and women such as these, and how desperately I miss them!

When it was reported that Jill was alive, we were happy campers, to say the least. However, I imagine that the Marines with whom she had previously been an "embed" (an embedded reporter) were ecstatic. All soldiers, especially Marines, would see it as a personal failure if they couldn't find her and bring her back alive.

Jill talks in her interview about once having casually asked the Marines to whom she had had been attached what would happen if she were ever kidnapped. She was assured that a "whole platoon" would comb the country to find her. I *know* they would, and there is no doubt that she endeared herself greatly to them while she was there. How could anyone not love Jill?

Interestingly, that was the effect she had on her captors as well. Whether or not it was a ploy, her lead captor mentioned to her that "everyone loves you" and told her that other muj cells knew of her captivity. That had to have been weird. I would have thought, "Right. You-love-me-so-much-that-you-are-going-to-kill-me-at-any-moment-because-I-am-part-of-the-Great-Satan-but-in-the-meantime-you'll-let-me-play-with-your-kids." (The children of the muj cell were her chief comfort and source of sanity during her captivity.)

What her story flawlessly illustrates is the complete polarization and therefore instability in the minds of jihadists. She'd be subjected to a vehement tirade regarding all the evils of America and the need to wipe it off the map, followed by more contemplative musings and discussion about how eventually there could be trade with America for oil, their children could be sent to America to go to college, and that would be OK. I wonder if it ever occurred to them that if they wiped out America, there would be no colleges to get a degree from and no one to buy their oil.

While I had been aware of this flip-flop as far as men were concerned, I was not prepared for her discussion of the pregnant would-be suicide bomber. One of her guards was female and pregnant with her fourth child. Her husband, Jill's lead captor, told Jill that his wife was planning on being a suicide bomber one day, beaming as though she had just been accepted into med school.

When Jill casually said, "Oh. I didn't know women could be suicide bombers," she was given a detailed explanation of the inexplicable by the husband/captor. The mom would have to wait until after the baby was born, as it is against Islam to kill an unborn child. Ironically, her husband wanted a whole bunch of kids. I don't think Jill ever heard what had been planned for taking care of this crew after Mama embraced "The Final Exit," put on her wired vest, kissed the kids goodbye, and detonated her way into untold delights.

No one has ever explained to me what the women get if they self-martyr. Are there seventy-two male virgins waiting for them? The seventy-two-virgins thing is a real incentive for male would-be bombers, and self-martyring is the only absolute assurance of heaven for either gender. I can't help but wonder if there isn't a "cha-ching" for the gals somewhere that serves as a comparable motivator.

Apparently, among Al-Qaeda cells, destroying a fetus is forbidden, but destroying an infant is not. Remember the terror scare involving flights leaving out of the UK the summer of 2006? Public service announcements indicated that if you had an infant with you, you had to drink some of whatever baby formula was in your diaper bag, in front of security, before you could get on the plane. This policy was enacted because a *woman* had hidden liquid explosive in her baby's bottle and was planning on blowing up her own family, including her husband, as well as everyone else on the plane for the glory of Allah and the furtherance of jihad. This makes me sad and angry, and the only way I can deal with it is to talk to my Maker about it, *lots*.

Jill says that although she had been raised a Catholic, it wasn't until several weeks into her captivity that she prayed. It often takes a crisis to provoke what is supposed to be indigenous to humans: communicating with their Maker. The cliche "there are no atheists in foxholes" may be frayed from overuse, especially in a combat zone, but it is nonetheless true. What I found particularly touching about Jill's prayers was that she asked for strength not only for herself, but also for her family. As time wore on, she really had no expectation of living, and she wanted comfort for her family. I would be curious to find out someday if the timing of her beginning to talk to the only Friend who knew where she was coincided with when the soldiers decided to fast and pray themselves.

Jill's captors threatened her with death even while taking her to freedom. She forced an anything-but-heartfelt laugh, as though they were joking, and said, "Abu Rasha, you're my brother! You wouldn't do that!" He laughed and replied, "You are right; we're not going to kill you." They did, however, give her several hundred dollars for her "trouble" and a gold necklace with a pendant as a gift. I could envision a Jay Leno monologue: "Here, infidel honey, me and the muj went in together to get you this as a little going-away gift. Just a little something to remember us by."

As touching as it was to read the story and see the pictures of Jill's reunion with her family, it was the actions of the soldiers who picked her up once she was free that reduced me to my now nearly daily tears of gratitude. Jill had been so psychologically punched out by her captors that she was afraid that if she went with the soldiers, the muj were watching and would get her for sure. Unless someone has been subjected to this kind of abuse, whether it is something as spectacular as being held captive by Al-Qaeda or slowly dying in a domestic violence "cell," it is hard to understand being afraid of those who would do you well. Truly, if every bit of fear spoken into her had been materialized as physical blows, she would have been black and blue from head to toe and probably unable to walk. That she is as whole as she is, as quickly as she is, is straight up miraculous.

The Marines got her safely into the Humvee and sped off in a large convoy toward the embassy. There were three guys sitting near her. The first took her picture out of his wallet and handed it to her, telling her that he didn't need it anymore. The second reached over to his right shoulder, removed his American flag patch, and handed it to her. Who knows what holding that flag in her hand did to help her trust again as she bounced down Baghdad's potholed streets?

The third said, "We've been looking for you for a long time." That's the statement that got me. There is a Soldier's Creed that I know applies to Marines as well: "I will put the mission first. I will never quit. I will never accept defeat. I will never leave a comrade behind." Jill, in my view and no doubt theirs, more than qualifies as a comrade, and I am glad they never gave up.

People sometimes ask me why I wasn't afraid much while I was in Iraq. The biggest reason was my faith, but right next to it was guys like this—guys who would carry around a picture of a young woman, not because she was their sweetheart, but because protecting her and others like her is what gives them breath. These guys made me feel safer than at any other time of my life, even when we were all in danger.

There is only one part of Jill's story that made me want to howl with disagreement: her feeling that in any way she is responsible for the death of her journalist friend and interpreter, Alan Enwiya. He was an unarmed man murdered right before her eyes. She was an unarmed woman who wanted to tell a story. She blames herself, saying she "should have seen it coming," that if it weren't for her, "he'd still be alive." No, honey, no. You didn't kill him; hate did, just like it killed Margaret Hassan.

My dear, dear Jill, I am sure you have heard it a thousand times from everyone from Army shrinks to your dear twin, Katie. What you are wrestling with has a fancy name, Survivor's Syndrome. You ask over and over why you were allowed to live and he wasn't. I don't know. That stuff is way above my pay grade, but I do know that one day all of it will be explained to you to your satisfaction by the One who loves you the most. Until then, I pray you are completely healed from everything you went through. Thank you for gifting us with your tender heart, quick wit, and sweetly sassy tale of freedom lost, found, and cherished.

CHAPTER 13

Stellar Soldiers

As I put my heart to paper regarding the military men and women I encountered in Iraq, I wonder how I will even begin to tell their stories and faithfully illustrate their complicated strength and beauty. I also fear that I will forget to mention one of these innumerable shining ones from my recently discovered personal galaxy. I know they'll continue to shine in spite of my gaffe and forgive me if I had a senior moment.

Sadly, in the America of early 2008, organizations are re-emerging whose spirit reminds me of my gladly escaped past. These days the Berkeley City Council calls the Marines "uninvited and unwelcome intruders."[17] A Code Pink activist describes soldiers as "killers, trained to kill, ready to kill, willing to kill."[18] Last year a really messed-up fellow who was a guest on FOX actually said he rejoiced every time a U.S. soldier was killed! The soldiers and I watched in disbelief, and I was reminded yet again that willfully ignorant ingrates such as he are among those for whom soldiers sign on to die.

I would like to take "Ms. Pink" and set her down next to Tom as he tells in tears of a burned kid he took care of in the Abu Ghraib hospital. A faulty furnace in the child's home had exploded in a non-combat-related accident, and it fell upon Tom to be the one to have to scrape the child's burns as part of his recovery.

Then there is tenderhearted Zach, who used to spend his time on Saturday nights praying and weeping over Iraqis. He wanted to volunteer to go outside the wire "just to tell the people how much they are loved."

Perhaps she should have been present when Mark C. came flying into MWR in the middle of the night to e-mail his wife: "Please clean out the closets and send shoes. There are kids out there who don't have shoes, and it's thirty-two-degrees outside."

Or maybe she could have agonized with Arnie, a respiratory therapist who had wondered if he had arrested the right guys. "They claimed to just be farmers, and their kids looked so scared." Turns out they were bombers and had the incriminating residue on their hands. Maybe the Berkeley City Council should sit next to Arnie as he shows the pictures he took of adorable Iraqi children and has to stop to gain his composure. "She looks so much like my daughter," he says wistfully. Or perhaps they could have looked into his face as he mourned over a gate guard who had affectionately named himself after Arnie and who was blown up by a VBIED (Vehicle Borne Improvised Explosive Device—a car bomb) that shook our camp.

Arik used to give heartfelt pep talks to the Iraqis not to back down, to do whatever it takes "to build an Iraq that is free and peaceful for you and your children." They would erupt in cheers. He also was one of the organizers of the Hawaiian National Guard unit's distribution of soccer balls to Iraqi kids at Christmas. To this day Arik and I talk about how much we love and miss Iraq.

"Onion," whose real last name was Huynh, was originally from Viet Nam. When he was three years old, he and his mom were escaping in a boat, and she accidentally got left behind. Several days later the captain discovered that the little boy was now without anyone to care for him, as the Viet Cong had killed his dad and they were not going back to Viet Nam any time soon. The boat captain raised Onion for several years and then finally found his grandma in the States. Onion's mom is still in Viet Nam, and the grandma and an uncle raised him. He has seen his mother once since then and sends her a sizeable part of his not–so–sizeable Army paycheck. This boy understands terrorism and what it takes to defend liberty, and he plays a pretty mean game of Ping-Pong.

"Corndog" was in a heavy metal band and attending an exclusive eastern college when his best friend was killed in Iraq. He upset everyone in his life when he said, "I will honor his memory by going to finish what he started, to set people free." He left school and all that was safe back home and enlisted, and he could make me laugh till I cried. So could Jarmon and Jordan; Jordan is now recovering from taking an IED to the head after volunteering to go back to Iraq for the surge. Amazingly, he still has his sweet sense of humor.

There was "Uncle," a Hawaiian who I am sure was really a noble chieftain in disguise and who watched over his men and us with a father's heart. Identical twins from Hawaii, Peter and Paul, were so fun they could make us forget we were in a war. Gabe, a warrior's warrior, was an assistant camp mayor and would do everything he could to make the guys' lives better. Rebecca was a re-up officer who collected Avon products and toiletries to give to Iraqi women at the women's shelter, and Rainer designed and produced the coolest t-shirts and gave them to members of the Iraqi Special Forces and to me. George left a stable job in the States to reenlist in military intelligence so he could come over and help both the Coalition and the Iraqis.

An older Guardsman nicknamed "Old School" was an MP who would encourage young detainees to "straighten up and fly right"; some thanked him for it. He was a "plat daddy"—a papa—to the rest of the MPs, too. Merrill, whom I called "Cuz" because my maiden name and his were the same, and Sgt. V, who came to MWR to pour out his grief over the loss of a young soldier in his group, always checked to make sure I was OK. They were determined to see to it that my every need was met and nobody messed with me. Batemon made me a bracelet out of parachute cord for my birthday, and I don't intend to remove her handiwork from my left wrist until they have all come home safely for good.

Li'l T, a beautiful young African-American, was called up from the National Guard just before finishing college. She told me, "At first I was so mad, having to interrupt my life and come over here, and then I got here and saw what was really going on. Now I am glad to be here, to be a part of this. Ali, please tell our story, cuz they sure won't hear it any other way back home." Will do, li'l T. David Shinn, a second-generation Korean, was an excellent Christian rapper who had the soldiers on their feet cheering.

One Sean gave up being the military editor for a major New York publishing house in order to keep protecting us; another Sean was a lawyer who dispensed financial aid in the Green Zone. One Joe had been a television actor and was now a chaplain's assistant, and another Joe was the quintessential Irish cop who cracked us up with his Irish brogue and jokes. Irish Joe is now with the FBI. Mervin was the Manhattan bus driver who had come from Puerto Rico, and another New Yorker had been a firefighter at Ground Zero and had lost men there. The Fighting 69th had been on constant duty since 9/11 and made our lives a joy.

One man, a single dad, had an autistic son at home being cared for by the man's parents. One woman had left her children in the care of her husband; he developed a drinking problem while she was in Iraq, and she was worried sick about her boys.

Michael had saved the life of a battered child in the States and had so much pure brotherly love for our whole praise and worship team that any of us would sign up to go back and serve with him, anytime, anywhere. I get e-mails from men and women that say "I miss Michael." "Yeah," I write back. "I know how you feel. I miss him, too."

AA, who had been brought up in an orphanage, became my first "soldier son." He taught me karate and relentlessly challenged me to think, grow, and forsake my stupid personal fears, all of which he was a master at exposing. If I had a motive toward anyone or anything that wasn't spot on, he would call me on it, and for this I love him deeply, even though the process was not fun. Steve would back up AA's admonitions when I would tell him of our conversations. "Busted, huh, hon," he would lovingly chuckle. AA was the first of many who inspired me to "soldier up and quit whining."

This has become one of my chief takeaways from my time in Iraq; I have made "no whining" a permanent personal goal. Lord knows I have done enough whining to last a lifetime, and the example of these soldiers puts me to shame.

One day I walked into the MWR to start my shift and beheld a curious and endearing sight. Three huge African-American warriors were sitting on the couch, their weapons at their sides . . . watching *Sesame Street*. At first I thought they were just being incredibly polite in obeying the sign on the wall that said "If you wish to change the channel, please ask the MWR staff." Fascinated, I tiptoed up and said, "Guys, you don't have to watch *Sesame Street*. I'd be happy to change the channel for you." "Oh no, ma'am, we're fine. We're just sitting here pretending we are with our children."

Nick would tear up when he talked about the birth of his three-year-old daughter. Nathan would tearfully talk about his little Cora and how she had stolen his heart. N was working through the rage that he felt over the fact that his daughter had been sexually molested back in the States and he wasn't there to protect her. Nothing but trained killers, Ms. "Pink"? I don't think so.

Perhaps the guy who is glad when soldiers get killed would feel differently if he had been in Douglas Woods' shoes. Woods was an Aussie contractor who had been kidnapped and held hostage in the summer of 2005. He appeared on a muj video shown on Al-Jazeera, with two weapons pointed at his head while he read a demand for Australia to withdraw from Iraq. He might very well not be alive today if it weren't for AA, who was on patrol and making house-to-house checks. "There was just something about this one house," AA told me. "We had passed by it, but I just 'knew' something was going on there." The rest of the unit was further down the street, and out of nowhere he cried out to his five-guy, team, "Stack on me!" (This means to get into quick entry formation.) He kicked in the door, his guys close behind him.

He went straight like a locked-on missile, guided by an unseen force, into the next room where there was an object under a blanket. Those in the home first said that it was their ill mother, then their ill father under the blanket, and not to disturb him.

AA partially peeled back the blanket and asked, "Do you speak English?"

"Oh yes, mate!" came the hearty and distinctly "Down Under" reply.

"Do you want to go home?"

"Oh yes, mate!"

"Go get in the truck," AA told him, and Douglas Woods quickly complied.

Now here's some irony for you. Mr. Woods was so effusive in his praise and thanks toward his rescuers that he became downright amusing.

By contrast, AA told me that the hardest people to rescue are American women "because they don't like being told what to do." Oy vey! The most unstable and dangerous part of a rescue is at the very beginning, when the situation is being resolved and the most important thing is to get the noncombatants out of harm's way, pronto. So you are going to tussle with your rescuers, either verbally or otherwise? Are you nuts? "GO GET IN THE TRUCK!!!"

Another soldier son who shall remain nameless also spoke of that eerie sense of "just knowing" that something wasn't right, and he could have gotten in big trouble for what he did. A local couple was being searched and questioned, and this very gentle soldier was trying to follow all the rules regarding cultural sensitivity and respect for women. He was just about to let them go, when something told him to check her bra. He did so quickly and found explosives hidden in a place where everyone knew "the Americans would not check because they have been taught to respect our women." Ever the gentleman, he blushed as he told me this story. I asked him, "What did the woman do when you searched her?" He said, "She just looked at her husband like he had betrayed her." I would love to send this story to the National Organization of Women, just so they might understand that something that is clearly justifiable lawsuit material in one context can save lives in another.

Saul, a medic from Hawaii, could probably have been a concert pianist and wanted to do combat medicine with Special Ops Delta. He would send me care packages from Hawaii loaded with healthy treats. Once Cindy Sheehan, the now-famous war protester who camped outside President Bush's ranch in Texas, went to Hawaii to protest the war, and Saul went to the rally wearing his Army PT (official workout t-shirt.) He politely asked to speak to her after the rally and told her that he had been in Iraq and had a very different perspective than hers. Saul said she seemed interested, but he was not able to converse with her. Saul, my dear tall one, you have just summarized the theme of this book for your Jewish mother bear. My mantra is, "I have been in Iraq, and I have a very different perspective from what you are used to hearing." Now perhaps you are starting to see why.

The summer of Hurricane Katrina, we were sitting outside of Uday's hotel-turned-Dfac in weather that was upwards of 125 degrees Fahrenheit. Pedro was inside a Humvee, dressed in IBA (Individual Body Armor), which made it at least ten degrees hotter for him. Things were crazy in New Orleans, and Armed Forces Network (AFN) was playing an audio clip from inside the Superdome. A man was yelling, "It's ninety degrees in here! It's ninety degrees in here!" Pedro robotically looked over at us and with a straight face and a monotone quipped, "Cold snap." We fell out laughing. Laughter was abundant, as were truly gifted comics. Sloopy could do impersonations that were spot on, and Gozzo's political humor should be registered as a concealed weapon.

Things were going so well in the town where Josh was stationed that he didn't need to wear his IBA, and he played soccer all day with the kids. He conducted an anonymous survey of the townspeople, and out of 4,200 surveyed, only two people said they wanted the Americans to leave!

Col. Steve knew everything about explosive ordnance and was a gentle dreamer. Marc was a passionate philosopher, the son of a legendary Chilean officer who had immigrated to the States. B had done covert ops in the Colombian jungle trying to keep drugs out of America. Alan, who was a Command Sergeant Major, agonized over the new generation of soldiers who had grown up without fathers. Cecelia, a nurse/captain, wept over losing a medic who was killed in action just before he was due to go home.

There are a few ex-mil guys who deserve to be mentioned as "stellar soldiers" because they functioned with the same valor and selflessness. Big Pink had just gotten out of the Army, had come right back over as a contractor, and took it upon himself to inform his Iraqi workers that women were not to be hit, period. Marty had recently gotten out of the Army after twenty years and would tear up over the plight of some of his female Filipino workers who had abusive alcoholic husbands back home. Ty was an ex-Marine and would walk with me at night to keep me safe. All three were fiercely protective of me and would make me laugh when my work situation made me want to whine and weep. Talk about a Band of Brothers!

Michele was a beautiful intelligence officer who is the most conscientious person I have ever met; her presence humbled me. Latrice was my very first soldier friend and made me feel as welcome as you can to a war zone. Terri, Karen, Nancy, Margie, Regina, Cecelia, and Heather treated me like a sister, and not just a civilian. We played together, prayed together, and laughed and cried together.

The chaplains deserve their own chapter—their own book, actually. Chris was a former soccer player who had become a detective. He had four children and a wife whom he dearly loved. Sharp as a tack, he would patiently explain all kinds of things to me about the Army when I first got in country and he was furious with the way my boss was treating me. Chris was more than ready to confront him, and I have no doubt that had I given him the go-ahead, the job would have been done handily.

Dixey was the Papa to all of us, terps included, and everybody went to him for counsel. He is the one who encouraged us to fast and pray for Jill Carroll when she was held hostage, and he had a deep heart for the Iraqis. Megan was the mom to her unit, and I took it as a high compliment when a young female soldier said to me, "You sound just like Megan."

Kevin, who had a very ill child at home, struggled with finding a way to help the SEALs, who were a tough group to minister to. Dave, a former history teacher who brought his love of his ancestral Ireland into everything he did, fumed over judicial activism and dereliction of constitutional duty. He once told me, laughing, "Your pedigree as a former liberal is impeccable," and he gave me wonderful Irish tea as a parting gift before he rotated out.

John (Chaplain "Hacky-sack," as we called him) played his bright blue violin during church services. Chaplain Haa, an intense Korean, could play Olympic-level Ping-Pong. Nobody could beat him.

Jim had a child with Asperger's syndrome, and Lonnie had a disabled adopted daughter who suddenly became ill and died while he was home on leave. Matt was a searcher as well as hilariously funny, and he has no idea how he encouraged me when I needed it the most. Every one of these chaplains had a full plate at home, and yet they poured out themselves for the soldiers and the rest of us day in and day out.

These are just a few of the soldiers who will be a part of me forever. A book the size of *War and Peace* would have to be written to record every cheerful greeting, e-mail, note of thanks, hug, door held open, and every time I heard, "Ma'am, you have no idea how much we appreciate you" or "We just came to see you and check on you to make sure you're alright. Gotta take care of Mama." Then there was the hardest of all: "We had to come and thank you one last time and say goodbye before we go home."

Oh, my special, stellar soldiers, if there were just some way I could thank *you!* The only way I can get any release from how much I miss you all is to tell your stories over and over again. I not only owe you my personal freedom, but you ganged up and "flat sprung me" from a set of lies about the likes of you that I had lived with for forty years, and you did it with grace and humor. I love you more than you'll ever know.

You staged a powerful nonviolent revolution that Martin Luther King would be proud of, and you did it with your M16s and sidearms ever at the ready. I owe you a permanent, unpayable debt, and I will gladly spend the rest of my days "paying it forward."

The Berkeley City Council may have been so delusional as to say that the Marines are "uninvited and unwelcome intruders," and I pity the Berzerkers. Perhaps someday they'll understand that if it weren't for the "unwelcome intruders," the folks in Berzerkeley wouldn't even *have* the right to insult the very people who recruit other people to take their verbal abuse! The Code Pink gals would be wearing mandatory burqas, and the guy who celebrates soldier deaths wouldn't be alive to rejoice over the deaths of his very protectors.

If I were Queen of the Universe, I would send these folks on a mandatory field trip to the Great Sandbox to see the Marines and the rest of the service branches in action. Perhaps then the City Council, Code Pink, and the "rejoicer" would end up singing a different tune.

I do know this. If Berzerkeley and crew never change their tune, the Marines will calmly continue to do what they have always done: protect the uniquely American right to willfully sing off-key.

CHAPTER 14

The Day Saddam's Air Conditioner Went on the Blink

am sure that it is difficult to believe that Saddam ever provided comic relief to Americans in Iraq, but he did, and I want you to know about it. If you are anything like me, you could use a therapeutic laugh after wading through the man's black waters. Truth is often stranger than fiction, and the extreme improbability that something like this could actually occur makes this story even more remarkable. Though we were not able to actually observe the incident, I and about six or seven others listened to the eyewitness account just moments after it occurred.

It was a Friday night in late winter, and our praise band was practicing in the fishing lodge for Sunday service. "Mr. X"—a curious, bright, tenderhearted,

searching, wonderfully musical warrior-brother who had not been a believer long—
burst in, his brown eyes as big as proverbial saucers. "You guys, you are *never* going
to believe what just happened!" We hadn't heard any mortar or VBIEDS; there was
no news that Osama had been caught, no cameras smuggled in by foreign visitors
to treat us to shots of Saddam in his tighty whiteys. None of us could imagine what
could have so animated our dear brother "Mr. X."

To get the full impact of this divine irony, you need a little background on
both of the players. Saddam was phobic in a Howard Hughes kind of way. He
was terrified of being poisoned as well as of the germs that naturally occur in
creation, and he went to obsessive lengths to avoid both. He also had a vitriolic
antipathy toward "flies, Persians, and Jews," which will play nicely here in our
little impromptu comedic vignette.

He was also obsessive about controlling indoor temperature. He would spend
part of his day planning the level of temperature in various meeting rooms to
produce a desired psycho/physiological effect on the specific meeting attendees. Too
hot, and you were in trouble with the Uncle; too cold, same thing. Comfortable,
and things were OK, at least for the time being, but that could change on a dime. If
Saddam's air conditioner anywhere ever went out for very long, heads were going to
roll, if only figuratively. Even Coalition heads were at risk. In spite of Saddam's claim
during his trial that he was being kept in a "cage" where he was "tortured," great
efforts were made to ensure that his air conditioner was always functioning and that
he was in all ways at all times comfortable. This, in Mr. Hussein's mind, resulted in
the universe continuing to exist with him comfortably ensconced in its center.

Now for a bit of background on our dear Mr. X. His parents were born in Central
America, and he was born in the States. He had trained as a sniper with the Marines
and nobly served our country in Desert Storm. At one point he actually had Saddam
in his sights. He could have taken him out, and the world would have been spared
a great deal had he been allowed to fire, but it was not to be. Mr. X kept confirming
to his superiors that he had the shot, but they denied him permission to take it, as
Saddam and the doubles had been deemed off limits. God only knows why, and

when I think of what Saddam was able to "accomplish" after Desert Storm, I cringe. Bottom line, Mr. X obeyed, and the rest is history.

Fast forward fifteen years, and our two players are about to meet face to face.

X had returned to Iraq as an HVAC (Heating, Ventilation, Air Conditioning) contractor, and Saddam was in need of his expert services. X had to fill out about seven pages of paperwork prior to going in the cell, so he figured that whoever was inside with the broken AC had to be in the Magnificent Seven (Armyspeak for the top seven most wanted out of the Deck of 52 of Iraqi government war criminals). He had absolutely no idea it would be "Melvin" himself (as Saddam was sometimes referred to).

Dear X was in the cell minding his own business, just doing his job, and in came Saddam, escorted by his guards. Saddam was told to stand facing the wall at the opposite end of the AC unit from X—a distance of about 3–4 feet. Unbeknownst to the Butcher of Baghdad, it was his former would-be assassin working diligently on the all-important AC, and the converted sniper was eyeball to eyeball with his potential hard target from a previous lifetime.

X looked up, saw who it was, inwardly freaked out, and went back to his work. The irony of the moment was not at all lost on our Mr. X, who realized that if he had been allowed to shoot the now-handcuffed man only a yard away from him, no Americans would be in Iraq in the first place.

Saddam turned his face toward X and began speaking to him in Spanish. (Saddam was a brilliant man and spoke several Romance languages as well as Russian.) The guard who had been left in the room with them did not know Spanish, which put him in the position of being the foil for the comedy that was about to unfold. All workers and guards were cautioned against getting into conversation with Saddam, as he was a master manipulator and loved toying with people. Saddam assumed that X was Mexican, but X explained that his family was from Central America. The following conversation ensued, in Spanish.

"Do you hate me?" Saddam asked.

X looked at him and said, "No, I don't hate you."

"Are you a Christian?" Saddam queried.

"Yes."

"Are you Catholic?"

"No."

"What are you, then?"

"I am a Baptist," X told him, continuing to fix the AC.

"What's a Baptist?" asked Saddam.

"I believe that Jesus is the Son of God, died on the cross for our sins, and was resurrected after three days," X replied.

Saddam scoffed in both Spanish and bodyspeak, then decided to change the direction of the conversation toward something more like small talk. He actually could be quite amiable at times, as is the case with many sociopaths, and prided himself on his wise discourses. However, his charming veneer would soon run even thinner with just a little help from the intrepid X. With one flick of his wrist, Saddam's world was about to be turned completely upside down.

X had contracted with some local Muslim jewelers to custom make a gold Star of David for him to wear on a gold chain under his shirt. Risky business, this. That they were willing to do it at all is surprising, but there are several possible explanations. They might have been some of the Jews in Baghdad who only appear to be Muslim, just as there were Jews during the Spanish Inquisition who appeared to convert to Catholicism to avoid the Iron Maiden. It's also possible that they just needed the money badly. They also could have been so grateful that the Butcher was no longer able to get them that they made the Star, even though they had been taught to hate and fear the people who carried the flag bearing it. We will never know. They did a beautiful job on the piece, and X wore it always.

Saddam asked X about his family, which is classic conversational etiquette in the Arab culture. While their backs were to the gringo guard, X had pulled his necklace out from his shirt; as he began to tell Saddam about his wife, kids, and parents, he casually leaned forward to let the Star of David dangle in plain view. He now moved in for a different type of kill than the one that had presented itself fifteen years earlier. He let it slip that his grandfather had immigrated to Central America from—you guessed it—*Israel.*

At this point, according to X, Saddam began to beat his head against the wall! Apparently he couldn't bear to have his precious AC repaired by someone who had Jewish blood ("pig's blood," to Saddam's ilk) flowing in his veins. The guard leaped up, restrained Saddam, and asked X, "What did you say to him?" "Nothing," X replied innocently. "He was just asking me about my family."

The MPs (Military Police) had everything on video and played and replayed the questionable scene from "The Saddam and Mr. X Show." Finally the officer in charge asked the right question, and X was not going to lie, so he told him what had happened. X was then taken off the approved Saddam list, never to return to face one of history's most evil men for any purpose. X had to wait fifteen years to take his shot at Saddam, but I have no doubt that it was worth the wait, even though he got in trouble.

This was yet another time in Iraq when we were virtually incapacitated with laughter and incredulity; our praise band practice came to a screeching halt. Telling this story has brought mirth to a great number of folks, both soldiers and civilians. Since I'll probably always see MWR as a permanent assignment, I hope that I have succeeded in raising your morale with therapeutic laughter at the Amazing Air Conditioner Caper.

CHAPTER 15

The Unholy Ghraib

A bu Ghraib Prison. It is the blight of blights on Operation Iraqi Freedom and will forever live in the annals of bad U.S. military history. What happened there has been heated and spun to the point of becoming a bitter foam on the top of a scalding, nasty, tongue-burning latte. I was still Stateside when the endless digitized photos of naked prisoners in human pyramids were paraded before us on the nightly nag. Like most other Americans, I was furious that something like this could happen on our watch and was relieved to know that those responsible were going to be prosecuted. I just never dreamed that I would become friends with someone who would be prosecuted but was not responsible. Thankfully he was found innocent, and some of his story is contained in this chapter.

Abu Ghraib under Saddam rivaled the evil of Auschwitz, Dachau, Ravensbruck, Bergen-Belsen, and Treblinka. It should have been called Saddam's Center for the Study of Sadism. It would not surprise me at all to find out that Saddam actually studied what was done to concentration camp victims in Nazi Germany and made it SOP for Abu.

One day when I was working at Saddam's hunting lodge, I talked with three soldiers who were just finishing their tour of duty and were getting ready to go home. They had arrived in country just after the assault phase and had been assigned to Abu Ghraib. What they told me they had found there made me want to puke. It can be summed up in seven words: *three vats of acid and a chipper.* In addition, there was a room where whatever was done was so horrific that no one could totally figure out how it was done. There was so much gore and it was so impossible to clean it sufficiently that they just walled in the doorway and sealed it off forever.

I briefly worked at a camp staffed by soldiers and contractors who had been at Abu before it was handed back over to the Iraqis. In the early days of OIF, they had been significantly under-resourced, had to wear their Kevlar and body armor every day, and were constantly under mortar, rocket, and automatic weapons fire. In these conditions they cared for local Iraqi children and ran a hospital where they treated everyone—no matter what their injury or who they were. For the first five months or so they had only one hot meal a day, and things like cold water and laundry soap were hard to come by.

One man told me that he had seen a succession of jail cells, each smaller than the previous one, where condemned prisoners were moved daily as their rendezvous with death drew nearer. The last one was so narrow that it forced the condemned to stand continuously. The last cell was also located right next to the death room, where everything that occurred could be heard by whoever was waiting his turn.

Iraqis who were incarcerated there but later released have told of hundreds of hangings during a two-to-three-day capital punishment frenzy. I don't think that they had received trials of any sort. There was also a surgical room where the condemned's organs were automatically harvested following execution. I sincerely doubt that either the condemned or their families were given an option; "organ donor" never appeared on a driver's license.

My coworker Frank Sorbin told me that because Saddam allegedly didn't believe in "torturing" women and children, he had specially designed drowning pools created for them. Yes, that's correct; there was a specific one for the kiddos. I wonder what Saddam's response would have been if someone had suggested that a fitting sentence for him would have been to be drowned in the kiddie pool rather than hanged. I am still amazed and encouraged by the fact that he had a trial at all, given all that he had done, and yet many folks feel that his hanging was done improperly because some invectives were exchanged.

So what's my point? Am I trying to say that the actions of a few U.S. soldiers should be given a pass because those actions pale in the presence of what Abu was designed for in the first place? Not at all. As I said at the beginning of the chapter, I was pretty hacked at our soldiers' behavior and would have been personally dismayed if they *had* been given a pass. However, there are a few things that need to be examined more closely for a fuller picture.

The first has to do with defining torture—the subject of an ongoing debate throughout the duration of OIF. It is true that after the Abu Ghraib debacle, the U.S. military changed its definition of torture to include the offenses that were prosecuted in the various Abu-related trials. However, comparing torture as it has been historically understood to what happened at Abu is a classic apples-and-oranges comparison. Both situations are wrong, but one was much more like a hazing.

In my mind, torture is the stuff made famous during the Inquisition—things like the rack or the Iron Maiden. It is like the Japanese slitting open men's testes and then lighting them on fire during WWII, not pointing at them and grinning in a picture. As one Iraqi man said, "If the American idea of torture is having a female officer fondle my genitals, then sign me up!"

I have no desire to be coarse here in citing the Iraqi man's statement. But the fact of the matter is that according to detainee testimonies gathered by interrogators and terps at one camp where I worked, no one in the Arab world looked upon what happened at Abu on our watch as being torture. They were absolutely shocked that we would think it was and were even more amazed that we would prosecute for it. Their idea of torture is consistent with the things Al-Qaeda does, like inviting a family over for dinner and serving their child as the entrée to keep them from cooperating with the Crusaders. It is not, as a JAG officer alleged on TV, putting a detainee in a cold room and playing Red Hot Chili Peppers CDs until they break down and tell all.[19]

True to form, Al-Qaeda turned our concern for prisoner treatment against us. They were the embodiment of the famous quote from Shakespeare's *Hamlet*, "the lady doth protest too much, methinks." According to detainee reports, their outrage was feigned and designed to sully us. It was a near-perfect psy-ops move on their part.

Trying to arrive at a global understanding of what constitutes torture is not the point of this chapter, and I doubt that there will ever be a global standard codified by a globally recognized revision of the Geneva Convention. Even if there were, I doubt that terrorists would do much more than laugh at such a definition.

There was one positive result of the Abu Ghraib scandal that is considerably less known than the torture debate. Some detainees *actually flipped—turned toward the U.S.—because of our concern for them.* They were so unsettled by the fact that they were not about to lose digits one by one that they "sang." Who would have thought it?

Furthermore, I was privileged to observe firsthand a story of personal redemption in connection with Abu Ghraib. When I was in my first official hostile work environment, it was very clear that I was not welcome in the MWR office or anywhere else in the building, for that matter. Whatever I did seemed not to be the right thing, and I had to find something worthwhile to do and lie low until I could be transferred. I spent my days organizing the MWR library, which took days due to the number of books that had been sent from the States.

It was during my own "lemons-to-lemonade" exercise that I met Lt. Col. Steve Jordan. He was one of the highest ranking officers to be associated with the Abu Ghraib scandal, and the only one to face a possible court martial and prison time if convicted. He began to come into MWR prior to redeploying home to his family and waiting while the Army decided how it was going to proceed. While he was in legal limbo, I would find books for him written by authors that I knew he liked. We began to chat bit by bit, and I enjoyed his acquaintance. It looked like he was going to be indicted, and while he was very careful not to discuss the details of the case, it was clear that he was about to face his personal lion's den.

I would listen to him as he struggled to make sense of all that was going on. I had no idea if he was guilty or not, but it did seem strange to me that any soldier could be held responsible for the wrongful behavior of other soldiers that he did not command or supervise. From what I understand, primarily Military Police soldiers did what we saw on the news, and it occurred outside Jordan's sphere of responsibility and without his knowledge. In fact, Lt. Col. Jordan was not even assigned to any of the Army units associated with Abu Ghraib, though initial reports stated he was somehow "in charge."

Ever the blunt one, I told him, "Colonel, if you are in fact guilty, then I hope you are found guilty, and I hope that your sentence will be just. If you are innocent, then I hope that you are found innocent and that you'll be exonerated. Whatever happens, though, if you let it, it will make you a better man than if Abu had never happened." We remained friends in spite of my boldness—perhaps because of it. I was just glad that I was a civilian and didn't have to ask permission to "speak frankly" and that Steve wasn't offended.

He knew that I played keyboards for the Sunday evening church service, and I invited him to visit. I knew that Capt. Chris Bassett, a most excellent chaplain with a shepherd's heart, would be able to help Steve Jordan get through the days ahead. As the heat turned up in his life, he would visit me at MWR almost every day, even if only for a moment to say, "Please pray for me and the other soldiers," meaning all who were involved and had been indicted. He told me that he had been raised in a Christian home and that his mom and family in the Midwest had been faithfully praying for him for years. However, as a young man he had rebelled and decided to check out life in the land of the prodigal; now it looked like his family's prayers were lovingly backing him into a corner.

The day finally came when he attended our church service, and I could tell he was enjoying the music as well as Chaplain Chris's message. Watching him as he surrendered his life to his Maker is one of my dearest memories of my time in Iraq.

Yeshua fished Steve Jordan out of the drink that beastly hot night and began to cleanse and heal him from the effects of being backslidden for decades, right in the middle of Saddam's old fishing lodge.

I know the cynical would sneer, "Yeah right, jailhouse religion." Think that if you wish. All I know is that the man walked out of the building changed. He has his struggles, as do we all, and he is refreshingly honest about them. I know that he wanted to see justice served, as we all did. That night he became ready to face whatever was coming down, and all he asked was that we would pray for him to get through it honorably. Not long after that eventful Sunday night, he returned to the States to "face the music."

As he opened up more during fellowship after services, it was interesting to hear what had caused him to put his focus back on God. It was not just the mess at Abu Ghraib. He told about being wounded by mortar fire and spoke with obvious grief of two young soldiers being killed in that same firefight. Any officer who has a heart will always feel the loss of fellow soldiers, and Lt. Col. Jordan is no exception.

There were numerous other times when he felt he should have been wounded or possibly killed. "Why did I live, and the other guy didn't?" It's a question that every soldier who survives wrestles with. Steve was having a difficult time over the loss of soldiers and Iraqi civilians as well as the negative press over Abu Ghraib that at times seemed to be attempting to implicate him. I suspect he'll have his own book to write on that score; I sure hope so. I can say from experience that the man described in the Abu archives is not the man who became my friend in the Sandbox.

Most of all he was concerned about his family, and the load was taking a physical toll on him as well. Through it all he never quit soldiering, and now he had some new hope and extra help in facing all that was ahead. He has told me that he has a special gratitude for Chaplain Bassett and fond memories of the military and civilian congregation who gathered for worship in a building once owned by Saddam.

As the months then years wore on, Lt. Col. Jordan was finally charged in the late spring of 2006 and was reportedly facing 47½ years at Fort Leavenworth, Kansas, if convicted on all counts. In October 2006, an Investigating Officer dismissed some of the initial charges. As further judicial hearings were held, the truth began to materialize, and when it came to trial in late August 2007, Lt. Col. Jordan was found innocent of having anything to do with detainee abuse at Abu Ghraib. He was initially convicted for failing to obey a general officer order not to discuss the case and was sentenced to a Letter of Reprimand. However, upon final review of all evidence and the questionable memory of a specific general officer, the Army dismissed the guilty charge. Lt. Col. Steve Jordan is free at last, his record clean. I believe that we got our hearts' desire that the truth would come out and justice would be served.

On 10 January 2008, Steve Jordan sent an e-mail that struck me. He notes, "I recently read that . . . 'wounds do heal, and that the friendship of old comrades breathes meaning into life.' . . . The nearly four years of the Abu Ghraib saga have taught me that I am little without your friendship or support."

I contacted him to proof this chapter and see if he objected to anything that I was detailing about him or his Army tribulations. He replied with the following, and I so appreciate his candor and transparency regarding his struggles to walk the walk and not just talk the talk.

I am indeed blessed in all that has happened in my life, including the Abu Ghraib saga, though I am unable at this time to fully discuss the events. I do want everyone to know that yes, at one point I returned to the Lord. Honestly though, residual Abu Ghraib issues tested that faith and I have lost that battle, for now. Just know that there was divine intervention in US vs LTC Steven L. Jordan that is easily attested by the final positive and truthful legal results. I am confident that it was not my doing but the prayers from Christians as Ms. Turner, CPT Bassett, my mother and family members, fellow Soldiers, and Prayer Warriors everywhere that sought the Lord so that truth and justice would prevail.

I believe that divine intervention likely began as I encountered deployed Christians along my patrol path to trial. People such as Ms. Turner, Chaplain Bassett, and others, including CPT Jamie Boston of my legal team, and his pastor-father, fought for me with their prayers and counsel. I am not sure if I am a better man following the Abu Ghraib ordeal as Ali promised I would be that dusty, incredibly hot, and bleak Iraqi summer day. I do know that I have a very unique understanding of what others may face in life, and I believe that you can make it, even if it takes 47 months.

I did renew my belief while in Iraq, but my faith is not yet where and how I want it to be. To those that believed in and supported me, my ability is inadequate to properly express my deep heart-felt gratitude. To those who believe in falsehoods, misperceptions, and government conspiracies regarding Abu Ghraib, you too have my gratitude as well, because it makes knowing all others unlike you so much better. SLJ

If I had been through what Steve Jordan went through, I would be sorely challenged to forgive. My personal struggles in the Sandbox seem silly in comparison to facing nearly a half century in jail for something I didn't do. Forgiving others who seem bent on destroying you can be a lifelong challenge, but I am confident that he'll come through it. I also have a firm hope that when we are indeed old, we'll look back on the outer and inner struggles of Iraq with gratitude, having had friends "to breathe life into us" and wounds that did indeed heal.

CHAPTER 16

Bart Simpson Is
Sleeping with Your Wife

A legend that was especially popular amongst the psy-ops guys in the Gulf War continues to bring a chuckle. The story goes something like this: Baghdad Betty, who allegedly served in the same capacity as Tokyo Rose in WWII to injure the morale of U.S. soldiers, broadcast the equivalent of a loop tape (that plays continually) over the wall to the Joes, stating, "GI, you should be home. Why? Because while you are away, movie stars are taking your women. Robert Redford is dating your girlfriend. Tom Selleck is kissing your lady. Bart Simpson is making love to your wife."

In 1991 *The New York Times* quoted Betty's buglings as being *true*, and as it is tough to get urban legends to die (I think CBS has cancelled *Touched By an Angel* each year for the last seven years because of its reference to God), many still believe that Baghdad Betty actually depicted a little yellow-haired cartoon character as the Casanova that is sullying the virtue of American wives.

Johnny Carson claimed that his staff were the true authors of the Baghdad Betty spoof, and Snopes.com (the plucky resource to which I look to discover just what, in fact, are the chances of my getting bitten by a brown recluse spider while using an airplane toilet) went to great lengths to prove that Baghdad Betty was never really involved in this brilliant example of psychological warfare. Apparently the original gag was to have named Homer Simpson, not Bart, as the culprit. I had read the story years ago in a "World's Stupidest . . ." book and was slightly saddened to find out that it was only a folktale.

Near Christmas Day 2005, an opportunity presented itself that I simply could not ignore. I had temporarily moved into the hooch of my dear roommate Nikki while my lodging a few doors down was being arranged. On the top of Nikki's bookcase was a stuffed Bart Simpson doll. We giggled as I explained the story, and she accommodated my request to take a shot of my arm around Bart while I "slept." Steve was already aware of the Bart story, and I sent him the picture to prove that both Bart and Betty really were indeed alive and well in Baghdad, but his wife's faithfulness had emerged unscathed despite their best attempts.

The Bart Simpson story is simply amusing, but the secret role of stuffed animals in the lives of soldiers and contractors while downrange bears looking into. Stuffed camels are exceedingly popular and can be really elaborate; my hoochmate Beverly gave me one for my first Christmas in Iraq. Karen and Terri, two female officers who were a part of our praise and worship team, gave me a floppy-eared stuffed hound named "Mama Love," and they said I reminded them of the dog. I took that as a compliment, and today Mama Love is perched on the headboard on my side of the bed, reminding me to remember all the brave ones whom I love so deeply.

Stuffed animals (most often Garfield) would show up lashed to or peeking out of soldiers' backpacks (although they were temporarily kenneled for required ruck marches) as well as on the hoods of Humvees. Sometimes kids back home sent stuffed animals so their parents wouldn't be lonely, and soldiers often sent stuffed animals to their kids to hug when they missed their mommy or daddy. The sight of tough-guy soldiers standing in line at the PX to buy stuffed animals for themselves or others is still a sweet memory. I suppose the possibility of hugging a stuffed animal in secret qualifies for "don't ask, don't tell," so I won't.

No treatment of the role of toys downrange would be complete without a lively discussion of the G.I. Joe Hostage Doll Incident, the topic of the next chapter.

CHAPTER 17

A Hoot
of a Hostage Incident

here were times in Iraq when things happened that were so funny that we'd just about slump across stuff and laugh till we wheezed. As I would look at myself acting so silly, I would also realize that my laughter was at the very least cathartic and hopefully therapeutic and that while the level of my hooting was disproportionate, it was as delicious as it was necessary.

Not long before her release from an Al-Qaeda cell, Jill Carroll's captors forced her to make yet another DVD. This time instead of denouncing the U.S. or demanding the release of female prisoners, muj vitriol targeted a sheik from the United Arab Emirates. Jill, who knew some Arabic, was trying to do the broadcast in Arabic with her captors' coaching. The sheik's name was long to boot, even if it had been in her native tongue, which obviously it wasn't. She couldn't get the name right and kept messing up. She finally got so tongue-tied that she started laughing uncontrollably, like you would see in an outtake clip or a blooper show.

She managed to get her captors to crack up, too. Part of it was the actual humor of the situation, and part of it was the stress she was under. Though my tough times were minuscule in comparison to hers, I experienced that type of laugh a few times while in Iraq. You begin to feel a bit out of control, and after a while it's not even funny anymore, but you can't stop. I am about to describe to you one of those very incidents, but before I do, please humor me just a bit.

In the Theater of My Scampish Brain, I envision a Jill Carroll Bloopers DVD being produced by her captors as a fundraiser. Maybe they could charge a few more dinar if she autographed it. Perhaps we could go live to the set and watch in anticipation as they cry "Roll 'em" and snap down the arm on the black-and-white thingy that always appears at the beginning of filming a scene. "Jill Carroll anti-sheik promo, take two." Then the inevitable "Cut!" Then it's, "Now Jill, read my lips as I walk you through this part. You're doin' real good, honey, and we're almost done." And finally, "Cut!" "That's a wrap, everybody, and thanks! Shukran! See ya tomorrow!" "Jill, sweetie, you did just great, just great." Who knows? Maybe Jill will become a cult movie queen among the muj.

One of Jill's captors actually had a copy of Dale Carnegie's *How to Win Friends and Influence People.* No, I am *not* kidding! Maybe they could toss in the Arabic version of Carnegie's classic as a bonus with the promo DVD, beautifully gift-wrapped and with free shipping. "Operators are standing by. Call 1-800-MUJ-DVDS in the next ten minutes to claim your free bonus. Have your credit card ready!"

Humor plays a role in all of life that is designed to keep us well. This is now documented by medical science, and I have seen it used up close and personal as a therapy for cancer. I suspect that the more critical the situation, the greater its healing properties.

I remember when I was a kid and *Hogan's Heroes* first came on. This was about twenty years after WWII ended, and some vets of the Greatest Generation were very offended that anything about a stalag was being portrayed in a humorous fashion.

Truly I can understand their objection. If the antics of Colonel Klink and Sergeant Schultz, with his iconic "I know nutheeng, nutheeng!!" sputterings brought back PTSD symptoms to someone who survived all that, then indeed the show should have never been produced in the first place.

But I wonder now, having been in the midst of such insanity for nearly three years myself, if one role of humor as it pertains to adversity or adversaries is to laugh away some of their hold. Does laughter lessen their ability to rob of joy and thus their control? Does evil lose some of its power when it is laughed at? I know for sure that it does when it is loved at.

I was told once by my dear friend Norm, a Jewish Christian, that the guy who played Colonel Klink on the venerable sitcom was himself half Jewish. Werner Klemperer was the son of a famous symphony conductor, and his Jewish mother was an accomplished soprano. His *Halbjude* heritage would have been enough to get him killed for drawing breath in Hitler's Germany. He escaped Nazi Germany with his family in 1933 and had a long career as a concert pianist, violinist, actor, and conductor. He joined the U.S. army to fight in WWII and later spent time traveling and entertaining the troops.

At first I was kind of taken aback at the idea that someone who would have been exterminated on the watch of the *real* Colonel Klinks would choose to be a caricature Nazi. Then Norm explained to me that the only condition under which Klemperer would take the part was if Hogan and crew *always* bested his character. *Hogan's Heroes* went on to win several Emmy awards and is a cultural reference point for all American Baby Boomers. I hope that there were dads who survived the stalags who got together and watched it weekly. Group therapy was not big back then, but I hope they received a hearty dose of cinematherapy.

I would love it if someday we get so far away from this muj madness that, just as *Hogan's Heroes* hit our corporate cultural funny bone in the sixties, someone will create a comparable foil that will be routinely outsmarted, as was Klink. I know some folks won't think poking fun at stuff that went down while we were in the Great Sandbox will ever be appropriate, and I hope they can forgive those of us who find lots of stuff to laugh at. We mean no harm; we're just trying to get through.

Solomon said that a merry heart does good like a medicine. I watched the soldiers visibly brighten as the tale I am about to tell you circulated through the camp. One guy laughed so hard I was sure he was going to start crying. He turned bright red, and his shoulders shook. I know the laughter it brought me was certainly needed at the time, and I hope you at least can crack a one-sided smile. For those who were there, it is a fond memory of Morale being lifted, Recreation being spontaneous, and Welfare definitely being increased for all of us. Here goes.

On 1 February 2005, just after the first election, the *New York Times* printed an article stating that a Coalition soldier had allegedly been kidnapped the day of the election. Ostensibly this was a psy-ops move on someone's part to dampen the spirits of the Coalition, who had just been the attending physicians and midwives at the birth of the New Iraq. However, no known group was taking credit for it, and there had been a theater-wide accountability check, with everyone present and accounted for. No commander was missing anyone anywhere.

A picture of the "missing soldier" was on the desk when I came to work that night. Something about it was odd, even to rookie me. The soldier of African descent had a weird, empty look on his face, and his gaze was at the wrong angle for the picture. Behind him was the typical curtain present in most hostage videos, with "There is no God but Allah, and Mohammed is his prophet" written on it in Arabic.

He sat awkwardly on the floor, and he was wearing a vest that certainly wasn't part of standard-issue IBA (Individual Body Armor). His face bore camo paint, which was not needed in the desert. Off to the right was a weapon pointed at a strange angle at his head, but no hands were shown holding the weapon. M16s and sometimes M4s are used throughout theater, and I am told this wasn't exactly either. "Hmmmm, that ain't right," I'm a-thinkin'.

Sgt. Walter N., my friend from Puerto Rico, came in to the MWR center, and soon we discovered the poor guy's true identity. Now Walter and I had had many a hearty laugh prior to this night. He would come in and play Yahtzee, Trivial Pursuit, and other board games, and he had a great sense of humor. However, what we were best at was coming up with zany improv scripts in Spanish while watching

Arabic soap operas with the mute button on. Soap operas in any culture tend to be over the top, and Arabic ones are in a class by themselves. We would come up with instant, convoluted plots about "whose-daughter's-lover's-evil-twin-had-just-come-back-from-the-convent-pregnant-with-triplets-conceived-in-a-test-tube-and-implanted-in-vitro-against-her-will-by-an-evil-scientist-in-the-convent-dungeon" type of stuff. We would play all the roles and change our voices for each character until the wheeze factor kicked in so hard that we couldn't do it anymore. Daytime Drama Emmy Award material for sure, and in Spanish, even.

Well, ladies and gentlemen, the "hostage," whose picture had now been circulated around the Net and apparently also by some news outlets in the States, was none other than an *action doll* named Special Ops Cody. Whoever made this little set and placed him in there must have been registering their displeasure at the success of the election and wanted to demoralize the soldiers. It quickly became known on the Net as "The G.I. Joe Hostage Doll Incident." After we composed ourselves and wiped the tears from our eyes, we began to formulate plans to "get after it" and find our "missing man."

Walter made copies of Cody's ransom picture and posted sign-up sheets for those interested in going outside the wire to rescue the doll from a fate worse than death. A true live extraction mission, and anyone could go! As we showed Cody's picture to soldiers who came in the MWR center, the reaction was predictable and glorious. We got positively punchy over the imperiled Cody. I watched in delight as, for a moment, the exhaustion from being on duty during the election left our guys, and they were as playful as pups.

Now remember, this was at the SEALS / Special Forces / Iraqi Special Forces camp, so these guys were really good at making up stuff as they went along and quick at coming up with particularly daring plans. The doll was going to be beheaded soon, according to the jihad grapevine, and they were going to have to move fast. After all, by now we had found out that the "Mujahideen Brigades" had posted the following on the Internet: "Our mujahideen heroes of Iraq's Jihadi Battalion were able to capture American military man by the name of John Adam after killing a number of his comrades and capturing the rest."

In addition, John Adam was going to be beheaded within seventy-two hours.

By morning, it seemed the whole camp knew about "Joe," as we were still calling him, and bloggers from all over the world had gotten into it. Their involvement didn't have anything to do with Walter, but they were trumpeting this poor guy's situation all over cyberspace, and the comments took on a life of their own. Eventually there were over *51,000* entries in the blogosphere. *Jihad Watch* had a Barbie doll dressed as a princess/mother pleading for the life of her son. *Daily Farce* showed a Barbie doll as the pregnant wife of Cody, agonizing over his possible fate. My personal fave was, "If Joe gets blown up, does he get seventy-two Barbies in paradise?"

The next day, 2 February 2005, the perpetrator of the scam issued an apology to the Arab world, although I did not discover this until November of 2007. I had assumed that whichever cell had produced it was so embarrassed by how badly it had backfired that they were too ashamed to come forth and take credit for their cleverness. If only they had known how much joy they had brought my guys and soldiers everywhere!

It turns out that the "group" responsible for the Cody caper was just one twenty-year-old Iraqi, whose e-mail handle was "al-Iraqi4." He apologized and admitted that the picture was created with a toy he bought for $5.00. He declined to provide much information about himself, explaining that it "might jeopardize my life and the lives of my family."[20] I don't think it was "al's" intention to give my guys such a bwah-hah breather, and apparently he managed to really tick off some of the meanie mujahideenies. According to the now-defunct SITE Institute, a Web site that monitored jihadist chatter, some people "prayed for the hoaxter's guidance toward righteousness and resorted to God for judgment, others were furious at him for 'demoralizing' the members."[21] Lesson learned: Muj ain't playin', so don't mess with him.

Well, this thing was not going to just go away, as there was still some fun to be had.

Three days later, in the 5 February 2005 *Stars and Stripes,* the military newspaper circulated throughout the armed services, there was more "in-depth coverage" of our kidnapped comrade. It appeared in the European edition, and Ward Sanderson was the "correspondent reporting from in the field."

Turns out that Cody had been specially commissioned by AAFES, the suppliers for all the PXs (the stores where military personnel make their discretionary purchases), to be made by a company called Dragon Models USA. This meant that Cody was not available for purchase by John Q. Public. True to the nature of the free market, Cody—who could originally have been "ransomed" off a PX shelf for a mere $39—was now going for somewhere between $100 and $230 on eBay! The Dragon Models folks got millions of hits on their site, and all twelve phone lines in their office were jammed with calls from people who wanted their own Cody to give a good home and coach through combat stress. After all, the seventy-two-hour deadline had come and gone, and the little guy was looking at getting his head popped off if someone didn't do something soon!

Good news, though! Another Special Ops action figure was on his way to the rescue. None other than Colonel Danny McKnight was fixin' to deploy and be "boots on the ground" real soon to go after our guy. No doubt he conferred with Walter, and the two of them likely came up with an extraction plan that was so solid and secret that it is now in the Delta training manual available at the Camp Liberty PX.

It was only a few days before Cody was safe back in his plastic packaging "hooch" with all his accessories neatly tucked away in their assigned cubicles. He has had extensive combat stress/PTSD help and is recovering nicely, although his face still retains that weird, blank look. He also doesn't want anyone to touch his face and remove his camo paint; it's kind of a security blanket for him. You can visit him at www.snopes.com/media/goofs/gijoe.asp, but he has strict visiting hours. Please, don't make any sudden movements, point anything at his head, or yell in Arabic. He's been through enough, and we don't want any relapses.

"Al," if you are reading this, thanks for the memories.

CHAPTER 18

Have Yourself a Merry Little . . .

C elebrating holidays in a war zone was bittersweet. I found a new appreciation for *all* holidays that, like just about everything else in my life, I used to take for granted while safely and comfortably living out the American Dream.

People went out of their way to wish one another Happy Thanksgiving, Happy Hanukkah, Merry Christmas, Happy Valentine's Day, Happy Whatever Day. It was refreshing that there was no workplace mandate against greeting people at holiday time. When I was still living in Seattle, one year the King County Executive's Office actually sent out a memo forbidding employees to wish each other Merry Christmas. I don't recall any free speech group protesting that this was a constitutionally guaranteed freedom, and back in that day it never occurred to me that it was *soldiers* who protected that right.

For each holiday in Iraq, our MWR department planned activities such as races and tournaments, and the food service crew decorated the Dfacs with props that had been sent to us as well as ones that we made. There were streamers, posters, sculptures, theme cakes, and sometimes candles and centerpieces. A couple of times there were two real beers per soldier, closely monitored. There has never been a wartime situation where there were so many homey touches, and I was glad we could help out. The best part of all holidays was that the palace was opened up to everyone for services and prayer, music, reflection, and encouragement. The services were always packed out, and we invariably emerged energized and grateful for all that we had, both in Iraq and back home.

The first American holiday I celebrated in Iraq was the Fourth of July in 2004. Iraq had just been turned back over to the Iraqis, and Independence was about to be birthed. We had no end of "fireworks," courtesy of Baghdad Bob.

On Labor Day of 2004 it seemed like the whole base came to the barbecue at the MWR center. It was just a mellow time, like you'd have back home in your own backyard. I still think with fondness of Prince, my MWR boss of African descent, Andrew, a dear guy from the Philippines who worked with us, and Manuel, a Latino kid from Houston, cooking over a hot fire in 125+ degree weather. Three guys from three completely different backgrounds sweatin' for the soldiers. Very cool.

One Halloween my coworkers Beverly and Dasheen decided to throw a party for everyone at the Rec Center. Beverly had candy sent over from the States to give to the soldiers and Iraqis. Dasheen was feeling particularly brave (either that or completely insane), as he came dressed as Osama Bin Laden. Seeing "the world's most wanted man" handing out Ping-Pong paddles and balls, checking out movies, and signing folks in and out of the computer lab in a place where Iraqis were training with Navy SEALS provided some welcome comic relief.

In Iraq I realized that some of our national holidays that had been designed to express gratitude to our service members had been almost completely stripped of their significance. All they had ever meant to me was the chance to have some time off to just do my thing as a typical American woman. I was completely disconnected from the whole point of the holiday as well as from the people who gave themselves so I could have the freedom to go where I wanted and do what I wanted. In Iraq, Veterans Day and Memorial Day took on meaning for the very first time.

Thanksgiving Days were my favorite, probably because the name of the day lit up in neon the continual process that was occurring inside of me. Thankfulness seems to take on a power of its own when you have no idea if your next breath could be your last. Also, there is no commercial confusion attached to Thanksgiving, and it was my dad's favorite holiday.

In 2006 the first person I was able to wish a Happy Thanksgiving was a full-blooded Navajo who was a member of the firefighter team. I thanked him for being willing to risk his life for us. (Can you imagine donning thick gear and fighting fires in 130-degree weather while being shot at?) I repented to him for whatever my people may have ever done to his people. I don't power down daily megadoses of great white guilt; I know now that I am not responsible for what my ancestors did, although there was a time when I thought that I was. However, I have found that genuine repentance usually brings reconciliation—something I would love to see more of between people groups. The firefighter grinned and thanked me and wished me a Happy Thanksgiving as well.

On that particular day, I had an urgent need for mass quantities of toilet paper— another thing I used to take for granted before I lived in Mexico. The porta-potties in Iraq were often out of supplies in the morning, so I was relieved to discover just enough in the unit that I hastily scurried into. "Lord," I prayed, "On this Thanksgiving Day I would like to give thanks for toilet paper, right here, right now. I mean it, Lord. Thank you."

DD, the Dfac manager from India, greeted me warmly at breakfast and wished me all the returns of the day. Such sincere good wishes from someone from a completely different culture that doesn't celebrate the American Thanksgiving filled my heart, especially when he must have been exhausted and the day had only begun. The food service crew had worked hard for us to have a feast that greatly surpassed anything many folks would have gotten at home.

At dinner I sat with a young American man who had decided prior to coming to Iraq that he wanted out of the gay lifestyle. He had already shared his story with me, and I felt honored that he trusted me. His courage touched me to the depths; his commitment to change was awe-inspiring; and his humor and transparency were positively refreshing. As we held hands that day to give thanks at the table, I felt like I had no more room to contain blessing. It was a Thanksgiving I'll never forget, with a diversity that no change agent could have possibly finagled.

At Hanukkah and Christmas, the American people bombarded us with blessings. There was candy, homemade fudge, greeting cards by the hundreds of thousands, books, tapes, CDs, toiletries, hot chocolate, cookies, and more—a veritable invasion mounted by thousands of individuals and groups back home. My mom sent wondrous tea in brightly colored packets. Friends sent me so many packages for the soldiers that I could hardly get in and out of my hooch. A single mom who is homeschooling her four sons and another friend who has a heart to take care of everyone on the entire planet sent boxes filled with marshmallows, graham crackers, and Hershey bars for the guys at the Entry Check Points (ECPs). It can get down to freezing in Iraq, and on 11 January 2008, it actually snowed. The ECP guys kept warm on night shift by building fires in fifty-five gallon drums from whatever scrap they could find. It was delightful to see their grins when I alerted them to get ready for "some serious s'more action" and handed out the goodies.

I also enjoyed helping soldiers shop online for their wives. One soldier, Dave Smith from Niagara Falls, was one of those "salt of the earth" guys who would always make sure we had hot food on third shift. He and I were both new to online shopping, but together we found totally cool stuff for his wife, whom he called "Princess Di," and his mother-in-law, who had truly been a mom to him. I found out one night that "Smitty Jingles," as we called him, had guarded the area where my sister Kathy and her family live in Manhattan after 9/11. I was glad that she, my brother-in-law, and their family had had someone like him looking out for their safety.

One year we had a Christmas party for both Coalition and Iraqi soldiers, and it was a blast. Mercy and Marly, who were from the Philippines, and Beverly and

Elizabeth, who were from the States, made decorations such as paper snowflakes that took hours to cut and foil-covered Ping-Pong balls. Mercy took apart a New Year's noisemaker and turned it into an angel for the tree. Their ingenuity knew no bounds. We strung popcorn and lights on an artificial tree sent from home and had hot food trucked in from an adjacent camp for the party. The Iraqis were thrilled, and no one seemed to have a problem with getting into the season that is supposed to be about the Ultimate Gift. Elizabeth, who was Jewish, had taught English in the Middle East for fifteen years. Gutsy gal. She made sure there was a menorah on the event calendar for the month. There was also a *big* menorah inside Saddam's palace—something I don't think he would have handled well.

As always, the holiday services were filled with both joy and aching. We had real candles, sang completely politically incorrect Christmas carols, and became like family. I wanted to be back in Iraq for Christmas last year, as odd as that sounds. I wanted to pack up my whole family and take them over there so they could taste what I had been given. Nowadays, Christmas just isn't Christmas for me without the Joes and Janes.

In 2005 on New Year's Eve, NBC came to what had been Saddam's hunting lodge to film and interview the soldiers and then broadcast back in the States. We were having a dance with food—something that didn't happen all that often, and the place was wall-to-wall bodies. The marble walls greatly amplified the noise, and it was complete pandemonium as everyone yelled "Happy New Year!" I was hugged, picked up, swung around, and kissed on the cheek, and the New Year was rung in in no uncertain terms. What would it hold for us? Who knew, with a newly elected Congress that was so sour about everything that was going on in Iraq that it seemed it had been baptized in lemon juice? For the moment, we didn't care.

Valentine's Day saw the inundation of the PXs with those rather garish heart-shaped boxes of chocolates and the predictable huge, flowery, lacy mushy cards. Back home, the wives would get dressed up and send TV messages courtesy of AFN: "Happy Valentine's Day, baby! I am so proud of you," they'd say, gowned in the little black dress. "Can't wait till you come home!" Meanwhile, AFN broadcast spots that reminded soldiers to remember their loves on the home front. The soldiers would stand outside the post office in long lines to mail their cards and chocolates back home in time to get to their sweethearts by the fourteenth. Once again I got to help Smitty pick out flowers for his wife, mom, and mom-in-law, as well as to be his scribe for the e-cards he sent with the bouquets.

Soldiers did their best to be romantic on the phone, despite all the other people in the room. There was also quite a waiting line to get to the phones. I don't think anyone back in the States minded being awakened in the middle of the night to be reminded they were loved, though they may never understand just how physically tough it was at times to communicate. The soldiers would also instant message mush and gush, and Steve and I used the "falling hearts" IM wallpaper with all the hugs-and-kisses emoticons. Sometimes I would sing to Steve from inside the phone booths, and if the American Dfac manager was on the line to home and was able to hear me, he would tell me how much it touched him. I had always taken telephones for granted before Iraq, but I became deeply grateful for them during the holidays. The lines to use the phones were long and the calls short, but being able to say hi, even if briefly, to my family wherever they were together eased the ache that invariably came on those days.

For some soldiers, Valentine's Days were sheer torture. More than one had gotten a Dear John or Jane letter while in Iraq, which is painful any time, let alone in the middle of a war. Sometimes the Dear John/Jane letters originated from the Sandbox, but thankfully far less often due to the soldier care given by the chaplains.

Holidays in the midst of hostilities become more precious due to the precariousness of the situation. Pushing away that precariousness for just a moment to celebrate is heady, rejuvenating stuff—something I hope I never forget. The freedom in the first place to celebrate anything, even in a makeshift manner, becomes the most precious of all. I hope I never get to the place that I ever sit down at home on Thanksgiving, surrounded by people whom I love, where there isn't a significant part of me that wishes I was in a Dfac in the Sandbox with the Joes and Janes.

CHAPTER 19

The Dance
toward Democracy

The night before the first Iraqi election, I had the distinct impression that I was about to experience what the ancient Greeks referred to as a *kairos* moment. The Greeks had more than one word for time, just as they had close to a dozen words for love. *Kairos* is difficult to translate into our idiom, as it has the idea of "time between time," or at the very least, a "special time." *Chronos* is the other Greek word for time, and it is our etymological source for English words such as "chronological" and "chronometer." In contrast to *kairos*, *chronos* is the practical, quantifiable stuff of seconds, minutes, and hours.

I knew that what I was about to encounter as I waited for Voting Day to arrive was the proof that once again I have been privileged to be an intimate observer of an inarguably remarkable quest for freedom, and I wanted to record it carefully. The

151

MWR was slow that night, as everyone was gearing up to go out and protect the voters come morning.

To preserve the authenticity of that *kairos* moment, this chapter consists of two journal entries which I sent home as newsletters—one written just before midnight on the eve of the election, and the other written on election day itself.

JOURNAL ENTRY, 29 JANUARY 2005

In fifteen minutes, it will be January 30, 2005, and the Iraqi Dance toward Democracy shall begin on a grand and official scale. The prayers of millions in the States and all over the globe shall be answered with what will no doubt be endless stories of courage under fire, both from the military and civilian side. My heart tells me that liberty, though purchased with blood, will be born here. In our species, all natural births involve some blood, but the cost is nearly always greatly outweighed by the joy and the new dance of the heart. So it is in the affairs of countries. There shall be a bawling, hollerin' brand-new nation! Someone new to dance with! We are on tiptoe, waiting. Some of us are pacing outside the birthing room, and some are in the midst of the inevitable mess, keeping watch and cleaning up afterward.

The Dance has begun in the States. The now-famous footage of two Iraqi men in America, who having just completed their absentee ballot began dancing in celebration in the parking lot of a polling place to music provided by a car stereo, has been broadcast around the globe.

We decided to start early here in Baghdad by having a swing dance at the Morale, Welfare, and Recreation center where I work. We put up posters all over camp with pictures of Fred Astaire and Ginger Rogers, announcing the time and the date. The invitation said, "Let's Face the Music and Dance. Celebrate the Iraqi elections the way Fred Astaire would." "Face the Music," of course, was a reference to whatever Baghdad Bob had planned for us. We'll have to ride that one out, and tremendous precautions have been taken to make sure that Bob's bombs are a bomb.

The swing dance was a successful event, with the consensus being that we need to do this much more often, and so the Baghdad Swing Society was officially born.

Although I am sure we will increase in our level of skill—guys will get better at leading out on the dance floor, and women will become more skilled in reading their cues and following—tonight will always have a special place in my heart. This is because it will forever be tied to a most important birth—that of a new nation which, contrary to what naysayers back home are warning us, has great potential to be an example to its neighbors and whose rebuilding is being realized quite speedily.

Senator Ted Kennedy says we are bogged down here in a "quagmire" and our presence here is "the problem." I disagree. Consider this: there is more stability and progress being made in postinvasion Iraq than there was in post-WWII Germany, when the French and the Russians were in the reconstructive mix. It took three years to establish a new bank and print new currency in Germany, but it happened here within two months. It took ten years to start training a new German army, but a new Iraqi army started training here within just three months. I have personally seen the look of pride on the faces of the Coalition soldier "papas" as their local guys are getting ready to graduate from boot camp. Most likely the children of these Americans get the same "attsa-mah-boy" grins when their dads are home coaching Little League. Their dads and some of their moms are here, and they continue to amaze me.

Here, after two months, there were municipal councils in all major Iraqi cities, but it took eight months to achieve that in Germany. There are more positive statistics, and it needs to be remembered that there was also insurgent terrorism in postwar Germany. I wish Senator Kennedy could be here for this. I wish he could hear with his soul as well as his ears the voices of Iraqis all over the world who are forever grateful that they are getting a chance to "breathe free," as the Statue of Liberty so poignantly invites, and that we will ultimately be safer ourselves. Do I believe that? Yep. It has taken about thirty years of colliding with concepts which I never had considered as well as being over here seeing this firsthand to convince me.

Chris Matthews of MSNBC said he's praying for the safety of a fellow newsman broadcasting from Iraq. Wow. Appealing to Someone greater than ourselves? On a mainstream newscast? Cool. Hope no one sues him.

ABC reports that 80 percent of Iraqis are planning on voting. One eighty-year-old woman said she'll buy a coffin just in case she needs it, but she's voting. Let's talk about the women for a moment. If the recent elections in Afghanistan can serve as a benchmark, the women could very well be the deciding factor in the Iraqi elections. Women in Afghanistan walked through mine fields in order to vote. Ohhh, Americans, listen up! We did way better than usual in our own recent presidential election as far as showing up at the polls is concerned. But walking through mine fields? Just to choose? Would that we had that passion!! There is a tangle of candidates on tomorrow's ballot; some no doubt are scalawags. Yet the people will risk their lives to choose whether scalawags or saviors will speak for them. I am sure that when it's all over, some pricey Havana cigars will be passed out over here by the folks who are here making sure Iraqis get their chance to choose.

I would love to tell you about one of them. Arnie is from New York City, and for him—as for most of the New Yorkers here—this campaign, this war, officially began on 11 September 2001. His background is nuclear medicine, and then he made a huge career "lane change" and became undoubtedly one of "New York's finest," a comfortable term for a police officer. He did it because he wanted to help more people than he was helping in his medical career. His heart is captured by children, and he has brought me precious photos of Iraqi kids that he's taken while out on patrol. He also has a father's heart, something of which there is such a dearth in our current largely fatherless American culture. He is what is known as a "plat daddy," a father to the guys in his platoon, and he carries his guys in his heart in ways that probably no one besides his Maker fully sees.

Arnie recently came in to our MWR center, and it was clear that the wind was out of his sails. They had just had to do some door kicking. The guys they encountered were farmers, seemingly. Traces of nitrogen found on their hands indicated of one of two things: either they were farmers using fertilizer to fortify their crop yield, or that was their cover and they were busy making bombs. Maybe both. The men were arrested. One was weeping because he had to leave behind a sick child, and the families of all three had been disrupted due to the portending absence of the menfolk. And here was Arnie, agonizing over the decision to bring them in, over the plight of the sick child. "Did we do the right thing? Did we just make new terrorists [referring to the children] because we arrested innocent men? What if we were wrong?" These are the times when I feel like I have nothing to say that could help; I have no answers or wisdom.

What I do have is a cheap guitar purchased here at the bazaar, which, like all guitars of its caliber, has a B string that steadfastly refuses to stay in tune for more than ten seconds. So, I got out my guitar and began to sing to Arnie of the only One who could help him. "Who is refreshing, as water in the desert, lovelier than all things here below"—a song written by my deceased friend Sheila. "Farther along, we'll know all about it; farther along, we'll understand why"—another, written by an old black Southern preacher who had just been through the kind of hell that crushing loss can etch on a soul if it is allowed to—operative word being "allowed."

Turns out, Arnie played the guitar himself as a kid and hadn't played in twenty years. He politely asked if he could play, and to his delight, his fingers remembered what to do. A slight smile returned to his face. The burden was not totally lifted, but there had at least been a reprieve, thank God. I hope he will borrow my modest guitar as often as he needs and wants to. It turns out they were right. These guys had been making bombs. Intel was good, the mission was a success, and Arnie himself can now "breathe free" over this incident in the same way we are waiting for Iraq to take its first, crucial breath tomorrow and the next few days.

Why are guys like Arnie so important in my life? Because I grew up with the memory of the My Lai Massacre in Viet Nam and had so handily come to believe that soldiers were "baby killers," just by virtue of being soldiers in the first place. While I know there are jerks to be found anywhere, what my life here in Iraq affords me, day after day, is exposure to guys like Arnie—men with father's hearts, men who have been used to change me.

As surely as I believe something will be born in this weary nation tomorrow, I know that something has been born in my formerly weary and cynical soul, for which I am grateful. I have an appreciation for liberty that could have been obtained in no other way than getting to be here for this birth. There is cause to dance! As I work nights, I often go up on the roof of our building at dawn to welcome what for everyone else is the beginning of a new day and dance my thanks to the One who made it for me. If you are in my 'hood, you are welcome to join me; if not, then begin to dance yourself, even if no one joins you. The Lord of the Dance will, if you ask Him.

JOURNAL ENTRY, 30 JANUARY 2005

Our baby is here!

Few days have meant so much to me; few days have brought such unchecked joy and the tears thereof. There are no words to express how wildly grateful I feel to be here in the middle of it, and even though I was only in a position to personally celebrate with one Iraqi, his smile said it all. The barber, who risks his life just to be a barber here, came in looking like he had just gotten married, or his wife had had a baby, or he had won the lottery, or sumthin'! We all got around him, pouring out congratulations, thumps, and handshakes. I wanted to hug him, but of course, that would not be appropriate here.

Not long after the barber (whose name I can't mention), the guys who helped make it happen started to stream in. They had been out all day protecting this Iraqi democratic "mother" as she bore down giving birth, and they were pooped. Happy, but tuckered out. Captain Sean Michael Flynn, of New York's Fighting 69th (and author of a book by the same title), sat down in front of the TV with cable access to watch the history he had just helped to make and promptly fell asleep in the chair, his M16 right next to him.

One soldier had to go right back out on a mission, a "snatch and grab" of a bad guy. He had little time to let down long enough to celebrate, but his tired smile said it all. As I watched the news, I would leap up and shout from time to time, knowing that no one in the center would think that I had gone off the deep end any more than they usually do. I hooted, hollered, and jumped in response to what I was seeing and hearing. There were so many scenes—the dancing in the streets, the lines of people waiting to vote, the Iraqi soldiers dancing, families at the polls.

However, there were two images that wiped me right out. The first was of a ninety-four-year-old woman, a little raisin of a human, being brought to a polling place in a wheelbarrow with what was probably her great-great-grandbaby in the wheelbarrow with her, voting for what could be the only time in her life. Then there was the couple standing in the street showing their "purple badges of courage," the index fingers which had been dipped in purple dye at the polls after they had voted to insure that no one would vote more than once. Do we realize what guts that took? They could still die for their choice. I wonder what would happen if we did this in the States each November when we vote?

As an American, I took great pleasure in watching the reporters who are over here. They didn't even try to subdue their elation. They had been out risking their lives to film history, and they were most definitely like proud new papas, reporting the ecstasy occurring all around them. When one was asked if the Iraqis, as had allegedly been reported, felt that this was just a show, that the elections were simply an expression of Western arrogance, he said, and I paraphrase, "That is the biggest bunch of crap I have ever heard. I was there, they weren't, and I was moved to tears twice with what I was seeing. You had to have been here." I laughed heartily, as this is solidly and consistently what my experience has been since I have been here. I am glad that this guy was able to sing my tune and send it all over the planet.

Undoubtedly rough times are still ahead. Retribution could be intense. However, the picture that I hold in my heart is that of people who were standing in line and who stayed put when a suicide bomber went off (literally), waiting for their turn to choose while the pieces of violence that ultimately failed on every front were picked up and taken away.

Oh, day of days! Oh day of joy, hope, newness, freedom, and answered prayer! May it be the harbinger of more to come.

With General George Casey, Commander of the Multi-National Forces in Iraq from 2004-2007 and current Army Chief of Staff.

My first Black Hawk flight. I couldn't stop smiling!

Pre-convoy briefing prior to returning from the Red Zone to BIAP.

Brave members of the Iraqi Special Forces.
They adopted me as their little sister and gave me an official ISF t-shirt.

Medic Saul McGirr and I celebrated Voting Day III with members of ISF.

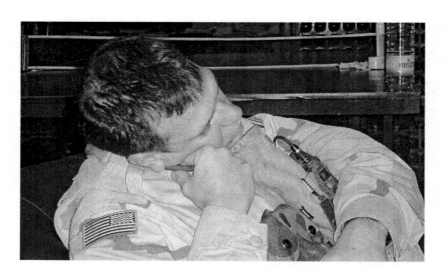

Captain Sean Flynn catches a quick nap in the MWR
after protecting Iraqis all day so they could vote.

*Saddam would have croaked if he knew that a menorah
was lit in Al Faw, his former Birthday Palace.*

*Near the crematorium at Dachau Concentration Camp, Hannukah 2006.
The inscription reads "Remember How We Died Here."*

Cpl. Adan Magana, one of my guitar students and one of my heroes.

Church services for everyone were held in Saddam's former fishing lodge.

Worshipping warriors—making war in the heavenlies. From left: Maj. Bob Isaac, CW01 Phillip Weller, Sgt. Michael Helmen, and Sgt. Zacharie Da Schiell.

"R" being baptized by Col. Dixey Behnken in Saddam's former swimming pool.

"Z" the terp, one of our beloved "adopted twins."

Getting ready for the coin toss at the Army-Navy Football Game.

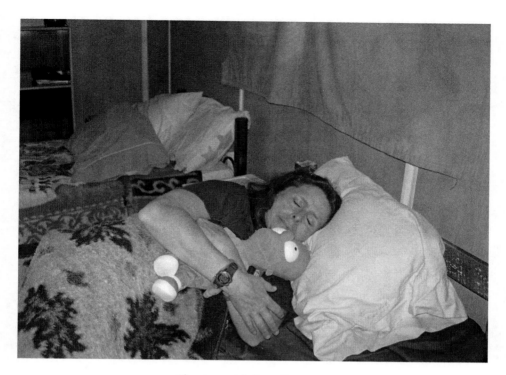

Sleeping with Bart Simpson.

Dancing in Uday's hunting lodge.

Some of my faithful, hard-working, affectionate staff.
From left: Raju, Jaddi, me, and Aida.

Floating in the Dead Sea in Jordan, June 2006. It's really true: you cannot sink!

Sgt. Kandy Ray Flores. This sweet woman risked her life every day to take care of our freedom as well as the teeth of those who would have liked to cut her head off, literally.

My "B52" (52ⁿᵈ) birthday party. Back row, from left: Capt. Derrick Biggs, Chaplain Matthew Atkins; front row, from left: Maj. Karen Little, Maj. Teri French, Tyrone Penn, me, and Sgt. Zacharie Da Schiell.

Sisters on Saddam's Throne.
From left: me, Phoebe Diana Akankunda, Capt. Rachel Park, and Juliet Kwagze.

Hawaiian National Guard members
prepare to take soccer balls to Iraqi kids at Christmas.

Teaching a Ugandan soldier to play the guitar.
Teaching music was one of my favorite pastimes.

One of a handful of female members of the Iraqi Special Forces as of 2005.
She would come in for tea and was lovely in every respect.

Christmas 2004 in Uday's former hotel. We sang "O Holy Night" for the soldiers. From left: Dfac Mgr. Cheryl Moses, Cpl. Mervin Rios, and me.

CHAPTER 20

Stetsons for Terri Schiavo

The first duty of government is the protection of life, not its destruction.
The chief purpose of government is to protect life.
Abandon that and you have abandoned all.

— THOMAS JEFFERSON

A young soldier who is trained as a scout and sniper has told me that the hardest part of being hidden in a country to get the lay of the land is not being put in mortal danger; for some guys that can be kind of a rush. Rather, the hardest part is observing an attack upon an innocent and not being able to step in to "protect and defend." If they blow their cover to save the one, they may end up causing thousands of others to lose their lives. Soldiers face impossible choices, the pain of which is only known by their Maker. The liquid

171

brown eyes of this soldier whom I have come to love as a son flickered with a pain that I knew was not mine to try to probe or relieve. I had the feeling that he spoke from experience.

Furthermore, he said, the fastest, fullest way to break a normal man in interrogation has nothing to do with causing him physical pain or inducing fear in him. Rather, it is to bring in a woman, rape her while he's forced to watch, and then to really finish *him* off and break *him*, finish *her* off and kill *her*. Unless they are bent, men are indeed hard-wired to protect and defend women. Living in the midst of soldier-men confirmed this to me every day, especially as I observed their reaction to the execution of Terri Schiavo, the brain-damaged Florida woman whose husband Michael had her legally starved and dehydrated to death in 2005. Having lived amongst hostiles for three years, I use the word "execution" without a smattering of apology. The surprising parallels between Terri's captivity, torture, and execution and terrorists' treatment of hostages are described in this chapter.

To refresh your memory, Terri Schiavo collapsed mysteriously in 1990 and suffered brain damage.[22] The cause of her collapse has never been completely determined, but it was alleged that her cardiac arrest was prompted by a possible eating disorder that was overlooked by her doctor; her brother Bobby Schindler tells me it was actually a low potassium level. Many, including law enforcement and medical professionals, suspected foul play on the part of her husband.

Her husband, Michael Schiavo, won a malpractice suit worth two million dollars, mostly designated for her care and rehabilitation. In the beginning of her mysterious disability, and while the two malpractice lawsuits were being fought in court, Michael was the model of the devoted husband. His court statements expressed a tearful desire to even become a nurse so he could take care of her for the rest of her life.

Then, for reasons that no one understands, he began to change. His relationship with Terri's family was severely strained and then broke completely. In the early nineties, he forbade all rehab and physical therapy protocols from continuing, including the brushing of Terri's teeth. In 1993 Terri got a urinary tract infection, and Michael tried unsuccessfully to block treatment that would prevent sepsis, which is often fatal. After the nursing home intervened on Terri's behalf, he posted a "Do Not Resuscitate" sign outside her door, which is a strange thing to do for a patient who is not dying. In addition, he tried to hide his actions from her parents, and they had no idea she had been ill. In the meantime, several women—including friends, dates, and some of Terri's caregivers—made affidavits and statements in court as to his lying, abusive, controlling behavior. According to the Schindler family, Michael moved out of their house where he had been living after Terri's collapse and in May of 1992 moved in with his girlfriend, Cindy Brashers (now Shook).[23] He met Jody Centonze in 1993 and fathered two children by her while still married to Terri.

In 1998, with the help of lawyer George Felos, a euthanasia advocate, Michael began to try to have Terri killed. In 2000 Michael announced that in the mideighties Terri had once allegedly expressed a desire to die rather than live disabled. With only verbal testimony as to her wishes, two unsuccessful attempts were made to starve and dehydrate her to death. A long, fierce legal battle between Michael Schiavo and Terri's family, the Schindlers, ensued.

There were those who would testify that Terri wanted to live, and others who would say that she wanted to die. There were many doctors who went on record saying that she could learn to swallow and talk again, and others who implied that she was beyond any hope of rehabilitation. There were nurses who testified that Michael was abusive to Terri and the facility staff members.

Though her family fought valiantly to protect her from having her feeding tube removed and they successfully won two stays of execution, finally on 31 March 2005, Terri lost a third political, culturally divisive three-week fight for her life amid a media circus and died in a Florida hospice. The shock waves from the incident were felt strongly in Iraq.

If there had been any way to pull it off, there were American soldiers in Iraq who would have commandeered a Black Hawk, stormed Woodside Hospice, rescued Terri Schiavo, helo'd her back to Baghdad, and kept her safe. She would have had a better chance at life, liberty, and the pursuit of happiness in some med tent in Baghdad, Iraq, than she did in fancy Florida in the U. S. of A.

The men I spoke to would have seen it as their *duty to rescue her*, as they promised when they enlisted, to protect the Constitution from "all enemies, foreign and domestic." They would have put their lives on the line in the process of freeing her because that is what they do *on principle as men*. They routinely volunteer to put themselves in harm's way in order to protect the weak, the helpless, the defenseless. You can call them cowboys; I don't care. They would have put on their Stetsons, saddled up, and rescued the maiden who was truly in distress. It would have been the stuff of legends, and I know guys who have the skill, experience, and heart necessary to have successfully pulled it off. Instead, by way of satellite, they were subjected to the "scout" scenario discussed above.

I truly cannot imagine what every member of Terri's family went through, especially her father Robert and her brother Bobby. Nor can I imagine what it must have been like for her lawyer David Gibbs and his legal firm's team of lawyers who had to watch while the spirit of the rule of common law as set forth by our founders was gang raped. Being designed to defend and yet not being able to is like being condemned to a room with the oxygen sucked out of it. Their breath these days is to fight for and rescue others from the same fate as Terri. May their cause bring as much healing to them as it does life to the ones for whom they fight. For more information on the Schindler family's efforts to protect the disabled, please visit www.terrisfight.org.

I would submit that, allegorically, Terri Schiavo was raped, but without the sexual element. Experts such as forensic psychologists, detectives, and therapists agree that rape is less about sex than it is about power. If rape is about overpowering someone, if it is about using a human for one's own release, if it is about proving oneself or exercising control or power over someone against their will, then Terri Schiavo was "raped" by several men, including her husband. Legally.

Then she was tortured. Legally. On several occasions.

Then she was murdered. Legally.

This, ladies and gentlemen, is what terrorists do. They subdue or permanently silence the defenseless. This did not sit well with our fighting men and women.

For the time being, Terri's killers walk free. But this I know, and this is what comforts me: in many religious traditions, there is a concept of "what goes around comes around" or "you reap what you sow." I have no doubt that her killers will have a rendezvous with Justice that will settle the matter to Terri's satisfaction. In addition, if we who mourn her death defeat the temptation to give in to the cowardice of hatred and bitterness—if we make forgiveness our aim and leave final judgment to God—then Justice will be served more quickly. Good *will* triumph over evil to the satisfaction of her family, her nation, and the soldiers who would have rescued her if they had been allowed to.

I must confess I was a latecomer to understanding Terri's case. I had been vaguely aware of what I *thought* was her situation, hearing little sound bites on the news and reading the one-liner news blurbs on the Internet. I honestly thought that it was a simple case of "end of life issues" that sadly hadn't been hammered out prior to the need and now it was a mess in the courts. The media had done a masterful spin job on me.

The same "soldier son" who taught me about what happens to men when they cannot protect happened to be from Florida, and he had followed the case for years. As I tumbled off the spin docs' version of Terri's situation, he deftly deflated every one of my talking points, and I realized that I needed to look into this more deeply for myself. If what he said was true, then we were about to watch an execution worse than if Florida's Ol' Sparky had misfired and, worse yet, the one strapped in to the electric chair had, by everyone's agreement, committed no crime whatsoever.

As I dug into it, I began to experience the same sense of horror and outrage as I did years ago when I discovered that I had been lied to big-time about abortion. I would sometimes smack the desk in anger, and it was much tougher to be the cheery little "MWR lady." What really did me in and got me crying so hard that I was glad I was working graveyard shift and MWR traffic was light was listening to talk show host Glenn Beck's eighteen-minute broadcast on 10 October 2002 as he described his own "paradigm shift" regarding Terri.[24] Like me, he had bought into what David Gibbs calls "The Big Lie," the idea that Terri was a vegetable who had previously indicated to her husband that she wouldn't want what are called Heroic Measures in order to be kept alive past her natural time to go. The other part of the lie was that Terri was on "life support" (which normally refers to a ventilator) which if turned off would simply cause her to slip away peacefully and painlessly. Beck described his own shame at having been casual about Terri's situation and, through tears, told of his painful turnaround. A weeping man is sometimes the strongest man.

For the record, I am passionately pro-life, but I don't have an inherent problem with DNR (Do Not Resuscitate) or NHM (No Heroic Measures) orders, as long as the person's wishes are inarguable and death is incontrovertibly near. Terri had left no such instructions in writing. More importantly, she wasn't dying. If someone is *organically* terminal from a disease or injury, natural death is imminent, and they wish to go, then let nature takes its course. I believe the body will give way when it is ready to. I do, however, have a huge problem with the belief that it's OK to intervene and speed along the process, either for others or for yourself.

The 1976 removal of life support from Karen Ann Quinlan, a young woman in a persistent vegetative state who surprised everyone by continuing to live for nearly another decade, upset Terri at the young age of thirteen. Five years later, in response to a TV show about Karen Ann, Terri reiterated her dismay at what had happened in the Quinlan case. If ever there were a hearsay indication of Terri's wishes, this was it, and it should have been given the same credence as the supposed testimony of Michael's family members that she would have wished to die rather than live in a disabled state. As a life-long Catholic, Terri was pro-life, and there was never any indication that she ever wavered in her convictions. To make the leap that a casual statement allegedly made to Schiavo family members while watching a TV program about someone on a ventilator constitutes end-of-life wishes is untenable, but it was enough for Judge George Greer.[25]

History shows that there is a crossing of a cultural moral line that without corporate national repentance can usher in the end of an entire civilization. If we didn't cross it with Terri by turning away in order to let her die, we came mighty close.

Our American death culture's shameful response to Terri reminds me of stories of German citizens' willful ignorance or denial of the Nazi death camps. The one that gets me the most is told by an ashamed Lutheran. His church was located near the railroad tracks on the way to one of the camps. Jews smashed into cattle cars could be heard screaming as they went past the church to their death. The response of the congregants was to "sing louder" so they wouldn't have to face what was going on in their land.[26] God help us, because we are going to need it. What we allowed to happen to a woman who was disabled yet sweetly full of life would have been unthinkable in post-WWII America. While there were those who fought nobly for Terri, there were way too many of us who basically ignored what was going on in a Florida hospice. We just turned up the volume on our iPods and, in our own way, "sang louder."

What is insane about this entire situation was that Terri wasn't dying. She was in good health despite being bedridden and not allowed to receive any physical therapy. While she was certainly disabled and needed considerable care, she was documented as being functional and responsive to *both* doctors and her family. She was breathing on her own and just needed some help with eating from a feeding tube, which was only connected three times a day. Hearsay statements made in a supposed conversation that her husband suddenly recalled years after she was disabled were essentially all it took to set in place the gruesome process which took her from her family. Michael Schiavo claimed that "she wouldn't have wanted to live this way." With no proof and no written documentation of her wishes, her life was taken from her. How could this happen on our watch?

Shedding innocent blood is a dangerous turning point for a culture. Many Americans already seem to think it's fine to stick scissors into the skull of a baby about to be born and suck out its brains. Are we becoming Nazis, boiling toward oblivion one degree at a time like the proverbial frog in the kettle? I shudder to think what will happen to us if we don't turn around, and soon. On 31 March 2005, the day tenderhearted Terri died, we demonstrated to ourselves and the world that there were those amongst us who had as much regard for life as Adolph Hitler or Saddam Hussein. That was the day we watched three men—a lawyer, a judge, and a husband—finally succeed in killing a woman by starvation and dehydration. Those of us in Iraq were ashamed, and the Iraqis were confused.

These three men had abdicated their manhood years earlier, the day they deserted their duty to defend and protect, and they'll never get it back. One got a lot of money from a fund originally earmarked for Terri's rehabilitation. One got the satisfaction of defying the president of the United States. One got money and the opportunity to marry, thus legitimizing the births of two innocent kids born out of wedlock. But they lost their manhood. If they had starved and dehydrated pet dogs, they would have been arrested, or at the very least pursued by PETA, or in pro football player-now-jailbird Michael Vick's case, the law and the NFL. Why aren't Terri's torturers enduring the same fate? As talk show host Rush Limbaugh said the day Terri took her last breath, it was the day "America hit rock bottom."[27]

Hasn't Terri's story already been hashed and rehashed to the point of pointlessness? Absolutely not! My purpose in this book is to tell stories about our soldiers and Iraqis that no one has ever heard before. The most die-hard right-to-die advocate needs to know what Michael Schiavo, George Felos, and George Greer did by *their* example to *our* soldiers and to the Iraqi people, as well as the response from those in the desert who were watching.

As I mentioned in chapter 11, when we contractors were given hostage survival training, the number one thing we were told to do in order to insure our survival was to keep our "human-ness" ever before our captors. For mujahideen to justify killing an innocent, or for a rogue government to make genocide palatable to its constituents, captives must be carefully, strategically, and systematically dehumanized. The skill with which this was done in Terri's case—over a hostage crisis that lasted from 1990 until it ended badly in 2005—is as noteworthy as it is diabolical.

Three excellent books written from three different perspectives about Terri's situation document this fact well: *Fighting for Dear Life: The Untold Story of Terri Schiavo and What It Means for All of Us* by David Gibbs, *A Life That Matters: The Legacy of Terri Schiavo* by the Schindler family, and *Silent Witness: The Untold Story of Terri Schiavo's Death* by homicide detective Mark Fuhrman. If you read any or all of these books, I don't think you'll be able to maintain the position that Terri was, as George Felos referred to her with classic dehumanization verbiage, a "house plant,"[28] nor that she was a vegetable who felt nothing as she was dehydrated to death. The truth about what really happened and how it was suppressed should touch all but the coldest heart and set the thinker on fire.

In brief, here are the cues that point to strategic dehumanization. These are the kinds of things that mujahideen do to hostages and that those who had a duty to care for Terri did to her.

FORCED ISOLATION

Humans are social animals, and an excellent way to wield power over them is not to allow social contact, either with humans or vicariously through media. At first, Michael allowed Terri to watch TV, although only one station, and listen to the radio, although again, only one station. He did not allow her to leave her room or have contact with other patients. Closer to the end of her life, the radio and TV were not allowed to be on at all. Why did this matter if she was a just a house plant? Her nurses and aides said in sworn statements[29] that, at the risk of experiencing Michael Schiavo's legendary wrath as well as losing their jobs, they would put someone on lookout to see if Michael was coming and take Terri out to the common area to be with the other patients. They also fed her gelatin and orange juice, which she swallowed (yeah, you heard me) and loved. My kind of gals.

LACK OF SUNLIGHT/SENSORY DEPRIVATION

Michael Schiavo forbade the curtains in Terri's room to be opened so sunlight could come in. Having worked in two nursing homes myself, I know that one of the first things you do to brighten your patient's day is to open the curtains and let the sun do its thing. In any good nursing home, there is a sun room, and you take your patients there because Vitamin D builds bones and sunlight chases away Seasonal Affective Disorder. Why would Michael want to block Terri's exposure to sunlight if he truly wanted the best for her? Depriving house plants of sunlight kills them. What normal person sets out to kill his house plants?

Corrie ten Boom, whose family hid Jews in their home during the Nazi occupation of Holland, writes eloquently in *The Hiding Place* of the day she was brought out of isolation at the Scheveningen prison and got to see the sky and have sunlight on her face. It was common Nazi practice to put people in a lightless "hole" or "box" to punish them. Was Terri being punished?

Jill Carroll, the hostage mentioned in chapter 11, writes in *Hostage: The Jill Carroll Story* of the lengths she would go to in order to get sunlight. Her captors figured out what she was doing and made sure she was deprived of it. Mercifully, one of her mujahideen captors who had once been in prison himself came in one day and pulled back the curtains so the sun could connect with her. "Sun," was all he said, and she basked in it.

SEIZURE OF PERSONAL EFFECTS

Nazis ripped the gold crowns out of the teeth of Jewish prisoners for their own personal use. Female prisoners used to try to hide their jewelry by placing it in their private areas, rectal as well as reproductive. Why go to such lengths to hold on to perishable trinkets? They keep people connected to a former life, the one their captors are trying to distance them from.

According to Terri's friend Jackie Rhodes, there is strong evidence to suggest that just prior to Terri's collapse, she was planning to escape from her marriage to Michael[30], but her rings were still hers. In 1992 Michael Schiavo took Terri's wedding set off her hand and had it melted down and made into jewelry *for himself*. His actions were understandably brought into question by the lawyers litigating the malpractice suit. His court statement, dated 19 November 1993, goes like this:

Q. What did you do with your wife's jewelry?

A. My wife's jewelry?

Q. Yeah.

*A. Um, I think I took her engagement ring and her . . . what do they call it
. . . diamond wedding band and I made a ring for myself.*[31]

"I made a ring for myself." Sweet. This is the same man who announced his engagement to Jody Centonze in the obituary of his own mother. This is the same man who had Terri's completely healthy cats, who were like her children to her, euthanized rather than giving them away to a good home. To me it was a prophetic gesture. Rather than "give Terri away to a good home" (her parents'), he had her killed. Was putting down the cats a run-up to the big one?

WITHHOLDING MEDICAL TREATMENT

The Geneva Convention prohibits withholding medical treatment in order to cause death, yet this is just what Michael tried to do to Terri. In Iraq when there are injuries, everyone gets scooped up and treated—enemy combatants as well as soldiers. My friend Theresa, who is a combat nurse, says you don't pay any attention whose side someone is on; you just give them the best care you can, and pronto. Medical kindness has had a profound effect on the Iraqi people, and I personally know of instances where insurgents have left the insurgency for this very reason.

Terri's family was not notified in summer 1993 when she was hospitalized due to a urinary tract infection (UTI). They also were not told that Michael had tried to get the hospital staff to withhold treatment. Heidi Law, one of Terri's nursing assistants said in a sworn statement, "When Terri would get a UTI or was sick, Michael's *mood would improve*" (emphasis added).[32] While in Iraq, I was told that Uday Hussein used to laugh when he used people for target practice. His mood improved, too.

Here is an excerpt from the 19 November 1993 deposition statement taken when Michael's fitness for guardianship was being contested:

*Q. And did he tell you what would occur if you failed to treat that infection?
What did he tell you?*

A. That sometimes urinary tract infection [sic] will turn to sepsis.

Q. And sepsis is what?

A. An infection throughout the body.

Q. And what would be the result of untreated sepsis be to the patient?

A. The patient would pass on.

Q. So when you made the decision not to treat Terri's bladder infection you, in effect, were making a decision to allow her to pass on?

A. I was making a decision on what Terri would want.

Q. Did you instruct the doctor not to treat the bladder infection?

A. Uh-huh. Yes.

Michael was told by the staff of Sabel Palms, the nursing home where Terri was at the time, that Florida state law did not allow lifesaving treatment to be denied.

Q. You did change your decision not to treat the bladder condition, correct?

A. I had to change my decision.

. . .

Q. Why have you changed your opinion?

A. Because evidently there is a law out there that says I can't do it. [33] *[Emphasis added.]*

That's right, Michael. There is a law that says you can't do it. So the only thing to do is to get one passed that says that you can. Of course, your law will be based on contemporary statutory law, the kind that is the product of the whim of capricious judges, and not common law, thus violating the intent of our whole judicial system, but that's another discussion.

WITHHOLDING FOOD AND WATER

The Germans withheld food and water from millions of Jews, and the Japanese from thousands of American soldiers on the Bataan Death March. This is what Saddam did, what the Viet Cong did, what mujhahideen do. This is what Michael Schiavo did to Terri. All of them did it within the framework of law. Shame on us for even remotely resembling the very ones our soldiers have died to protect us from.

There is a woman named Kate Adamson who survived the very thing that Terri endured (having her feeding tube removed by the hospital) and was starved and dehydrated in the same manner against the wishes of her family for eight days. She came out of her coma and lived to tell the tale. In her book *Kate's Journey: Triumph over Adversity*, as well as on national television, she has gone into great detail regarding not only the pain of having the feeding tube removed but also what it was like to starve. Unlike Terri, however, she had a husband who protected her. Of her ordeal she says, "The only difference between me and Terri Schiavo is that I had a husband who loved me and wouldn't give up on me."[34]

DEHUMANIZING LANGUAGE/ DISINFORMATION

Language is a very important component in the psychological system of dehumanization. In the Arab world, defining people as "infidels" makes it easier to kill them. Nazis called people of all types "useless eaters," and it was easier to kill them. Hitler killed thousands of folks who had nothing to do with being born Jewish. *He went after the mentally ill, homosexuals, and the disabled.* He forced women to have abortions if there was the slightest chance that the child would be anything less than Aryan perfection. In America, unborn children are called "fetal material" or "products of conception," which makes it easier to kill them. The rhetoric is repeated endlessly until death-thought invades a culture like a cancer and people actually believe that these government-sanctioned deaths are reasonable.

Terri was described over and over on blogs and in other media as being "a vegetable" or "brain dead." It wasn't true, but it sure made it easier to get us to buy into the idea that her death would be no big deal. When I spoke with Terri's brother Bobby Schindler while in the process of writing this chapter, he was working toward getting George Stephanopolous to correct his description of Terri as "brain dead." *The New York Times* and the TV news program *60 Minutes* spread the same misinformation. Not one doctor on either side of the battle for Terri ever, ever said she was "brain dead."

My question is: so what if she *was* brain dead? So that gives anyone the right to kill her? So *you* get to determine that her life is not worth living?

The most dehumanizing language of all was exposed in an affidavit made by Carla Iyer, one of Terri's caregivers, who claims that Michael Schiavo made the following statements more than once:

"When is she going to die?"

"Has she died yet?"

"When is that b_ _ _ _ gonna die?"[35] [emphasis added]

If this is true, then the fact that he relegated his injured wife to the category of a female dog ought to raise some suspicions among law enforcement officials, and it did.

As I was undergoing the process of changing from being vaguely aware of Terri's plight to wanting to get in a Black Hawk with the guys and go get her, I had the opportunity to speak with an expert in identifying criminal behavior through language. Like me, he had originally bought into the spin on Terri until he began to read some of Michael's deposition statements which I downloaded and printed out for him. The more he read, the more he began to feel like something was really wrong with Michael Schiavo's story.

When I told Bobby Schindler of this man's sense of things, he said, "I hope someone someday can professionally analyze the videos, the Larry King interviews. Many people have told me that they can tell Michael is hiding something, and they aren't even professionals." Detective Mark Fuhrman agrees and points out that there is no statute of limitations on murder. If it can ever be proven that Michael caused Terri to collapse, the fact that he actually killed her with a court order is obvious.

The roles of the other passionate and public accomplices, lawyer George Felos and judge George Greer, have been written about extensively, and I am only going to touch on them briefly. The issues include conflict of interest, the blatant need for recusal, and a preoccupation with death.

Judge George Greer never went to see Terri Schiavo for himself. He said there was no need to do so. He threw out the testimonies of forty doctors who felt that

Terri was either not in the condition Michael said she was or that she could have been rehabilitated. He threw out the testimony of eminent forensic pathologist Dr. Michael Baden that her bone scans indicated trauma.

What would have been the harm in erring on the side of protecting life? What *is* the harm in erring on the side of protecting life?

George Greer was kicked out of his church for his actions in the Schiavo case. According to one of the Schindler family lawyers with whom I spoke, the pastor of Mr. Greer's church had a daughter in a similar disabled state as Terri and would not allow even an implied sanction of such a hideous death to occur on his watch. Good for him. I am glad a real man stood up when it surely was costly.

By far the most unusual member of these three musketeers was George Felos. His spiritual beliefs regarding death are described as disturbing in two books by people of two completely different spiritual perspectives. David Gibbs, the lawyer for Terri and her family and the author of *Fighting for Dear Life: The Untold Story of Terri Schiavo and What It Means for All of Us*, is a Christian. In *Silent Witness: The Untold Story of Terri Schiavo's Death,* Detective Mark Fuhrman makes it very clear that he is not in any way a religious man. David Gibbs cites faith as his foundation and motivation for having fought so hard for Terri. Mark Fuhrman approached the situation as if he was investigating Terri's death as a possible homicide, a "just the facts, ma'am" approach.

Felos candidly describes his own spiritual beliefs regarding euthanasia in his autobiography, *Litigation as Spiritual Practice*. He believes that his mission is to help people die—something he's succeeded in before. David Gibbs says of Felos, "His cold clinical view of Terri's slow torturous death and his ongoing efforts to put a positive spin on her unbearable pain can be traced back to this first right-to-die case, that of Estelle Browning."[36] Felos believes that a person who wants to die communicates silently with him through "soul speak."[37] He claims that he silently asked Mrs. Browning if she wanted to die and that he heard Mrs. Browning's soul scream back to him silently, "Why am I still here . . . Why am I here?"[38] Interestingly, when asked, he never claimed to have "heard" from Terri that she wanted to die. He said that "it's a pending case."[39] I guess that means that he was still waiting to hear from "the houseplant."

On a larger scale, Mr. Felos's views on the Jews who died in the Holocaust are inarguably bizarre. He seems to imply that those who died as a part of Hitler's Final Solution somehow agreed to it long before it occurred and that the event needs to be seen on some level as "uplifting." In *Litigation as Spiritual Practice* he says:

> *The Jewish people long ago in their collective consciousness agreed to play the part of the lamb whose slaughter was necessary to shock humanity into a new moral consciousness. Their sacrifice saved humanity at the brink of extinction and propelled us into a new age. If our minds can conceive of an uplifting Holocaust, can it be so difficult to look another way at the slights and injuries and abuses we perceive were inflicted upon us?*[40]

Great. Felos says the Holocaust was "uplifting," and Ahmedinejad doesn't think it happened at all.

Given Mr. Felos's strange view of human suffering, I don't think it's too wild to at least ask whether Terri Schiavo was a one-woman "uplifting Holocaust" by virtue of being a human sacrifice. Did Terri agree long ago to be a sacrificial lamb? Is no one to be held morally responsible for her death when the premise of our culture is the inalienable right to life, liberty, and the pursuit of happiness?

Isn't the sacrifice of an innocent human—whether it occurs in an oven, in a gas chamber, on a jihadist Web site or, as in Terri's case, in a hospital bed—the very essence of terrorism? Weren't Mary—Terri's mom, Robert—Terri's dad, Bobby—Terri's brother, and Suzanne—Terri's sister, in fact terrorized as Terri was held as a hostage? Was not our very constitution terrorized? Is this the democracy that we are hoping Iraq will emulate?

Barbara Weller, one of the lawyers who tried to save Terri, told me in November of 2007 about the day she informed Terri that there was nothing more they could do. You know what "the houseplant" did? She got mad! She glared at Barbara, turned away from her, and would not communicate with her. Barbara is the one who told Terri she was going to have to convince someone that she wanted to live, and "the houseplant" gave it her all. "I W-A-A-A-A---" she yelled so loudly that the policeman on duty came in to see what was going on. But that wasn't enough, and some saw Barbara's testimony as perjurous—something that could have cost her the right to practice law.

George Felos said that he had "never seen such a look of peace and beauty" upon Terri as while she was dehydrating to death.[41] Barbara told me, "I was there. It was horrible. Some things I guess you just never get over."

In *Fighting for Dear Life*, David Gibbs describes in horrific detail how terrible Terri looked as a result of her "painless" process, as Michael Schiavo called it,[42] and the nightmare it was for him to be with Mary Schindler while she was with her daughter for the last time. You should make yourself read it and determine for yourself how to define "beauty." Terri had one tiny providential drop of water left in her body that manifested itself in the form of a tear on her cheek. She also sobbed silently, cheek to cheek with her mother, and then Mary had to leave for the last time.

When David Gibbs announced on the news that Terri had died, soldiers cried. I cried. Soldiers had prayed, and prayed hard. So had I. They wondered out loud what was happening to the country they were defending, let alone how to explain it to the Iraqis. The Iraqis were looking to America to be their guide as they built their brand-new nation, and we showed them that we do what Saddam did: we torture people to death.

I was visibly upset when Mustafa, a young Iraqi Special Forces Lieutenant, came into the MWR center that day, and I did my best to try to explain to him what had happened. He listened, then put his arms around me and, with a wisdom that could only come from having endured Saddam, said, "Ali, I am so sorry this happened in your country today." Me too, buddy. Me too.

Soldiers and citizens alike have wondered why Robert and Bobby didn't just bust her out of there. Answer: it was commonly known that there were snipers on the roof, and snipers don't shoot to wound. I have no doubt that the Schindler men would have been willing to put their lives on the line for her, just the same as the soldiers, but what would have happened is that their bodies would have been removed, Mary and Suzanne would have lost the Schindler menfolk, and Terri still would have been scuttled back in to face her execution.

Barbara Weller, who described Terri's last state to me, had a lengthy discussion with a soldier who was in the Green Zone during Terri's hostage ordeal and execution. He told her that the Iraqis who worked there watched the situation very carefully, and when it was determined that President Bush couldn't save her, they concluded that America was weak and not to be trusted; they left the base. An American soldier who wishes to remain unnamed, who was there and who helped me with this chapter, asked me to include the following comments:

> One thing that I might add is the effect the case had on the war. Many people never stop to consider how the two connect. If the president of the U.S. said he wanted her to live, and she still died, how can he possibly protect us way over here in Baghdad? . . . How can we trust that he'll stick by all of us Iraqis? Remember, we lost a lot of Iraqis over that, not to mention the devastation to the U.S. morale.[43]

So, Mr. Schiavo, Mr. Greer, and Mr. Felos, this may not have been your intention, but you just may have created some real live terrorists while you were busy acting like the muj. You also hurt our soldiers. All I can say is, may God have mercy on you. And, Mr. Obama, if you feel that your greatest mistake in your brief career as a senator was voting to save Terri Schiavo's life,[44] there is no way you are going to get my vote for president. As the Green Zone soldier who spoke to Ms. Weller said so simply and eloquently, "We would have died trying to save her." It's true; they told me so themselves. They would have died to save Terri Schiavo from those who were once men.

CHAPTER 21

The Iraqi-Coalition Soccer Tournament

$\mathcal{J}$n the spirit of team building and goodwill that the Olympics and the World Cup stand for, in the fall of 2005 I began to do a survey amongst Americans and Iraqis to see if there would be any interest in organizing an Iraqi-Coalition Soccer Tournament. If we were going to do it, we were going to do it right: it was going to be by the book, with regulation everything—coaches, refs, and uniforms . . . sorta. The positive response from both sides was overwhelming, and this time I sincerely hoped that the plug would not get pulled on my newest brain- and heart-child.

Because the tourney would be held on the restricted-access base where the Iraqi Special Forces trained and because it was way more important that their Iraqi battle uniforms take precedence over spiffy PT outfits, let's just say that other than the requisite brown t-shirt, PT uniforms for the Iraqi side were anything but, well, uniform. On any given day we would see all manner of wild striped shorts, stuff that looked like pajama bottoms, completely mismatched workout outfits, etc., being sported when the guys would run by in the morning on their PT drills. I am sure that some of them had pretty sharp soccer uniforms from playing on local teams, but it wasn't exactly like they could quickly zip home in the Red Zone and grab them after their moms ran them through the wash. Nevertheless, the guys in the clown pants were a force to be reckoned with, as we would soon find out.

Truth be told, there would be U.S. guys playing in their service branch official PTs, so our guys weren't going to be perfectly outfitted in the same colors either.

We had several planning meetings with the powers that be, and as always, security had to be considered. It is impossible to describe the continual balancing act of always making sure the troops are battle ready, yet trying to provide activities that are so fun that they forget for a while where they are and what may be going on down the block. One of the reasons I love these guys so much is their ability to do just that—to live life, to play with passion, and to switch gears when they had to if a situation arose. More than once I watched them empty an MWR facility in a heartbeat due to an emergency. One moment, My Space; the next, "Mount up!"

Unless you actually live outside the U.S.A., you probably don't get just how big soccer is for the rest of the planet. It's like the NFL or, especially if you live in the South, NASCAR. I was in Dubai for the last games of the World Cup in 2006, and it was multicultural mayhem of the grandest sort. Any TV in a public place was swarmed by passionate aficionadoes who probably would have sacrificed appendages in order to be at the actual match.

Planning went ahead in earnest, and Marcos and Kal, American terps from Iraq, volunteered to head up the coaching for the Iraqis. Kal had spent three days in the desert without water while running from Saddam, and then another three and a half years in a Saudi refugee camp, which wasn't much better. Keau, a female contractor from Hawaii, ex-mil and one tough athlete, was working in the Motor Pool. She was actually certified to referee soccer, so we had at least one part of the necessary "official-ness" covered. Unfortunately, Sal, the terp who had played soccer as a kid in

Baghdad, was going to be home on leave; I know he would have loved to coach the Iraqis. Sal was so good in his day that he would have been forced to play for Uday on the Olympic team and in fact did play on Uday's version of a Little League team, soccer style.

One of the funnest things about being in Iraq and working in conditions that didn't exactly accommodate a quick trip to Home Depot or Hobby Lobby in order to get supplies was seeing how creative people could be in order to get the job done. This was certainly the case with the soccer project. There were no soccer goals close by, so the logistics guys determined that one of the big trucks would transport the rather permanent goals from another camp to ours; our construction guys would get all the measurements so we could eventually make our own.

Ingenuity prevailed when it came to creating the set that we would eventually keep. Some SCWs (Subcontract Workers) and Freddy the Plumber (who was so funny that he could probably unseat George Lopez as the reigning king of Latino humor) put together some PVC pipe that been lying around out back, and we were going to use camo nets over the backs to keep the balls from flying where they might get shot down. The understanding was that if the plumbing needed to be fixed or anything needed to be covered in camo netting, the goals would be returned to their former use.

Transporting the borrowed goals had to be scheduled so it wouldn't interfere with any armored equipment going out, so you can begin to understand how complicated something as simple as a soccer game could become. Returning the goals was just as challenging. The next thing was preparing the field. Yikes—where did all the rocks come from? If we had been audited, someone who could not see the value in what we were doing for the long-term security and stability of Iraq might have fussed over the number of personnel hours used to get ready for our goodwill event.

I realize that some folks may scoff at the "soccer-game-resulting-in-the-defeat-of-Osama" idea. Perhaps understanding how I pitched my idea for the event to the mayor, or military leader, of our camp will help. What was my purpose, the mayor wondered in our meeting, in proposing our funky little tournament with its makeshift uniforms and borrowed goal sets? I told him I wanted to give the Iraqis a chance to shine, to give their U.S. instructors a run for their money in a totally different context than would occur in classes, to build friendships, to release tension, to be—if only for the moment—playing serious soccer as a gesture toward a day when they didn't need to worry that someone would blow them up while they played with their comrades. I wanted to buoy up their hearts and minds. He could see the value in my idea.

Who knew if someday down the road an Al-Qaeda recruiter would try to turn one of these guys toward terror and the memory of the fun of that day might keep them from being flipped? Someone could conceivably *not* buy into the ever-present refrain that America was the Great Satan just by being innocently boys-will-be-boys rough-and-tumble for a few hours on an October afternoon. I am fascinated by what is called the "Butterfly Effect"—the idea that a butterfly flapping its wings in the Amazon jungle can affect the tropical storms in Southeast Asia. Seeing my reasoning, and, I think, needing something for the whole camp to get behind, the mayor cleared our "butterfly" for takeoff.

The next challenge was chalking the field, and this is where Ervin and Jasmin, the Bosnians amongst us, came to the rescue. I downloaded the specs from the Internet to get the exact regulation measurements, and we discovered that the field was not quite regulation size. Ervin, Jasmin (Jazzy, as I called him), their crew of Filipinos, and my crew of guys from India (who sometimes got into it with each other because of caste differences) all pulled together to downsize the specs a bit and chalk the field. We were now ready to go.

A flawless fall Sunday dawned, and it was time to get going. The Red Cross/Red Crescent Humvee was present in case anyone got hurt. The welcome ceremonies were finished, and no, no one sang the national anthem for either country. The coin was tossed, the Iraqis won the toss, and it was Game On.

Our guys made a valiant effort and played well, but they were absolutely no match for the Iraqis. With a score of 4–2, it wasn't a complete rout, but it could have been argued that they at least partially mopped the floor with us. Iraqis hollered every good-natured insult in Arabic at the Coalition—the usual stuff like "Is that all you got?" "Go home; you're terrible!" and "You stink!" The terps would laugh as they translated for us. Whenever the Iraqis scored, they went completely nuts. They danced and drummed on the barrels that been put in place for field markers, getting into a rhythm reminiscent of Caribbean steel bands. Their celebrations were even more fun than the actual game.

When the game ended and the Iraqis realized they had won, you would have thought that they had indeed taken the World Cup. From somewhere on their camp emerged two odd open-top Russian jeeps left over from the sanction years, with what seemed like fifty people piled in, on, over, and around each of them. The rest stayed at their post as the steel band. Glorious pandemonium! They bounced down the field for a victory lap, and then, just when we thought it was over, they started again.

Maybe this was a bigger deal than any of us had thought. Maybe my little idea was paying off. God only knows. The best part was the presentation of the trophy. I had known that the Army was planning on getting something for the occasion, but I had no idea that it would be this cool. Someone had commissioned some Kuwaitis to make a commemorative trophy with an inscription about the Coalition and Iraqis being brothers in arms in the cause of bringing liberty and freedom to Iraq.

Iraqis beamed; I, of course, got teary while laughing; and Coalition team members took it all in good stride. Captain Mark Citarella, or Cinderella as we called him, got razzed by one of his Iraqi students, a little kid who was as fast as the Roadrunner. Just two years earlier that could certainly not have happened on Uday's watch. The look on all their faces and the utter though momentary suspension of conflict and grave responsibility, mixed with a delirious and sweaty peace, blessed and fed all of us. Game On, Game Over, and Afterglow.

These are the memories I savor, especially when folks insist that "the war is lost." Not.

CHAPTER 22

The Army-Navy Football Game

T here wasn't any gambling in the home where I was raised, except for once a year; I believe the permanent bet was one dollar. This "pool," if you will, was set up between my grandfather, Glenn Hersman, and my father, Roy White. Glenn, or "Gumbo" as we called him, was in the Army in WWI. My father, whom I called "Poppo" or "Whizzo" (after Supreme Court Justice Byron "Whizzer" White), served in the Naval Air Corps in WWII as a pilot.

This annual journey into high-stakes gambling would always occur in the fall whenever the Army-Navy football game was played. As a side note, my Uncle George had been kicked out of Duke University for painting the Navy mascot blue. He later served in the Navy, and I sometimes wonder if that were just in order to vex my grandfather—something George did often and with alacrity.

As I have said earlier, one of the many reasons I went to Iraq was to say thank you to both my father and grandfather for their service, so in their honor I decided to seek permission from the base commander to have an official Army-Navy game in Iraq on the same Saturday as the one back in the States. I hoped to promote just a smattering of friendly rivalry and a touch of home.

Permission was granted, and boy, howdy, it was Game On long before that highly anticipated Saturday rolled around. Cans of spray paint were mysteriously obtained for unofficial purposes, such as tagging the J walls (the waist-high concrete barriers) with "Go Army," "Go Navy," and some other slogans which I won't repeat. This went on for several miles down the road and near the entrances of adjoining camps. I remember thinking, "Yikes, I hope I don't get in trouble for getting this thing going!" Spray painting is, shall we say, frowned upon. Apparently the Navy SEALs were particularly ticked that the Army had managed to sneak into their part of the camp and do some pretty serious tagging under cover of night.

Because our camp was highly restricted, life there took on a small-town feeling where everyone knew everyone, and there was lots of contact with Iraqis. Iraqis are into soccer big-time, but they don't really get just what the big deal is with "Ameriki futbol." They did, however, come to watch and cheer for their favorites. Everyone pitched in to measure and chalk the field, clear the rocks, coach, and referee. As always, security was an issue. As I sat in the final pregame meeting in the palace that had been built for Saddam's mistress, I was, for the zillionth time, impressed that soldiers would pull guard so their buddies could participate in a time-honored tradition as safely as one can in the middle of a combat zone.

Saturday morning arrived with cool weather in the nineties, and these boys were pumped and ready to do whatever damage can be done playing flag football. As I had been "coined" (given a service branch coin as an award or expression of gratitude) by the Naval Criminal Investigative Service, the NCIS coin was used for the toss, but I made sure the Army knew I had no favorites here. I told the story of my grandfather and father and confessed that I had been the punk who had tried to shut down Wright-Patterson Air Force base during the Viet Nam War. So, in honor of Gumbo and Poppo, the game began, both sides playing valiantly. In Iraq the Army won, and back in the States the Navy won, so it all worked out.

That evening a young African-American soldier came up to me at supper and said, "Ma'am, don't you ever apologize for protesting. It is your right to protest that we are here to protect." I was, once again, undone. This elusive thing we call liberty—this thing that I had so dismissed while intoxicated by the entitlement mentality of youth—was once again being defended at any cost by complete strangers.

When my father and I would argue about the war in Southeast Asia, he used to tell me, "I may not agree with you, but I will fight like hell for your right to believe what you want to believe." Army and Navy both won on the football field that day, but I was won over . . . again, and I know I owe my Poppo, Gumbo, and my guys way, way more than a buck.

CHAPTER 23

Have Leave, Will Travel

I was eligible for a ten-day vacation every four months, with a few weeks at the end of the year. To remain classified as Foreign Workers, we had to make sure our vacations added up to being physically outside of the United States for 330 days per calendar year. When you work twelve hours a day, seven days a week, the prospect of taking a break makes your heart dance like a frisky spring calf. Here are the tales of some of my more interesting vacations; I promise not to hold you at gunpoint while I show you my pictures.

DUBAI AND MEMPHIS, TENNESSEE, OCTOBER 2004

My first break was in the fall of 2004, having arrived in country in June. I flew by charter from BIAP to Dubai and spent about thirty-six hours there before flying to the States. My trip coincided with my first Ramadan, and we had a sensitivity briefing in Dubai to keep us from accidentally ending up in jail.

During Ramadan, consumption of food or water during daylight is forbidden, and the feasting begins at nightfall. During the day, not only were we Westerners not supposed to be seen eating, but we could also get thrown in jail if there were gum or even a toothpick in our mouths or if we were seen carrying a water bottle. We women were also told to make sure that we wore long sleeves at all times. The hotel had arranged for us to be able to eat behind closed doors or curtains during the day, and at night the restrictions didn't apply. I survived the cultural immersion experience and anxiously awaited the prospect of getting Stateside.

I got through the fourteen-hour nonstop flight to the States but not without wondering if this is what it would be like to be reincarnated as a sardine. As I have a goal of getting to the place where I don't whine, I have to remind myself what people used to go through to come to America in the first place. Fourteen hours of intense population density was small potatoes by comparison. I landed, cleared customs, and seriously thought about kissing the ground in the airport. A shuttle flight later, and I was within striking distance of home. My friends Lyndon and Rita Campbell picked me up in Nashville and took me to their home, and Steve joined us the next day. Their daughter was away at school, and I was treated to a stay in her room, which has a lovely balcony overlooking a peaceful field.

The next morning I went out on the balcony. Morning mist and the gently encroaching sunrise made the scene perfectly pastoral, the potentially abundant subject of any aspiring artist. One problem, though: it was too quiet. Where were the soldiers? Was I indeed safe? There weren't any Entry Check Points—no one to greet me at the gate, clear me, and send me on my way. Man, at first it was so hard to relax without any visible reassurances of being protected. I came to reason that it is precisely because of the sacrifices of soldiers that our cities in the States don't have to have ECPs. It is because of them that the view from Jana's balcony was unbroken by barriers. I'll just happily and gratefully deal with the discomfort of having the sounds of silence yelling at me.

Once, during my third year in the desert, I was discussing reentry with a young, small, darling, feisty Puerto Rican soldier, whom I nicknamed Tru, as her unit was getting ready to rotate out. Her question reminded me of my musings on Jana's balcony: "How am I going to be able to relax in a room where no one is armed?" There was a time when I would have been freaked out being in a room where anyone at all had a firearm, but now it was just the opposite. The changes one goes through!

As a rule, my body clock would finally adjust to the local time zone the day before I was scheduled to fly back and mess it up all over again. I would also have the eerie feeling that I hadn't actually arrived all the way yet, like there was some part of me still back at the ranch. The easiest way to describe coming home to the peace that is ours in the States is to say that it is like viewing something on a split screen. My heart was always wondering how everyone was faring back in the Sandbox, as well as exulting in the fact I didn't need to keep my body armor within arm's reach.

During this vacation, I went to Memphis, Tennessee, for an annual leadership conference for my wellness business as a Juice Plus+ distributor. While it was truly delightful to see my colleagues, I had to face for the first time what our soldiers do their entire career: try to fit in back in the States when they have been living on Mars. One night a group of us were walking back to the Memphis Convention Center after having dinner at a crowded old haunt on Beale Street, the birthplace of rock 'n roll. Suddenly an SUV pulled up near us, and the occupants exited quickly. The heavy car doors slamming sounded like we were taking fire, and I immediately started to dive for the pavement. I caught myself at the last moment and was thankful I was at the rear of our group, where no one noticed me. This kind of thing happened over and over when I would come home. After a while I just laughed, but at the time it wasn't funny at all.

To be back in the arms of my man was an indescribable comfort, and not just for the reasons one associates with happily married folks. It was that he got it; he got "where I was at"; he got *me*. It was with Steve that I could finally, totally relax. A couple of days before I was due to return, an unexpected phenomenon occurred. Providentially, Steve discerned what was going on. We came to call it "Game Face" in ensuing departures.

I would find that, as I was gearing up to go back, I would start to "leave" before I left. Nothing was wrong; there was no desire to be distant or to shut down. It was just that preparing to leave my loved ones and to go back to others whom I had come to love took so much emotional energy that I had to begin the emotional wire transfer early so the funds would be available when I arrived. I am so glad that Steve was not hurt or miffed. I have said more than once how much my husband's support strengthened me, and this is just one of many examples.

My fall break also coincided with the 2004 presidential election, so e-mails of that time were often laced with political slogans and references to campaigns of bygone eras, former presidents, or quotes from our founders. When I got back to Dubai, I purchased computer time from the hotel business center and started to get caught up on e-mail. All was well until I tried to open one message forwarded to me by Steve. The world's biggest pop-up came on my screen, and no, it was not to announce that I was the 9,999th viewer and had a cash prize waiting for me. It said something to the effect of "the content of the e-mail which you have tried to open is offensive to either the religious, legal, cultural, social, or political beliefs of the United Arab Emirates."

I sat back, looked in disbelief at the screen, and tried again. Same thing. I thought to myself, "Turner, what in the world have you tried to send me?" I thought that maybe somehow in cyberspace his e-mail had gotten infected, thus demonstrating my high level of techno-ignorance. When I returned to Baghdad, I eagerly went back to his e-mail, knowing that there would be no problem getting it to open on the MWR computers, out from under the Big Brothers. Here are the "offensive" words, penned by the culprit Benjamin Franklin in 1759: "Democracy is two wolves and a lamb deciding what to have for lunch, and liberty is a well-armed lamb contesting the decision." This had been way too much for the powers that be in the sixteen sheikdoms that make up the UAE. I would hear on subsequent trips through Dubai that its residents would go to all kinds of lengths to get around the blocks so they could hear what was going on in the outside world.

My birthday fell on the day I returned to Dubai. As I was sitting in the hotel restaurant eating by myself, I received a deeply appreciated gift that lasted for approximately eight seconds. For reasons I cannot explain, out of the clear blue on the hotel sound system, the first line of "Have Yourself a Merry Little Christmas," complete with vocals, was piped into the restaurant. Then it was gone and the elevator music was back. For a moment I just sat there, and then a tear of gratitude came down my cheek, as to me this was a little proof of "Kiddo, I see ya and I got your back" from the One who loves me. You can think what you want, as is your delirious liberty as an American. Just be sure to thank a soldier that you have the freedom to do so.

For the record, I don't like Dubai. It gives me the creeps. It is lavishly beautiful, with the most remarkable architecture I have ever seen. While it is necessarily more relaxed than, let's say, Yemen or Bahrain, its flagrant courting of world money is brazen and yet quite seductive. Business is booming, and I have been told that many of the world's heavy-duty construction cranes are in Dubai to keep up with the building.

Beneath the glitzy, lavish, seemingly hospitable surface, however, is something truly sinister: a booming trade in human trafficking, sexual and otherwise. *Every single time* I went through there, workers from India and the Philippines would talk to me about the conditions and the despotic bosses; on more than one occasion they begged me to please get them out of there. One big problem, though: the companies often keep their passports so they can't go home. Oh, they return them to the workers when there are human rights inspections, and then the workers have to give them right back.

Every contractor working in the Middle East had to take TIP (Trafficking in Persons) training produced by the State Department so we could be a secondary watch-dog force regarding the foreign companies working in Iraq. In 2006, the State Department issued a report estimating that at least 10,000 women are ensnared in the TIP industry in the UAE. Dubai is known as "the pipeline," and, like I said, it gives me the creeps.

MOZAMBIQUE, FEBRUARY 2005

The February 2005 break arrived not a moment too soon, as was the case with all of them. Because of the Foreign Workers regulations, there were two times in the three years when I had to go for eight months without coming back to the States. Steve and I agreed that both of those trips were ones I needed to do solo, and we would save for a trip to Hawaii during our anniversary to renew our vows, which we did in November 2005. I hated not seeing my husband and was comforted only by the fact that both trips without him would serve to powerfully change my life in a most positive manner that I wanted him and everyone else to benefit from.

I taught at a private school in Seattle in the midnineties and went on to become the school's director before we moved to Juarez, Mexico, and started another school at an orphanage. One of my Seattle students, Deborah Haggerty, had gotten her nursing degree and had been working at an amazing orphanage where true, supernatural miracles take place. It's run by Iris Ministries in Mozambique. I had wanted to go there for ten years, and Steve told me, "Hon, I don't want to think about not seeing you for eight months, but I think this is your time, and I think you need to go."

I was ready for no bombs and a kid fix, believe me. One of the things I missed greatly while living on the various bases was the presence of children. Occasionally the children of Iraqi officers would come on base with their dads, and families would visit prisoners, but I didn't get much chance to interact with them. An artificially childless environment is strange and lonely indeed.

Again, I had to travel through my not-so-favorite-place, Dubai, to get to Mozambique. The tsunami had just occurred in December, and I asked a Sri Lankan woman who worked at the hotel if everything was OK with her family. She burst into tears and said, "Oh, Mahm, I lost so many people. I am here alone!" She sobbed like a child in my arms, and I was glad we were in the hotel bathroom where hopefully there are no cameras. If she had been caught on camera crying in the arms of a Western guest, I don't want to think what would have happened to her.

When I arrived in Johannesburg to catch my connecting flight to Maputo, Mozambique (or Moz, as it is affectionately known), I decided to treat myself to a massage while I waited in the airport. I was not at all expecting what happened next, but several friends who are massage therapists had told me that it is not at all unusual for someone who has been under protracted stress or has experienced trauma to store it in their muscles. Massage can apparently have a way of drawing it out, and that is exactly what happened.

I was under the strong, caring hands of someone who was very skilled, and as she began to work my muscles, I began to weep silently, seemingly for no reason. I could hear bombs going off in my mind, and if I hadn't already been aware that this not uncommon, I would have thought it was time to call the men in the white coats. "Madam, are you alright?" the therapist asked with genuine concern. I lifted my head and through a running nose and eyes explained that I had been in Iraq for several months. I told her that I truly was fine, that she was doing a great job, and not to pay any attention to my silent sobbing. Boy, was I glad she kept going. By the end of the session I felt like I had gotten all that stuff out and was ready for a true vacation.

My flight landed in Maputo, where Debbie met me with some of the kids from the orphanage. Although it was February, it was the middle of summer in Africa. Due to the humidity, it was a different kind of heat from an Iraq summer, but to me it was glorious. The east coast of Africa is dazzlingly beautiful, with the most amazing trees I have ever seen. No wonder Africa has endured such molestation and turmoil! Everyone wants her beauty for themselves.

When we got to the orphanage I saw and heard what my heart had cried out for. Kids—kazillions of them! Oh, what music to my ears and heart! At the time, Iris had about 500 children there, several of whom are HIV+. As I was introduced to the resident directors, Steve and Roz, who were from Australia, Steve looked at me curiously and asked, "Why would you come to an orphanage, of all places, for an R and R?" I laughed and said, "Just give me no bombs and a kid fix, and I'm good!" He laughed, perhaps because he knows all too well that orphanage workers tend to march to the beat of a different drummer.

My two weeks in Moz went speeding by, as did all breaks. I basically smothered myself in kids, cooked for some of the missionaries, went shopping, visited the AIDS clinic, ran errands, and helped out—basically the kinds of things I used to do in Mexico. This may seem strange, but another thing I missed while I was in Iraq was cooking. I know it sounds nice to many to have a three-year forced hiatus from cooking, but being able to cook again was actually a lovely part of this vacation, and I found it restful and satisfying.

The children made me feel normal again. They would wake me up in the morning with their singing of praises, and spontaneously drum and dance out in the girls' play area in the afternoon. I still had to deal with wanting to find a bunker whenever a car would backfire, which in Maputo is often. Thankfully I was surrounded by people who loved me and who knew I was not making it up.

We also took a few days to go to Kruger National Park in South Africa. Oh, to be in the midst of such animals, such beauty! Iraq and all its turmoil were in another galaxy. Elephants would decide that it was time for them to cross the road, and we didn't argue with them. There were anthills taller than I am. Monkeys were scampering down the road and warthogs ambling along. Giraffes, impalas, hippos—on and on it went. I felt like I was in the middle of *The Lion King*, except this was the real deal, not a cartoon. I was truly refreshed and ready to head back to my work in Iraq.

When I arrived back at camp, I learned some heartbreaking news. There had been a kidnapping involving twelve Iraqi soldiers-in-training. These guys used to greet me at the gate both coming and going, and now they were gone. It looked like an inside job, as twelve had been kidnapped but only eleven had been killed. The killers had sent the head of one of the trainees to his wife in a box.

I was worried that they had gotten Mr. Aram, one of my favorite terps, and I was so relieved to find out that he was OK. If it had been appropriate, I would have thrown my arms around him and given him a hug, I was so glad to see him! Instead, I told him how thankful I was that he had not been harmed, and a few evenings later he came to the MWR center and told me his story in detail, which is described in chapter 10.

SEATTLE, WASHINGTON, JUNE 2005

The R and R at the end of my first year in Iraq ended up being an adventure wrapped in a caper hidden in an escapade. I found throughout my time in Iraq that certain crazy, dangerous, or difficult situations caused instant bonding with near-strangers, and this was no exception. The trip included getting stuck in Baghdad, being rerouted to Kuwait, getting bumped in Kuwait due to overbooking, flying through Germany, being rerouted through Canada because no flights were available in the States, and finally ending up in Seattle, the city of my birth and where a good chunk of my kids and family live. All in all it took a week to get home in this day of speedy air travel.

The first hitch was that BIAP was closed because Global Security had gone on strike. BIAP was already the most dangerous airport in the world, so the lack of private security forces made it impossible to leave. Every day the would-be travelers were hoping that the situation would be resolved; meanwhile, folks who were streaming in from all over Iraq to head back to the States were starting to seriously overcrowd the Baghdad Transit Center.

Military flights, known in Armyspeak as Mil Air, were dispatched on a first-come-first-served basis, with troop movement having priority. We would muster for roll call, then "hurry up and wait." One afternoon we were assured that we were next in line and were taken out to the terminal. The hours passed; we grew restless; the plane didn't come. We flattened the cartons that bottled water was shipped in and slept on them on the ground. The summer heat made it still about 85 degrees Fahrenheit, so there was no need for a blanket. It was one of the most beautiful night skies I ever remember.

The C-17 we finally piled into to fly to Kuwait was from McChord Air Force Base near Tacoma, Washington. I thought of my dad and how he would have loved an adventure like this. My throat ached with missing him. I tripped and fell flat on my face while trying to take a picture of the big bird, and my skinned-up hands looked like they used to after a rough day on the playground.

We ended up in Kuwait at a transit center normally used for processing contractors out of Afghanistan as well as Kuwait. It was on the coast of the Arabian Sea. There was actual grass in which to let our toes frolic, and the smell of the seawater was a straight blast from my past playing on the beaches of Puget Sound and the Pacific

Ocean. I met wonderful people there: Robin and Sarah, the nurses, and Bobby, the operations manager. Instant friends, instant coping laughter. No, it wasn't as good as being home, but it surely could have been a lot worse.

My new ticket in hand, I headed to the Kuwait City airport, thinking that surely I would now be headed toward home at last. Not yet. This time Lufthansa had overbooked the flight, my camera and a leather hat from Africa which I had bought for Steve were stolen, and I was bumped from the flight.

It seemed that I would always make a travel buddy with whom to get through the challenges of modern mass transportation, and this time it was a coworker named Chad who had gotten bumped as well. Our ticket agent, whose name started with an A, stayed with us, worked to get us reservations, and asked us questions about the U.S. and Christianity all night long.

Chad, who was also a believer, and I basically tag-teamed A (at A's insistence) the whole night. A was shocked to find out that many Americans don't think it is good for a woman to look and act like a whore. We told him that movies are not at all an accurate representation of Americans and that lots of Americans don't like the stuff that comes out of Hollywood. He didn't think anyone felt that abstinence until marriage was important. He thought presidents were like kings and was fascinated to hear about how democracy works.

Most importantly, he heard that God loves him and wants to have a relationship with him—a concept that is completely foreign to Islam. I watched a miracle occur, even if only temporarily. While we weren't able to get him completely past his hatred for Israel, by the time the night was over, he looked at us, thoroughly puzzled. He said, "I should not be having this conversation with you. It is . . . wrong. But I know that you are true believers and that you are not going to hell."

Maybe, just maybe, this former Palestinian may remember this conversation when he thinks about America. He and we risked being jailed for having it, as such discussions are illegal in Kuwait, but to me it was utterly worth it. The loss of the camera and the hat were small compared to this.

I had to fly through Canada, as it was by now the Fourth of July weekend, and there were no flights anywhere in the States. I landed in Vancouver, British

Columbia, and caught an Air Canada flight into Sea-Tac International Airport in Seattle. Because I was originally supposed to fly into Huntsville, Steve had planned to pick me up there then drive to Seattle in our eighteen-wheeler for a family reunion. The change of plans made him miss my first day in Seattle, but oh my, was I glad to see him when he got there.

I loved being back in Seattle seeing family, kids, and friends, and I wished I could have stayed much longer. I wanted to hug my mom forever. I know that my being in Iraq was very hard on her, just as it had been hard on her when my dad was serving in WWII. I also know that she understands why I had to do it. I think deep down my son Gabe, who thought I was nuts to go, gets it too. It had to have been weird for him—for all our kids—to have their mom/stepmom voluntarily live in a combat zone.

When Steve and I had watched the movie *Black Hawk Down*, I wept all through it as I realized that it could have been our own two boys that went through such hell. Never in a bazillion years did I imagine I would live to have the sound of Black Hawks become not only familiar, but actually welcome. Never did I think I would come to love other boys like I do our sons. It is the others and their sacrifice that give my sons, daughters, and kids-in-law their freedom to pursue their dreams unhindered. They are probably going to have to put up with me telling them so for the rest of my life, too.

Hawaii, November 2005

Steve and I had decided that we would take one dream vacation while I was gone, and we chose to go to Hawaii. The Island Boyz on the restricted access base helped me plan it and told me all the cool places to go on Maui. Steve had done some work in the Islands before we were married and had loved Maui. We also had a friend on Maui, Nan, who had been with us at the lowest point of our marriage, and we wanted to renew our vows there and thank her for never giving up on us and for loving us both.

Steve and I rented a condo, and having a kitchen to putter around in and cook for someone I loved was utterly therapeutic. Even doing my own laundry was fun. Volumes have been written on the beauty of Hawaii, and they are all true. The lush foliage, the flowers, the ocean, and the laid-back, friendly people were all just as I had imagined. Truly the whole time was a dream come true.

We got up at 0530 the morning we went to renew our vows before God and each other. There was supposed to be a glorious sunrise, but instead there was a pretty hefty storm, and we got soaked. It didn't matter. We were just so happy to be alive, in love, married, blessed out of our boots, and free. We had breakfast in a charming local restaurant, and no one seemed to think it was strange that we were dripping wet. Hang loose, mahn, ya know?

However, one thing happened on Maui that has made my soldier friends howl with the laughter of familiarity and civilians just look at me as if to say, "What have you been smokin'?" Steve and I were walking at sunset along the road next to the beach at Kihei. It was classic Hawaii—lovers and tourists out for a stroll, the sun just starting to slip into the sea and giving off one last glorious gasp of color. Off to our right was a gentle slope dotted with apartments and condos. Suddenly out of the corner of my eye I saw what I reacted to as though it were an IED, and instinctively with one motion I shoved Steve out and away from it to "save" him. Never mind that I pushed him out into the street where he could have been hit by a car; I was going to save my man!

As Steve bounced back like one of those inflated toys that is weighted in the bottom and pops back up after you hit it, he gave me a puzzled look and gently inquired, "Hon, what are you doing?" I sheepishly replied, "Nothing," then pointed to the offending "IED," which turned out to be part of a row of automatic sprinkler heads. I suppose the only thing goofier would have been if I had thrown myself on the sprinkler head as though I were falling on a grenade. I explained that I thought they were IEDs, and I was dismayed that a bad word had slipped out of my mouth when I first saw them. Steve just smiled and shook his head, and we went back to walking. Then we started laughing. At times I wonder what it must be like for him to be married to me.

A Special Forces colonel once told me about a time he was with his family at Disney World shortly after coming home from combat. Every night in the Land of Disney there is a fireworks display, and the whistling sound caused him to go into instinctive, ultraprotective mode. He hollered "INCOMING!!!!" at the top of his lungs and threw himself on his wife and son, knocking them to the ground, covering them with his body. Never mind that it was Orlando, Florida, and they were on a family vacation; he was doing his duty, and his clan was going to be protected! His wife sputtered at him, embarrassed, but I understand his reaction. This is not something you plan to do while on vacation or any other time, believe me!

ALABAMA AND PHOENIX, ARIZONA, MARCH 2006

In March of 2006 I went home for what was supposed to be a normal over-the-road trip in our bright yellow eighteen-wheeler named Sunshine. However, it was anything but normal, as I had a horrible springtime allergic reaction which caused my eyes to swell shut. In spite of that, we had a wonderful time. I'll never forget the night before I was due to get on the plane. I was having to put on my "game face"—that bizarre, unmanageable process of "leaving" before you have actually left. As I lay on Steve's chest I began weeping uncontrollably with the pain of having to leave him. When I think of what military families go through in being separated time and time again for my liberty, I am more determined than ever to live a life of gratitude.

JORDAN, JUNE 2006

Being assigned to a new camp shifted my vacation schedule, but in June I was given a few days off to go to Jordan. Ahh, Jordan—the place that gives me the most hope for the Arab world. Mosques and churches stand right next to each other, and the late King Hussein's youngest daughter once wrote a beautiful essay about her desire for peace with Israel. I ate hummus till I could find no more room, got a hot stone massage, visited friends, and rested a few days.

I signed up for the tour that the hotel recommended, but the tour bus never came to pick me up, so the hotel provided a private tour guide for the same price. What a wonderful blessing that turned out to be! His name was Ibrahim, and prior to his retirement he had been an engineer, designing bridges in Jordan.

He took me to all his favorite places, some things I would have never seen on the hotel tour. Museums, ruins, all brimming with true ancient history. He told me all about King Abdullah and Queen Rania and beamed over the fact that they were so good for the people and the country. I put on a burqa designed for tourists and went in the King Hussein mosque. While standing there, I prayed that one day God's love would be their portion. The idea that God loves us fervently is not a tenet of the Islamic faith, and the idea of going without that experience makes me sad.

Ibrahim took me to the River Jordan, to the spot where biblical archaeologists feel Christ was baptized by John the Baptist. I was about ten feet away from swimming to where I could touch Israel. It would have been the last thing I ever did, as Israeli guards don't take too kindly to such antics, but oh, to be so close! I would have loved to go to Jerusalem while I was there; I could actually see the city from Jordan.

However, if I had tried to go back to Iraq with an Israeli passport stamp, I would not have been let back into the country. You can arrange to have your passport just scanned and not stamped, but I didn't know this at the time, so Jerusalem still is on my dream list. Dubai has the same attitude about Israeli passport stamps. The only way I would have been able to get through Dubai and back to Iraq after having been to Israel would have been to inform them ahead of time of my travels, and even then, it would still have been up to them. I decided to play it safe.

Ibrahim also took me to the Dead Sea, and I waded out to the water in my clothes, a Punjabi long tunic and salwar pants from India—perfect for adventures like this. I had heard from my brother-in-law Chuck that in the Dead Sea you absolutely cannot sink, do a surface dive, or do anything but bob like a cork, and it's true. Ibrahim took a picture of me floating on my back, with my feet out of the water, reading a book.

On the way back to the airport, I asked Ibrahim the question I had been wanting to ask all day. In the Arab world, something is happening that is sometimes spoken of in secret, and surprisingly often out in the open: Muslims are experiencing dreams and visions of Jesus. Muslims refer to Jesus, Yeshua, as Isa (EEH-sa), and people will ask others with whom they feel safe, "Have you had your Isa dream yet?" It is easy to see why this is so threatening to Islamofacsists, and the phenomenon seems to be growing. The first time I did an Internet search on Muslim dreams and visions of Jesus in 2004, there were about 150 results. As of the spring of 2008, there are over seven million and 1.5 million results respectively.

I took a deep breath, not knowing what kind of reaction I would get, but feeling pretty safe, both because of Ibrahim's sweetness and the fact that I was now quite close to the airport and there was no place to turn around to dump me in the desert. "Ibrahim," I said, "have you had your Isa dream yet?" He smiled shyly and said, "No, mahm, but I like Isa very nice, and I really like His Mother."

I smiled, thanked him for his wonderful hospitality, tipped him accordingly, and headed to the plane. "Mahm, please come back to us! I will take you to more places! Very nice, very nice, you, mahm!" He grinned at me, and I returned his grin. Again, if it had been appropriate, I would have hugged him goodbye, but I think he felt my hug in his heart.

GERMANY, DECEMBER 2006

Because my vacation schedule had been changed, this was the second time I had to go eight months without seeing Steve. I decided to go to Germany because the U.S. soldiers stationed there who had become so much like family had now been home a few months from their tour in Iraq and had settled back in. They had told me to visit if I ever got a chance, so I did. I was apprehensive about being in a new country close to the holidays, and I really didn't want to intrude on family time, but

I was to find that this vacation was nothing short of a series of gifts. Germany is the land of my mother's people, and I fell in love with it. My parents had traveled to Europe on more than one occasion, and Germany was always one of their favorites. Now I could see why.

There had been a mix-up about when I was arriving and where I would be staying, but a chaplain's assistant who had been part of our praise and worship team in Iraq came to my rescue and let me stay at her house the first night. Heather Frazier, whom we had nicknamed "Heaven," and her husband Aaron were finishing up their Army careers and were getting ready to go back to the States. This was the first of many reunions with soldiers, and I felt my holidays began that first night.

Heather took me to Darmstadt, where I was able to visit Michael and Aimee Helmen, Dixey and Jul Behnken, and Michelle Cedana, an officer originally from the Philippines. Michael had been the leader of our praise and worship team in Iraq, and Dixey had been our "papa" chaplain. We decided to have a reunion church service and made plans to fellowship, sing, and worship together. I couldn't wait to see the rest of the crew.

When Colonel Behnken came to pick me up after a few days at the Helmens', he told me he wanted to introduce me to some very special people. There is an evangelical community of sisters on thirty-six acres on the edge of Darmstadt. Their religious order was formed just after WWII to minister reconciliation to the world after Germany's role in the war, with specific focus on Israel. Their founder, a woman by the name of Basilea Schlink, had a vision to have a place where people could experience restoration, and the grounds of Kanaan are as strikingly beautiful as they are tranquil.

Colonel Behnken wanted to thank the sisters at Kanaan for praying for us while we were in Iraq. I fell in love with these dear women, whom we nicknamed the "honey-nunnies." I spent the next afternoon with them, going to a chapel service and having tea and stollen. I spent a long time touring the grounds and felt peace in a way that I hadn't in a long time. They wanted to hear our stories, and I theirs. They have written extensively, and you can peruse their booklist at www.kanaan.org.

As I was welcomed by and rested in the homes of these soldiers and their families, I thought about how it had only been a few decades since Germany had been overtaken by madness and how far away and long ago that dark time now seemed. However, I was sad to discover that the same madness is trying to rise again when the Behnkens and I went by train to a Weihnachtsmarkt in Frankfurt. The whole city turns out for this Christmas celebration of lights, decorations, food, music, hot spiced wine, and gifts. The night was perfect and unscathed until we came upon a madman standing on a raised podium spewing out hatred toward the Jews. My German is minimal, but I didn't need to know much to figure out that this was the same spirit that plunged Germany into insanity. It cast a shadow over the evening and made me wonder if it was an omen.

One day Michael, Aimee, the kids, and I bundled into their minivan and went on an all-day sightseeing tour which included Neuschwanstein Castle and the Nazi concentration camp at Dachau. Nothing could have prepared me for the beauty of the one and the horror of the other. The castle, built by mad King Ludwig, is the model after which the Disneyland castle and trademark are designed. It truly looks like the stuff of fairy tales, and if the weather is misty, the castle appears to be floating. Tucked up in the hills, it can be seen for miles.

The Dachau death camp, built by mad king Hitler, is so nondescript from the outside that it would be very easy to miss. Of course it has been sanitized of much of the traces of its previous purpose, but nothing—absolutely nothing—can prepare you to deal with what occurred there over sixty years ago. The original barracks are gone, but you can go into a replica barracks. The former processing center is now a museum. It has pictures of the medical experiments done on inmates, literal torture racks, old inmate uniforms, and hideous pictures. The painstakingly penned ledgers of the lists of inmates are still there, as well as pictures of the building, inside and out, when it was being used.

The crematorium ovens and the poison gas "showers" are a bit removed from the barracks, over a small stream and in an eerily picturesque part of the woods. To stand in front of the ovens, be in the shower room where people were poisoned, and try to take in what happened here is mind-boggling. It was pure xenophobia manifested with the fury of hate, the monstrosity of which I know will raise its head again and is starting to even now. I was badly shaken. There are no smiling faces among the tourists, and everyone is quiet. Trying to absorb such evil without choking takes all one's strength.

Unbeknownst to me, Aimee had purchased a poster for me as a gift. The contemporary painting depicts a hand and wrist in the sleeve of a striped inmate uniform, reaching up to the blue sky. The hand forms a dove, and barbed wire runs the width of the painting. It is the first thing you see when you walk in my door. We left Dachau at sunset on the first day of Hanukkah, and I came away with an even deeper determination to live in such a way that as much as possible, I would let what happened there change me for the better.

We had the reunion service in the chapel of the Darmstadt Army base, and the joy of making music and worshipping together again was deep. The "honey-nunnies" came to the service and enjoyed it as well. There was one tangible thing, though, that I wanted to take with me from Germany. I had trinkets from the castle, the poster, and a loose rock from the wall in Dachau, but I also wanted a menorah, the candlestick used at Hanukkah. Aimee and I searched high and low all over Darmstadt to find one, but to no avail. That afternoon before I left I went to Kanaan. Knowing of their reconciliation work among Jews, I asked them if they knew of any place I could buy one.

They gave each other a secret, knowing look. Sister Labona vanished, and came back with a silver menorah given to them from the people of Israel. I didn't want to take such a treasure from them, but to refuse would have been bad form. Humbled by their generosity, I tucked the small silver treasure into my backpack before boarding the plane to go back to Iraq, praying that no one in Iraqi customs would open my pack and seize it. No one did, and it is now safely back in the States with me, a reminder of love triumphing over torrential hate. This indeed was the R and R that changed me forever.

CHAPTER 24

Purple Pointers
for Freedom

here simply are no words to describe what it is like to watch a nation be born and to participate in it, even marginally. I have often said that every American should have a mandatory field trip to Iraq. The first reason is to become thankful again for all that we have and who it is that makes sure we have it.

The other reason is to experience hope in the air and to see faces absolutely jubilant with that same hope—faces connected to hearts determined to be free regardless of the cost. Once upon a time we were a nation with that kind of passion. I hope we can become that again. I know that for me and the soldiers who were there, the sight of purple pointer fingers on three different occasions is etched in our memories as one of expectation and delight. The first sighting of "The Color Purple" (which, incidentally, is a fitting video analogy of the determination to be free from

217

an oppressor) is described in chapter 19, "The Dance toward Democracy." This chapter concentrates on the third election, which occurred almost a year later

I got the idea of soldiers and civilians dyeing their pointers purple from something that Steve said was going on in the States. Bill Bennett, Sean Hannity, Lynne Cheney, Martha Zoller, and others encouraged Americans to dye their fingers purple during 12–15 December 2005 to show solidarity with the Iraqis. Shelby Dangerfield, a ten-year-old from Montana, had dyed her finger purple for the first election, and the idea had caught on. A Web site called PurpleFingersforFreedom.org was born, and people began to send their pictures to the site. There were pictures of individuals, families, classrooms, small children, the elderly, blacks, whites, all colors.

It was quintessentially American, and now that it is almost three years later, I am wondering something. What would happen in the American psyche if all of a sudden for the 2008 elections terrorists sprang up in our cities and threatened to kill us for voting? If we had to essentially sign our death threat by having a dyed digit, would we say, "Take your best shot," do the Founders proud, and vote anyway, or would we surrender our precious freedom to vote in exchange for safety?

Inspired by the courage shown by the Iraqis in the first two elections as well as the movement back in the States, I asked the base commander if it would be alright if we dyed our fingers. You might wonder why in the world I had to get permission to do something the Iraqis were doing, but our soldiers have learned from experience that the most innocent of actions or gestures can sometimes send the wrong message. Not long after the assault phase, our soldiers would give a thumbs-up sign to greet the ever-adoring kids, not knowing that in Iraq that gesture was the same as giving someone the finger. So here were these innocent little kids running around their houses showing their parents a thumbs-up, and their parents were aghast. It took a while for the message to get out that in America this was always meant as a positive greeting, an expression of affirmation, or an attaboy. I didn't want to inadvertently offend the very people we were wanting to affirm. After all, unlike the Iraqis, I wasn't risking anything to do it, and I was concerned that I might come off as a parasitic wannabe. There was also the ever-present security issue. A soldier who showed up outside the wire with a purple digit might show up more readily in a sniper's crosshairs.

The base commander gave his OK, and we took red and blue dry erase markers to our fingers. As I would be walking to work, truckloads of Iraqi soldiers in training would go by, and they would always wave, every day without fail. I remember with great fondness that during those three election days as I showed them my purple finger, their grins would get huge and they would show me theirs before they got out of sight. I would then give them the now-sanitized thumbs-up and point at them, grinning back. When they came into MWR at night after training, I took them to the computer at the checkout desk and clicked on the purple pointer Web site from back home.

I certainly didn't know enough Arabic to explain all the details, but it didn't matter. If ever there were a situation where a picture is worth a thousand words, this was it. They would literally ooh and ahh, and it was clear that they were touched that people who would probably never meet them were backing them in a tangible way. "'Sgood" (that's good), they would say in broken English. "S'ank you, mahm" (thank you, ma'am).

An Iraqi Special Forces colonel named Ali had adopted me as his little sister, always delightfully intrigued that we shared the same name. Oh, the look on his face when he saw the purple fingers on the Web site! His eyes twinkled and danced; he nodded his head and grinned; he gave me a hug and said thank you. No, bro, thank *you*. You let me see the human passion for freedom up close and personal on the big screen of your new nation's heart. I owe you, big guy.

CHAPTER 25

R and Z, Our Sunni Twins

e came striding up to the desk in the MWR tent and introduced himself. "Hi, ma'am," he said, "my name is Z." He was dressed in camos and had no weapon or identifying patches. While his English was beautiful, it was clear that it was not his first language. I instantly knew that he was a terp, and it became readily apparent that he was not at all of tired of talking for a living. He proceeded to regale me with his adventures and accomplishments and was an endearing blend of swaggering soldier, adolescent angst, and tenderhearted vulnerability.

He told me of how he had grown up in Baghdad, how his doctor father had been murdered by a thief, and how his face was on muj wanted posters "everywhere in Baghdad." He said he had taught Iraqi soldiers to shoot and was authorized to carry a weapon (most unusual for a terp). He would soon prove to be a source for a host of other war stories. Because the things he went on to tell me were so fantastic, I wondered if his stories had been enhanced. On the other hand, because life in Iraq at times was so unbelievable, his tales did not inspire any serious doubt.

He continually dropped the "F-bomb," to the point that I finally said, "You know, Z, this might come as a surprise to you, but there are a whole lot of Americans who aren't comfortable with every other word being the F-word. A lot of them are moms like me, so, when you are telling me your stories, which I really want to hear, pretend you are telling them to your own mother." "OK," he said, reddening. "I'm sorry, ma'am." "You are forgiven, bud," I replied, grinning. "Go on."

Z had grown up near Prime Minister Allawi's home in Baghdad, and his father and Dr. Allawi had been colleagues. Z's dad was Sunni, while Dr. Allawi was Shia, but prior to the February 2006 bombings at the Samarra mosque, differences between Sunni and Shia were largely ignored. According to Z, it was like Protestants and Catholics living together in the same American neighborhood. It was widely believed that al-Zarqawi was behind the bombing in Samarra and that his desperate move was designed to cause Iraq to spiral into chaos. Thankfully he is no longer with us, and thankfully Iraq's sectarian violence was short-lived—at least for the present.

Z told me of his "conversion" to being pro-American. Prior to the invasion, Saddam had put forth a great deal of effort to convince Iraqis that the Americans would rape, pillage, and kill anyone who got in their way. Baghdad fell on 9 April 2003, and we saw Saddam's statue pulled down and beaten soundly with the shoes of Iraqis. In the Arabic culture, showing the bottom of your feet or purposely touching someone else with your shoe is highly offensive. The fury with which Iraqi sandals were applied to the fallen bronze Saddam is indicative of the rage which had been pent up in the Iraqi people for decades.

The same day that Baghdad fell, Z—who was seventeen at the time—was on his way home from his math tutoring appointment and found himself in a scenario distinctly different from what Saddam had so passionately promised. As he rounded the corner, Z found himself on the sidelines of a firefight between Iraqis and Americans. The Iraqis were in a car, the Americans in a Bradley. Z noticed that the

Americans were not returning fire, and for the life of him, he could not figure out why. The Iraqis were clearly no match for the boys in the Bradley, and all of it could have been over in seconds.

Then he saw an Iraqi woman and her children who would be cut down in the crossfire if they made a move to get to safety, and Z realized that *the Americans were trying to protect her and her family by not defending themselves from enemy fire.* This was a mind melt for our Z-man, and he stood there immobilized. Then the Americans began to gesture wildly to the woman and call out in English for her to make a run for cover. She knew no English, they knew no Arabic, and she stood still, frozen in fear, clutching her children to her. Z then sprang into action and began translating what the Americans were saying to the woman. She was still afraid to move, so the Americans moved the Bradley around to make a shield for her. For Z, this was the knockout punch to Saddam's propaganda campaign. He was floored that American soldiers would put themselves in harm's way "just to protect a woman." The woman moved behind the Bradley, the Iraqis fled in their car, and the African-American captain calling the shots got out of the Bradley, came over to thank Z, and hugged him. Two days later, Z signed up to be a terp, and he has been at it ever since.

He then told me something that stunned me. When he was three years old, he met the love of his life. It rarely happens at such a tender age, but I believe he was telling me the truth. I watched him as he struggled with the rest of the story. When they were fifteen years old, he asked her to marry him, and she accepted his promise ring. They kept their engagement a secret from everyone.

She joined him in becoming an interpreter, and they went to help the Coalition in the brutal battle for Fallujah in November 2004. She took an IED, and his sweetheart was blown to bits right before his adolescent eyes. He identified her for the Coalition by the promise ring on her severed hand, which was about all that was left of her. He said that it was then that he knew he wanted to be a soldier forever and drive out of his Iraq the people who were annihilating the innocent.

I reached across the counter and took his hand. This was not exactly culturally correct, but I sensed it was the right thing to do. "I am so sorry, honey," I said. He swallowed hard a few times and continued.

"Thanks for you comes to Iraq," he said. "You're welcome," I said. "It truly is my honor, and I want to see the Iraqi people free."

He looked at me and asked, "What religion are you?"

"I am a Christian," I replied, thinking, "Oh, boy, it's on now."

"Catholic?"

"No. I just love Isa. I'm just a Christian."

"I respect that, even though it is against my religion."

"I appreciate that," I said, thinking that this would be the first of many interesting discussions; I was right.

"Are you Sunni or Shia?" I asked.

"I am Sunni."

"Please, would you explain the difference between Shias and Sunnis to me? I don't think I understand it very well."

He went into a very detailed history of Islam and explained that the division between Sunnis and Shias began after Mohammed's death. A dispute arose over who was supposed to be the next head honcho: whether it should be someone of Mohammed's physical lineage or one of Mohammed's followers. The "blood is thicker than water" group became the Shias, and the "may the best man win" group became the Sunnis. I was impressed with his grasp of this and other historical subjects and noted that he was a good teacher.

He continued, "We believe Jesus was a prophet, and we respect Him. We just don't believe that He was the Son of God or that He was raised from the dead."

"Ah," I thought, "the classic objections. This could get interesting, and I could get in so much trouble." I mused that the worst that could happen to me was that I could get sent home for "proselytizing" (even though he was the one who asked) and decided to take my chances.

"Well," I asked, "what did He say about Himself?"

"What do you mean?"

"I understand that this is what you have been taught about Isa, and I respect that, but what did Isa say about Himself?"

"I don't know," he said.

"Well, *He* said that He was the Son of God, and *He* said that if you destroyed Him, He'd still be resurrected."

"We don't believe that."

"I understand. Then I guess He was a liar, which makes Him not even a good man. Either that or He said things that weren't true because He was crazy. Either way, if He said something that is not true, then He can't be a true prophet as you have said He is. True prophets tell the truth. So why, if He was a liar and therefore evil, or crazy and therefore pitiful, would you think he was a prophet of God?"

He just looked at me, thinking. Our conversation continued and remained entirely friendly.

"Z," I said, "if you ask Him who He is, He will show you."

"OK," he replied.

"Ali," he said leaning across the counter as if to tell me his deepest darkest secret, "I have a Torah."

"Cool," I said, stuffing my surprise.

"And I am reading it." Now we were getting into really risky business. If any terp less open and searching found out that our Sunni boy had a Torah, it wouldn't take much to get him killed outside the wire or maybe even inside. What an impossible parallel universe this lad lived in!

"We have a saying that the Jews are our cousins."

"More like half brothers, Z. Read it for yourself."

He had to leave and thanked me profusely for the time I had spent with him. I asked him to please come back anytime.

"I need to bring R here to see you. She really needs to talk to you."

"OK," I said, and he began to tell me her story. They had known each other since they were little, but they were like brother and sister. She was a terp as well, and he brought her to see me a few days later.

"This is R," he said. Before me stood a young woman with some of the most amazing eyes I have ever seen.

"Hello," she said shyly.

"Hi, welcome. I am glad to meet you. Z has told me a lot about you."

She smiled again and said, "May I talk to you?"

I got the sense that she meant privately, and that was going to be a bit of a challenge. The tent was hopping—all the Xboxes were being used, the TV was on with the couches full of viewers, cards and foosball were being played, and the movie theater was full. One small table was vacant, so we headed over there.

We sat down, and she began to tell me about something that made me furious. An NCO had been verbally inappropriate with her, promising her entrance into the Army in exchange for sex, which she declined. She was really upset, as she should have been.

The first thing that I said to her was how sorry I was for the NCO's behavior, and I assured her that the Army had no tolerance for this kind of thing. I offered to help her file the report to get this mess taken care of, as our department had gone through the training on sexual harassment and I knew whom to contact. I also apologized especially from the standpoint of her faith as a Sunni, knowing that in her culture the guy could get killed for this kind of inexcusable behavior. The NCO's actions toward her were not exactly a good way to "win hearts and minds," and I was glad that the Army took this kind of thing seriously. I felt blessed to be a safe person in whom she could confide.

She told me that the NCO had already rotated out, and she didn't really want to pursue any official investigation. I decided to try to help her move toward forgiveness, which is the key to lasting recovery from any type of abuse or assault. I had not been explaining the power of forgiveness for very long when she stopped me and out of the clear blue said, "When I was five years old I had a dream. In the dream I was in a bed with no blanket, and I was cold. Jesus came to me and he opened His cloak and wrapped me in it. When I woke up, I was warm and full of light." Then she uttered the words that would change both of us forever: "And I have been looking for Him ever since."

R had grown up with absolutely no cultural reference point or contact with Yeshua, and yet she was desperate to find Him. I looked at her and said, "Honey, do you want to give your life to Jesus?"

"Yes."

I now felt like a firefighter or EMT doing an emergency delivery in the back of a taxi. This baby was coming fast, and about all I was going to be able to do was catch!

"OK," I said. "Here's what we are going to do. You and I could both get in so much trouble if we get caught praying; we are definitely going to pray, but we are going to keep our eyes open so it just looks like we are talking, OK?"

"OK."

"So just pray after me, but use your own words too, because He wants this to be from your heart."

She prayed, asked the Lord to forgive her for her sins, and gave herself to Him. I had not had any opportunity to tell her what it was like to experience Yeshua's presence, but she was about to discover for herself just how much her Maker loved her.

When we were through, she looked at me in wonder and said, "Wow, I feel like today is my birthday."

"It is," I said.

"And I feel so clean inside."

"You are."

And then she looked at me in complete puzzlement and said with a question in her voice, "And I love you more than my mother??"

I laughed. I was sitting in the presence of a miracle, utterly honored to be a small part of it.

We talked a bit longer while Z watched TV. R told me about how her father used to beat her badly when she was younger because she just didn't seem to be interested in "getting with the program" of being a dedicated Sunni Muslim. "I knew in my heart it wasn't true, the stuff he was telling me about Allah," she told me. This is not the first time I have heard this from a terp. I asked myself how in the world such a little Braveheart survived. I knew the answer: her life was a miracle, and nothing short of it.

She then told me about a time when she was in New York City with her family and someone on the street was selling votive candles with pictures of Jesus. She told the Jesus on the candle that she wanted to follow Him, and tears came to her eyes.

Her father looked sharply at her and asked her what was wrong with her. "Nothing, Papa," she said, looking down. "I just got something in my eyes." I was undone by such hunger and courage in the heart of a child. I knew I had to get back to the desk, so we ended our first meeting with heartfelt hugs, and the "twins" promised to come back and see me as soon as they could.

A few days later I encountered them when they had just come back from a mission. They were in sweaty ABUs, the all-purpose desert camo uniform, but I didn't care how dirty they were. I was just so glad to see them, and the only appropriate thing to do was to dish out a round of hugs. Being in the presence of twenty-year-old kids who are willing to take such huge risks for their country's freedom revolutionized my life, and now I owe terps as well as soldiers an unpayable debt of gratitude.

"We decided that you are going to be our mother," Z said. R smiled in agreement, and I said, "Fine by me." I am sure my grin went from ear to ear. This was the beginning of two relationships that I keep safely tucked away in my bag of heart-treasures given to me while in Iraq. When I get in touch with how much I miss these kids, I don't do very well, and yet the pain of being away from them makes me cherish them all the more.

Our fishing-lodge church was thrilled about what happened with R and warmly welcomed Z; we adopted them as our Twins. They were both very touched by their new family and began attending services. One night during testimony time, Z stood *and actually thanked the American people for invading his nation*! R was growing like a weed in her newfound faith, while Z was trying to figure out how to be both a Sunni and a Christian at the same time and was in a lot of turmoil. We in the West cannot imagine the dilemma that people go through when they are making a spiritual choice that could cost them their lives, especially when they have already made political choices that could easily do the same thing. Right now in America we have it ridiculously easy and our religious freedoms are largely protected, but I don't think that this will be the case forever.

Z and I continued to talk and work through his questions a bit at a time, and R—basking in the glow of being a newborn believer—was floating. A few days later our worship team did a song by the Newsboys entitled "He Reigns":

It's the song of the redeemed, rising from the African plain.
It's the song of the forgiven, drowning out the Amazon rain.
The song of Asian believers filled with God's holy fire.
It's every tribe, every tongue, every nation, a love song born of a grateful choir.

It's all God's children singin' "Glory, Glory, Hallelujah, He reigns, He reigns."
It's all God's children singin' "Glory, Glory, Hallelujah, He reigns, He reigns."

Let it rise above the four winds caught up in the heavenly sound.
Let praises echo from the towers of cathedrals, to the faithful gathered underground.
Of all the songs sung from the dawn of creation, some were meant to persist.
Of all the bells rung from a thousand steeples, none rings truer than this.

It's all God's children singin' "Glory, glory, Hallelujah, He reigns, He reigns."
It's all God's children singin' "Glory, Glory, Hallelujah, He reigns, He reigns."

And all the powers of darkness tremble at what they just heard
Cuz all the powers of darkness can't drown out a single word

When all God's children are singin' "Glory, glory, Hallelujah, He reigns, He reigns."
It's all God's children singin' "Glory, glory, Hallelujah, He reigns."[45]

"He Reigns" is one of those songs that grabs hold of you and will not let go. It played in my head for days after we sang it the first time, and it still turns me upside down. I did not, however, expect it to have that kind of effect on Z, who told me, "My mother, I just can't get that song out of my head. I sing it all day long. I sing it in my bed. I can't turn it off."

I laughed and told him that the same thing had been true for me. He asked me to print the lyrics for him, which I did immediately; then he asked me to explain them to him. As we went through each stanza, I explained to him that there were

Christians suffering for their faith in places like China and the Sudan, and they had to meet in secret. He seemed troubled by this. When we got to the chorus, he said, "My mother, what does Hal-le-lu-jah mean?"

"Well, my son, they are obeying the command to praise the God of Abraham, Isaac, and Jacob."

He stopped and looked at me. "My mother, I have a secret to tell you: *I love Israel.*"

"What?" I was thinking. "A person can't even get back into Iraq if he has an Israeli stamp on his passport." This admission on Z's part came as a complete surprise, but this was not the last time I would come across an Arab with an inexplicable love for Israel. Z had outted himself by telling a secret that could easily get him killed.

"Honey, if you love God, you will love Israel, not because Israel is perfect, because it certainly is not. But God made a covenant with Abraham, and He doesn't break His covenants. God said, 'I will bless those who bless you and curse those who curse you.' That's still true today."

"My mother," he said. "I have one more secret to tell you: I think I am Jewish."

Oddly, that didn't surprise me, now that I had recovered from his first confession, and I assured him that his experience was not at all uncommon. There are people all over the world who identify with Israel and the Jewish people even though they have no idea why. We ran into this when we lived at the orphanage in Mexico. I had a similar feeling when I was twelve years old, long before I learned that I had Jewish ancestors. It wasn't until the discovery regarding my lineage that I understood my desire to see Israel survive.

Two weeks later, R decided she wanted to be baptized. Several soldiers wanted to be baptized as well, thus making their profession of faith public, and Col. Dixey Behnken baptized them all in one of Saddam's many swimming pools.

Z came to see R's baptism, and he was in a state of complete inner conflict. First he'd bark at her in private about being a traitor to Islam, and then he'd encourage her to go for it. I think it's safe to say that he was wrestling hard with his own personal alligators. But as our team stood and faced the crowd to sing "He Reigns," I could see Z standing in the back singing at the top of his lungs and clapping.

One time a few weeks after the baptism, he lost an American soldier who had been his squad leader, and he took it very hard. He asked us to pray for him, and Dixey, who was like a Papa to all of us, went over and hugged him like a son. Then Dixey said from the pulpit, "Z, this song is for you." We knew he meant "He Reigns," and we sang it with passion. Although Z just sat and soaked it in, he told me later on the bus ride home that it really touched him that the Colonel would do that for him in public, "even in church."

"My son," I said, "That is the way it's supposed to be. That is what Jesus meant when He said 'Love one another' and 'Bear one another's burdens.' We all love you, Z, very much. And more importantly, honey, God loves you."

Yet he struggled. He told Dixey that he still wanted to be of both faiths, and while Dixey counseled him, he wisely knew that this boy needed time and space. This was something that he was going to have to come to on his own, or it would be meaningless.

On yet another bus ride home, he began to pour out his exhaustion. The kid had been in combat for years, had suffered horrific personal loss, and only took tiny breaks here and there. I was amazed he was in as good shape as he was. He just kept saying, "My mother, I am so tired. I am so tired."

"I know you are, Z." We sat in silence for a bit. I continued, "One of my favorite things that Jesus said is, 'Come unto me, all you who are weary and heavy laden, and I will give you rest.' Honey, He loves you. There are ninety-nine names for Allah, and not one of them is 'love.' Yahweh doesn't just love you; He *is* love." I watched his shoulders slump as he gave out a deep sigh. We got out at our bus stop and sat in the moonlight for a long time. I was way past curfew and could have gotten in a heap of trouble for being out so late, but I knew I couldn't leave him. I finally asked him the same question I had asked his "sister."

"Honey, would you like to give your life to Jesus?" He nodded. So we prayed, and he let Jesus love him for the first time in his life. There in that bus stop, he slid into home, and the Divine Ump hollered "Safe!" while the angels went nuts.

CHAPTER 26

Salt and Light

During my time in Iraq, spirited discussions about everything that our mamas taught us is a "no no" at the dinner table—religion, politics, sex, and philosophy—would spring up in the most unexpected places and times. The Dfac, the Post Office, the bus, and the MWR buildings were all scenes of lively, almost always thoughtful exchanges. Sometimes I would join in, but a lot of times I just listened. When I did get involved, it was out of the desire to fulfill what is referred to biblically as everyone's responsibility to be "salt and light" in the culture. Salt preserves that which is good, and light illuminates.

Just as in America, the Armed Services in Iraq gathered every type and stripe of person in one big proverbial Bedouin desert tent. There were Island Boyz who would just as soon surf all day and who would totally "hang loose" about all of life. There were career officers—Ivy League college graduates—who were so at odds with everyone and everything, including themselves, that we wondered what in the world they were doing pursuing a military career.

233

There were good ol' boys, gangstas, and Latinos who wanted Tejas and California to go back to Mexico. There were feminists who seemed to think that anything that looked or sounded feminine was completely taboo, and there were tiny female soldiers who seemed so delicate that I can't imagine them ever firing their comparatively huge M-16s, let alone slinging them over their shoulders and toting them everywhere.

The military finds itself in the difficult position of trying to stride the fence between being politically correct and having common sense. Posters in the Dfac celebrated Black History Month, Asian Pacific History Month, Hispanic History Month, Women's History Month, and Native American History Month; some guys wondered when there was going to be a Bubba History Month. Presentations were made for each people group, and TV ads for documentary programs were broadcast on AFN. I went to as many presentations as I could, and I always learned something.

Someone would point out with perhaps a touch of tongue in cheek that there are only twelve months in a year and way more than twelve truly-deserving-and-previously-unmentioned-and/or-disenfranchised people groups, so maybe we needed to go on a five-year rotation plan so that no one felt left out. The question that remained, however, was whether everyone would be willing to share or whether someone would feel duty-bound to sue the Army's EO (Equal Opportunity) Office for discrimination and marginalization.

The conclusion to these kinds of oh-so-weighty matters would always come down to one common denominator that defines so many things in a combat zone: at the end of the day, who in the world *cares* about being PC when the enemy sees *everyone* as infidels, wants to kill us all, and would feel blessed to behead us, either before or after we're dead? If someone blew up himself and everyone else in a Dfac (as happened in Mosul during Christmas of 2004), the "flavor-of-the-month" posters would go up in smoke anyway, along with the building. The continual threat of death quickly puts things in their proper perspective.

There is a marvelous quote from the film *The Four Feathers,* where a young British officer who has been blinded by a gunpowder explosion from his weapon speaks at a memorial service to honor his fallen comrades. He is a patriot, believes in God and country, is a true gentleman, and yet transcends those decent and necessary things to capture the essence of what being a fighter who protects his comrades-in-arms is all about. He says, with quiet passion, "In the heat of battle, it ceases to be an idea for which we fight, or a flag. Rather, we fight for the man on our left, and we fight for the man on our right."[46] It was exactly this context in which political discussions and even arguments occurred and what made such discussions so powerfully special.

Of course some soldiers have done bad things to other soldiers, but thankfully those occurrences are rare. Even during heated discussions of any type in Iraq, no matter what one's politics were, the soldiers' commitment to the Code and to each other kept things balanced and oddly beautiful. I found myself ardently wishing that this state of affairs could be transferred to the civilian sector. If comfortable civilians (who are comfortable largely due to the sacrifice of our soldiers and their families) would look at people with whom they disagree with the same protectiveness that soldiers show each other in a firefight, we might not be in a (so far) nonviolent cultural civil war in our own country. The problem is that it takes the physical threat of physical danger to forge the bond. I would not wish that danger on anyone, yet at the same time I am deeply grateful to have lived through it because of what it worked in me.

Let me tell you of a few notable conversations which transpired over my three years in Iraq.

In the spring of 2006, all across America there was a series of demonstrations allegedly intended to expose and wrestle with the problem of illegal immigration; at times the demonstrations got pretty ugly. One day a group of Latino soldiers came into the MWR to chill and talk. All spoke Spanish, some better than others. Some had been born in the States; some had emigrated from Mexico; some were the second- and third-generation offspring of people who had emigrated years ago. The discussion turned to the demonstrations back in the States.

They asked me what I thought, and I imagine my answer was not what they were expecting. I explained that Steve and I had lived at an orphanage in Mexico right in the middle of the turf of a powerful drug cartel. We had lived off grid, had power about two hours a day, and at times carried our water. Within ten miles of us, the FBI and the Mexican Federales had found twenty-two bodies of people who had been executed by the cartel for various "offenses."

I also told them that the orphanage was a place where people on a few occasions stopped on their way over the border illegally, and we gave them water for their journey. The summer before we arrived, over fifty people had died from neglect or at the direct hand of the "coyotes," the illegal "guides" who charge exorbitant fees to transport people over the border. One afternoon I found a young man who had been beaten up and robbed by fellow travelers and left bleeding on the hillside near the orphanage. We brought him inside, dressed his wounds, fed him, and prayed for him. He was still planning on crossing on foot, and we gave him some water.

At first the soldiers didn't exactly know what to think of me—not an uncommon state of affairs. It seemed strange to them that a middle-aged woman would choose to live the way we had, in poverty as well as danger. Just as my time in Iraq was some of the most fun I have ever had, living at the orphanage was supremely satisfying. I would gladly go back to either place right now if I felt like that was what I was supposed to do.

The soldiers soon indicated that I had their attention as well as their respect. They assumed that my taking care of the wounded man and the orphanage policy of giving water to travelers meant that illegally entering America was no big deal to me. I explained that while I understood why people would want to take the risks to make a new life for themselves in America, people were not entitled to come to America just by virtue of desire. Moreover, it was important for both the security of both the U.S. and Mexico that people enter *either* country legally. One soldier bristled, and the conversation narrowed to just the two of us.

"Mi hijo, let me ask you something," I said.

"What, señora?" he replied, his good manners being put to the test.

"If I am hearing you correctly, you are saying that Tejas, Nueva Mexico, y California should be given back to Mexico, si?"

"Si."

"Because we just 'took it away,' si?"

"Si."

"Those states belong rightfully to the people of Old Mexico, si?"

"Si."

"And in order to make amends to the Mexican people for past grievances, gringos in Los Etados Unidos should be willing to surrender the land and therefore their livelihood to the control of the Mexican government, si?"

"Well . . ."

"Si o no?"

"Si."

"Because gringos took it away from Mexicanos, no?"

"Si."

"OK, then, if we are going to use your plan, then the moment that Mexicanos have the land back in their possession, then they need to give it back to the Native Americans that they took it from, right?"

Silence.

"Right? I mean, if that is the way to fix the problem, you would then need to give all the United States back to the Native Americans, and the moment you are finished with that, you need to give Mexico back to the Taramuharas and the rest of the native tribes that Spain took it from, right, mi hijo?"

"Ummm . . ."

"Dude, she's right," another soldier interjected.

"Nah."

"No, Dude, she's right."

His face was perplexed; his buddies were chiding him; and we were going to have to come to some kind of peaceful resolution, because, after all, this was MWR, the place where everyone was supposed to get happy.

"Look, mi hijo, I don't claim to know what all the answers are, but, like you, I do want answers, and I do believe they exist. We just have to find them and make sure they are just. But before we do, I can tell you this: if we don't secure the border and if we keep leaving ourselves wide open to terrorists, we are not going to have anything left to give back to *anybody,* even if we decided that was the way we should go—which I don't think is the solution."

Our young social engineer indicated that he had enough to chew on for a while. One of his buddies later told me privately, "Oooh, Ali, you know you were getting to him, don't ya? He did not expect you to say what you said. You were right, too." I thanked him and reiterated that I *do* want to see the problem solved and for starters that would mean enforcing the laws that are already in place before making new ones.

Backing up a bit to the Presidential election of 2004, soldiers were deeply concerned over the prospect of having John Kerry as commander in chief. I cannot imagine what it would be like to face having someone who betrayed your warrior predecessors and lied about them as the very person you took an oath to obey, defend, and protect as commander in chief. Soldiers are also required to navigate the knife's edge when it comes to expressing constitutionally guaranteed freedoms of thought, choice, or dissent and not speaking seditiously about the president. Civilians can be as disrespectful as we wish, but the soldiers are utterly dependent upon the character of the person in the Oval Office to back them and give them everything they need for the job, especially after signing the papers to put them in harm's way.

I wonder what it must be like for Republican Presidential candidate John McCain to serve in the Senate with John Kerry, especially in war time. And what would it have been like for John McCain to serve in the Senate if John Kerry had been elected President? Thankfully we'll probably never know. I would hope, however, that if the two ever ended up in a foxhole again, one of them would be able to remember what it was like to "fight for the man on your right . . ."

One of the most powerful conversations I had in Iraq had to do with abortion. Nothing is more satisfying than knowing that because of a "thinking-it-through-all-the-way" conversation, the life of an unborn child might be spared..

On one of the camps where I worked, behind the laundry is a small, makeshift cross where a "little one"—a chemically aborted fetus—is buried. I don't know who the child's parents were; I just know that the Filipino laundry workers put the cross there. Sometimes, I am grieved to report, female soldiers will get pregnant on purpose just to be sent home, then have an abortion, thus buying some of what is deceptively marketed as "reproductive freedom."

One night the subject of abortion somehow came up at Midnight Chow—the meal for soldiers and civilians who worked graveyard shift. A beautiful, female African-American was eagerly curious to learn about the culture of life, so I began to expose some of the inconsistencies of the so-called pro-choice position.

"OK, you guys," I said, "let me make sure we are on the same page as far as the standard pro-choice arguments are concerned. A woman has the right to choose whether or not to terminate a pregnancy, at any point, and for any reason whatsoever, right?"

"Right," they said.

"And no one has the right to tell her what to do with her own body, right?"

"Right."

"All women, no matter who they are—women of color, white women, young, older, single, married, rich, poor—have absolute sovereignty over what occurs in their bodies, right?"

"Right."

"And that is going to be consistently applied to all women."

"That's right. Everybody."

"What if a woman is pregnant with a female?"

"What do you mean?"

"I mean, if a woman is pregnant with a female, why does the mother have the right to take away her own daughter's right to choose by killing her?"

"I never thought of that."

"If we are going to be consistent and believe in a woman's right to choose, then no woman has the right to interfere with another woman's right to choose, let alone a man. By your own argument, there really can't be any just application of 'choice,' because there is about a 50/50 chance of taking away the 'right to choose' of the woman inside of you. You'll have to explain to me why *your* right to choose trumps *hers*."

I let them think that over for a bit and maybe squirm just a touch.

"My girl, why do you think that Planned Parenthood clinics are most often located in black communities?"

"I don't know."

"Don't just take my word for it. If you do your research and search the Internet for 'African-American pro-life,' you'll see that the mission of inner-city clinics where your 'reproductive freedom is upheld' was actually born out of racism and eugenics."

"Eu-what?"

"Eugenics—the idea that there are races and people groups that are superior and should be allowed to flourish and inferior ones which should be eliminated. Margaret Sanger, the founder of what became Planned Parenthood, was a racist as well as a eugenicist. She wanted you eliminated, honey."

"What?"

"Yep, read it for yourself. Do the research. That's one of the things that changed me, and I was a hard core pro-abortion *believer*."

"You were?"

"Yep. I grew up in the sixties and was deeply involved in the Civil Rights movement, so finding out that someone was systematically trying to get black people to eliminate black people did not sit well with me at all. There were a whole lot of other things that changed my mind, but this was an important part. Just read what Margaret Sanger had to say about black people. Read her journals and read what she no doubt did not plan on having anyone else know about her feelings about black folks."

I told her the rest of my story about abortion, which is going to be the topic of another book, hopefully someday soon.

"Have you ever seen *Silent Scream*?" I asked.

"No, what's that?"

"It's the ultrasound recording of an abortion. It was produced by a guy named Dr. Bernard Nathanson, who either performed or supervised over 60,000 abortions and who was instrumental in getting abortion legalized in America. Then, mostly out of curiosity, he and a colleague filmed an abortion using ultrasound technology, which was pretty new at the time. You can actually see the baby screaming as they are cutting it up. Nathanson never again performed another abortion, and he became passionately pro-life. About fifteen years later, he became a Christian after having been a practicing Jew all his life."

Her eyes widened with horror. "Screaming?"

"Yep, but again, don't take my word for it, honey. You go online and do your own research, and we'll talk again."

She hugged me and promised that she'd look into it. A couple of days went by, and I saw her again at Midnight Chow. She came up to me, her eyes still wide as they had been the night we explored this together.

"Ali, I did what you said. I looked up that stuff about Margaret Sanger and Planned Parenthood, and I watched *Silent Scream*. I watched it for hours till about 0330 hours. I played it over and over again, and I completely changed my position. I am now pro-life. I will never, ever again be for abortion."

I hugged her tight and teared up. As I write this, the memory of our many conversations makes it very difficult to see the screen of my laptop because the tears are running afresh. These soldiers are so dear, and they are our future. I just hope we'll wake up and recognize it.

I told her, "Honey, if part of the reason that our paths crossed was so that you could change and go home and protect innocent kids—if just one life was spared because of our time together—it will have been worth it for me."

If you have been paying attention, you know that I have made that statement more than once in this book, and each time I have meant it from the depths of my heart. The truth is, even if I had *never* had a mountaintop experience such as this in Iraq, I would still say from my now much fuller heart, "It was worth it."

CHAPTER 27

Unsung Ugandans

n March of 2006 I was transferred to Camp Stryker, and upon arriving at the gate, I noticed guards of African descent who were not in any Coalition uniform that I had previously seen. Bennie, my new good-guy boss who had come to pick me up to move me and my stuff, told me that these guys on the ECPs were in the Ugandan Army and had been hired as part of the private security contractor force. At our camp there were about three hundred Ugandans—mostly men, mostly officers, and unfailingly wonderful.

Like the Filipinos, Indians, Nepalese, and Fijians, the Ugandans were indescribably warm, friendly, intense, and joyful. They would prove to be yet another expression of my Maker's love for me. Most definitely they helped to get me through my last year in Baghdad.

It was not uncommon for them to speak six or seven languages in addition to English. They had all kinds of stories about Idi Amin, the dreadful Saddam-like dictator under whom they or their parents had lived during his horrific reign of terror in the seventies. Clearly they were perfectly suited to help rebuild an Iraq which had likewise suffered at the hands of madness, and it was for that purpose that they volunteered to come here. A Ugandan officer told me that Uganda was the third country to volunteer to come to Iraq, after the UK and Australia.

The Ugandan soldiers' backgrounds were as varied as can be imagined. One was from a Christian family where there was a plural marriage, and he told me all about his upbringing (once he knew I wasn't going to freak out on him). Some had kinfolk who long ago had come to Africa from various European nations. One had an intensely protective heart toward Israel and longed to visit there. One had a child with cerebral palsy and a wife with a Ph.D. in zoology; he was earning money for his son's medical care. A female officer had been in the Ugandan Secret Service and had protected President Museveni and his family. One was getting his master's degree in finance. A few were Muslim; most of them were Christians. I see their smiles and hear their laughs with joy as I write this.

Many desired to actually join the U.S. Army as full-time soldiers. For a while I tried to get them hooked up with the recruiting officers, but the they would have had to go through the Red Zone into the Green Zone to the U.S. Embassy, and the travel was much too dangerous. You would have thought by their profuse expressions of gratitude at my paltry efforts that I had offered to donate one of my kidneys.

As the months went on they told me more of their stories. Two had lost their mothers to AIDS. One had an absolute gift at rapping and was fierce about keeping it clean. No potty-mouth for Kenneth, who in every respect was a delight. Kenneth used to text-message me just to say hi. "Hi, Mama Ali Tunner. God bless you today!!" often showed up on my cell phone screen. Sometimes when he was in a hurry it would just say "Hi, Tunner."

Diana had eyes that another contractor named Ty said "you could see the whole universe in." Juliet often sent me e-mails thanking me for "loving the Ugandans." What's not to love? Robert still faithfully e-mails me, and all of them beg me to come and visit them some day in Uganda when this is all over. God willing, I will.

Sometimes at night they would meet in a ditch by the road to pray and sing. They would pray for Iraq, pray for America, pray for the Coalition, pray for each other, and I heard later, pray for us, their American "family." When they would get in the vehicles to go out to the ECPs for shift changes, they would pray for everyone's safety. Being politically correct was not in their vocabulary, and no one raised a fuss. Novel concept, this.

If I was walking along the road and they saw me from their vehicle, they would hang out the window and wave vigorously like I was some kind of celebrity. Oh, the effect of being loved and protected like this is simply impossible to describe. It turns you upside down and shakes you. It makes you want to be a better person.

Once Chaplain Behnken mentioned in service that there was word amongst the insurgents that there was "a force field around the airport" that could not be penetrated. It certainly seemed to be the case. Mortars would land in the dumbest places and not go off. RPGs (Rocket-Propelled Grenades) would go through hooches like a BB through a soda can, but no one would be hurt. Incoming mortar and RPGs would land out in the middle of a field or even blow up before it got launched. I cannot prove it, of course, but I personally believe that the God of Abraham, Isaac, and Jacob was answering the prayers of those from a nation whose people not too long ago had hid in the bush begging Him to deliver them from evil. Idi Amin was defeated, and man alive, were the praying Ugandans ever on a roll in Iraq.

There is a little-known fact about the nation of Uganda, the turn it has taken for the better, and how it began to rebuild after Idi Amin was ousted. On New Year's Eve of 1999, as we in the U.S. were wondering what was going to happen with Y2K, the Ugandans brought in the New Year and the new millennium with something we desperately need: national repentance. An all-night stadium event in Kampala was attended by thousands, some of whom were now in Iraq at our camp. The president and the first lady told God in front of everyone there that they were sorry for the horrible things that had been done to Ugandans by Ugandans. They also dedicated the nation to Him and invited the people present to join them in this repentance and declaration, which they did with abandonment.

Thinking of this, I chuckled and groaned, wondering what kind of firestorm would be created in my own country if our president and his wife were to go to

Texas Stadium and repent by proxy for racism, genocide, and the murder of over forty-five million "little ones," which is what the word *fetus* means in Latin. What if they were to dedicate our country to God for His purposes? Perhaps if something this "outlandish" were to occur, we might see the same kind of turnaround that Uganda has. It sure couldn't hurt.

Sometimes these Ugandan treasure-people would sing on the way to the Dfac, and it was beautiful to listen to. Sometimes I would sit at their tables or walk behind them closely just to hear the sound of their language as they would chatter away. They would come and visit me at work, and I taught some how to play guitar. I have mentioned how unsettling as well as spoiling it was to have folks fall all over themselves with gratitude at the slightest expression of thanks or affection, and these guys were some of the chief "offenders."

Once we piled into a borrowed truck and visited an all-BIAP service held in the Birthday Palace, which they had never seen. We all smashed on to one of Saddam's former thrones and grinned like you do when you are in an instant photo booth with your best friend.

Almost always I was greeted at the ECPs with grins and "God bless you!" Sometimes they had to be more formal as they checked the buses and their occupants before letting us through. They took their job seriously, and they yet did it with love. When I grow up I want to be just like them.

Recently I got an e-mail from Robert, who had been transferred to Ramadi. Following are his kind words, exactly as written, which are a picture of how I was treated by all the Ugandans the whole time we were together at Stryker:

> *Hulo, my dear sister in Christ, How are you. im relocated to Fallujah, Iraq, and life here is very fine with many Marrines who are doing a good job, very friendly to many Ugandans.*

I responded and told him that I was including a chapter on the Ugandans in my book. He wrote back:

> *Hullo, my dear Turner Thanx for the quick response and your strong Courage to recall Ugandans in your book, im so grateful to hear that, wish all other*

Americans cld [could] share that. Did you know that Uganda and America share one Important country Motto, In God we Trust, and For God and my Country, those who trust in the Lord are like Mt. Zion . . . bye bye.

Bye bye, my dearest Robert, Diana, Juliet, Joseph, Simeon, Kenneth, Nicholas, Norbert, and all the rest of the crew. May our paths cross again, and may you know that your love for me was a shelter-tent in the spiritual sand storms of the desert. Thank you forever. All my love, Mahm Ali Tunner.

CHAPTER 28

The Bluez Brothers

hroughout my extended Iraqi field trip, I was providentially sustained and buoyed by joy to an extent that unnerved some and annoyed others. Still others felt that my psychological coping mechanisms kicked in to such a high degree that I only was succeeding in rafting down "dat River in Egypt, DeNial." I have been called crazy and other things. Oh well, it's not the first time, nor will it be the last. What was different in the Sandbox was that I was never really alone. Other rafters seemed to float near right when I needed ballast, throw me a line, and keep me from flipping when the water got frothy.

What you have before you is an account of a brief but intensely black mood experienced in February 2007. I survived the assault by hanging on to my faith, being nurtured by those around me who would speak into my abyss (often unknowingly), and the continual wise and loving presence of my hero/husband, Steve. There was also a bevy of people back in the States who consistently prayed for me and had the most amazing timing when it came to e-mails and care packages. Such support was my mainstay, and this bout with the blues became one of the many times I wondered how people stayed sane in this kind of stuff without telecommunications. Those who have gone before me are of a mettle that currently I only dream of possessing.

Who knows why a funk like this hits so hard? I think it is appropriate to say, only God. Maybe the blues bit because there was someone whose path I needed to cross and whose life I needed to speak into, and something evil wanted to abort that by driving me out of the Sandbox before it was my time to go. Maybe it was that something broken in me needed to be exposed and mended, and such mending often requires being backed into a corner where you'll either thrash around and wear out yourself as well as everyone else or you'll crash into the arms of grace and say, "Help! I am out of strength; I am out of 'gas'"

Man alive, did that "I'm-outta-gas-I'm-outta-here" thing hit hard. It came on like a snarly squall, and for a while I felt like I wouldn't even bother packing my stuff to exit awkwardly. I'd just say "bye," take my backpack, and head for home by way of Europe. For days I forced myself to smile and countered the standard polite query of "How are you?" with, "Hey, how are *you*?" because I just didn't want to answer.

I would hide in the porta-potties and hug myself, telling myself: "This is only a test." "The storm is passing over." "Sometimes God calms the storm; others He calms the child." "All things work together for good." "Viktor Frankl endured Dachau and came out of it a better person; you will too, if you choose to." All true, but when you are in the middle of a deep blue funk, these comments seem about as helpful as some of the insipid posters you can order from a *SkyMall* magazine.

I got so low that the only thing I could hang on to was that I knew I was loved, I knew I was forgiven, and if I wanted to be forgiven, I was going to have to forgive. I also knew that I couldn't do it myself. "Yeshua, I feel like I am going to jump on a table in the middle of the Dfac, thump my chest like King Kong, holler out my frustrations, and do something that is going to embarrass us both, so please help me, like yesterday."

As the "MWR Lady," it was my job to be up, stay up, and help everyone else up. As with all of the helping professions, I didn't have the luxury of being down. However, in the few times that I waded through the Self-Pity Swamp which paradoxically exists in the middle of the Iraqi desert, I found without fail that alligator wrestlers who would rival the late Steve Irwin were always sent to me, and never a moment too soon. Such was the case this last time around. I was in physical pain from what I was feeling and just wished I could puke it all out, get cleaned out, and be done with it. I felt like I had the emotional flu caused by a spiritual virus. At times I felt like I might faint—just keel right over. I felt like I was heading for the ground and my parachute was not opening. Something needed to happen immediately!

I knew that exercise is crucial in dealing with stress, that water is an absolute must, that sunlight is part of the Rx, that complete and total honesty with one's Maker is a no-brainer, and that it was time to plead my case. One morning I told my guys that I was going outside but would be close by if anyone needed anything. My cover story was that I was going to pick up the trash, which I did. I don't think I have ever been so glad to see cigarette butts in my life, as they gave me a truly justifiable reason for going out.

"OK, I am in trouble, here," I told God while picking up the butts. "I need help right now. Inside I feel like I am really only about five years old, I am lost and terrified because I got separated from my parents in the mall, and You are my only hope." Or, as it has been said, almost all of prayer can be reduced to three profound utterances: "Help," "I'm sorry," and "Thank You." I finished making my deposit in the Angst of the Ages Fund, set my jaw to do my job, and went back inside, but I still felt like I had a hole in my chest.

Only five minutes later, in they walked—my Helpers from on High. "Hi, guys," I said, in my best teeth-gritted cheery li'l voice. "How *are* ya?" One replied, "Blessed and highly favored, thank you. How 'bout you?" Stunned, I nearly asked them if they were angels, but thought better of it for the sake of my coworkers; they had enough trouble with me as it is. "Well," I said, "I have been feeling like I'm in utter meltdown mode, and I just got done asking God for help about five minutes ago. And here you are."

And here you are. Sometimes we have to wait for way more than five minutes, and sometimes we don't even get the chance to ask for help, as goodness and mercy are chasing us down at warp speed. But help *always* comes, and it always does the job. Both of them had things to say that had been lovingly cooked up in the kitchens of heaven, and I could tell that that I was starting to get unstuck.

Before the arrival of my African-American angels, I had briefly spoken with Steve, unloading my woes, as was and is my custom and his insistence. He listened, and then said, "Hon, I think you are supposed to journal this. I think it is supposed to go in the book. I think people need to know that there were times that you didn't know how you were going to make it. You are in a funk right now, and you know you'll be OK, but I think they need to hear it."

So, dear readers, here it is: a blow-by-blow account of a dalliance with depression in a combat zone. You want to know why it is hard for me to let you read it? Not because I am ashamed that it hit me. Depression is known as the common cold of mental health, and it attacks everyone at some point. It is just that by contrast I was surrounded by people who were outside the wire everyday, dealing with people who wanted not just to kill them, but to mutilate them, put their heads in a freezer, or parade their entrails through the street. Now *that's* a reason to sing the blues.

My struggles seemed so paltry by comparison, which brings me back to the theme of this Ballad. It is because of the warriors whom I hugged everyday that I even have the luxury of momentarily contemplating the fuzz in my navel. If it weren't for them, I wouldn't now be licking the wounds of being misunderstood for supporting the war in Iraq; I'd be figuring out how to survive being sold into concubinage, as is still the case with my Sudanese sisters. May they someday have the same blessing as do I, to be protected and free.

CHAPTER 29

Every Dog Has His Day

hat Saddam Hussein had anything that remotely resembled a trial as set forth by the constitution of his country is a testament to how well the country that he molested is functioning. On purpose I do not use the phrase "*his* country." He only *thought* Iraq was his, but Iraqis are proving him wrong, step by step.

That the trial went on and on due to Saddam's tantrums was no surprise, and it was also no surprise that there was bloodshed. But that doesn't mean that justice wasn't served, despite the naysayers on the evening news wringing their hands and declaring that nothing in Iraq was working. Those of us who had the privilege of observing from close range knew that the trial was the acid test of the new country's judicial endeavors. I believe they passed the test, and they will pass subsequent tests with higher marks.

Some people claim that the trial was just a matter of revenge and that there was no due process. If it was just about revenge, then why go through the motions of having any trial at all, especially when being involved in the judicial process to try him cost lives? Why not just shoot him, as did Mussolini's captors, transport Saddam's body to Baghdad, and hang it upside down on a meat hook, as was done to Il Duce? You might argue that the Iraqis never had the chance because Saddam was in American custody. But trust me on this: if the people of Iraq had really wanted nothing but revenge, they would have turned all of Baghdad into a mega-IED smoking wreck just to make sure that Saddam never got a chance to torture them again.

In an odd twist, the very fact that judges resigned and defense lawyers were killed and yet others kept stepping up to the plate to defend a man who passionately justified his involvement in mass murder *is* the proof that something was right about the process all along. In my view, they were willing to put their lives on the line for the very thing the man they were defending denied to millions. A judge actually recused himself after finding out that one of the codefendants might have been involved in the murder of his brother. That speaks volumes.

When Saddam was first arrested, close to 1,500 lawyers were retained for his defense. The one that stood out in bizarre bas-relief was former U.S. Attorney General Ramsey Clark. Mr. Clark has also been involved in the defense of such charmers as Yugoslavian brute Slobodan Milosevic, the "blind sheik" Rahman who planned the 1993 WTC bombings, PLO leaders who had been sued by the family of Leon Klinghoffer (the elderly wheelchair-bound Jewish-American tourist killed and thrown overboard from an Italian cruise ship by Palestinian terrorists in 1985), and one of the leaders who orchestrated the genocide in Rwanda.

In his article "Why I Am Willing to Defend Hussein," Mr. Clark stated that the United States had "engineered the demonization of Hussein."[47] No, pal, Saddam managed to demonize himself quite well on his own. He really didn't need any help from George Bush, as your article alleges.

The fact that someone didn't murder Ramsey Clark while he was in Baghdad is also a testament to how well, under the circumstances, things are going in Iraq. Mr. Clark had in days gone by been in cahoots with Senator John Kerry, who is not exactly popular with the soldiers for his vilifying of their Nam brothers and the resultant increase in torture of POWs in North Viet Nam. Because the soldiers are who they are, however, they essentially protected Clark's right to his own warped concepts of freedom and justice. That was asking a lot of the soldiers, but they did it, and I am glad they did it. Mr. Clark would not have the opportunity to see the evil of his ways and turn from them if he were dead. While I passionately resent his effect on Iraq and the soldiers, I wish him no harm.

Another indication of how well the trial went was the judge having the courage to eject Mr. Clark from the courtroom, apparently not impressed with his title of former Attorney General. Mr. Clark had the audacity to accuse a judge—whose life was on the line every day that he showed up in court—of "making a mockery of justice." The judge, Raouf Abdul Rahman, hollered at him in Arabic and English, saying, "Out! Out! You come from America and ridicule the Iraqi people!"[48] Well said, sir. Thank you for protecting us from one of our own.

I came very close to being able to go to Saddam's trial myself. An advisor to the prosecution said he would get me clearance and I could go with him. My boss at the time said he'd let me go and would give me the day off to do so. It was not to be, however, as I was transferred to another camp just before the trial. It would have been the second time in my life that I would have had the chance to personally see justice finally served in a landmark case.

My first opportunity was in 2001, at a different trial for murder by terrorism. I sat in on the court proceedings of Thomas Blanton, one of four KKK terrorists who blew up four little girls in a Birmingham, Alabama, church in September 1963. Blanton's courtroom demeanor could not have been more dissimilar to Saddam's. Thomas Blanton had turned from a swaggering, self-confident young buck into a rumpled, frightened-looking, confused old man. I can't help thinking that maybe the horror of what he had done had eaten him alive for close to forty years, that there was some regret in him somewhere for killing children who came to Sunday School to love God. That was not to be the case with the Terrorist from Tikrit.

Saddam's antics in court eventually became boring, as we had seen this behavior before, starting with the fit he pitched at his first arraignment at Camp Victory in the summer of 2004. However, a few of his more notable rantings need to be underscored in order to illustrate just how out of touch he was with what he had done.

One day he complained of not having a shower and access to his usual exercise facilities; he said, "This is terrorism." No, Mr. H., terrorism is three vats of acid and a chipper in your pre-invasion Abu Ghraib.

Another time he complained of having to walk up four flights of stairs due to a malfunctioning elevator. Looks like he got his exercise that day.

He threw himself around in his cell before American guards could restrain him so that he would get bruised and look like he was being abused. He rolled up his sleeve in court to prove it. Did he really think that with the international scrutiny of the U.S. and with Ramsey Clark there to make sure that he got a fair trial, any soldier was going to choose that time to rough him up and then face a court martial?

On and on it went, outburst after outburst. Pepperings of "Go to Hell," clearly his favorite phrase even until his last moments of his life, abounded. Saddam asked one of the witnesses who had previously been hidden behind a curtain something along the lines of "How do you remember all this?" The witness looked at the Butcher and allegedly said, "Some things you just don't forget." How glad I am that the witness had the opportunity to look Saddam in the eye and confront him. I know that it couldn't make up for all that happened, but I can only hope that something healed inside of him that day as he could safely tell his story and know that the Republican Guard wasn't going to toss him in the chipper or hook electrodes to his testicles.

As a woman who has counseled sexual abuse victims, I was glad that a woman got to confront him about being the "feast," as she described it, of her Saddam-sanctioned captors. She could not come out and use the word "rape," but it was clear what she was referring to. In the Arab culture, being raped is so shameful that in some quarters it is thought to be a rape victim's duty to her family to commit suicide and thereby cleanse their sullied tribal honor. How glad I am that she lived long enough to confront her ultimate abuser, who, according to witnesses, just sat there and blinked. The whole Arab world got to hear the voice of consummate courage . . . and it came from a woman who in one brave, true moment triumphed over the man who physically and emotionally sired a rapist and who himself in every imaginable way raped a nation.

In the summer of 2006 Saddam was hospitalized to have a feeding tube put in. This occurred about 500 feet from where I worked, and the extra security blocked the entrance to the bus route right outside our building. Supposedly Saddam had gone on a hunger strike to protest the death of one of his defense attorneys. That may be, but it is entirely possible that he was slimming down for his execution. Saddam was incredibly vain about his appearance, and he developed a passion for Doritos and Raisin Bran Crunch while he was incarcerated. He might have gotten a little chunky and wanted to make sure he was looking sharp as he was heading toward the gallows floor. This is pure speculation, mind you, but I wouldn't have put it past him.

During the time Saddam was temporarily our "neighbor" while in the hospital, al-Zarqawi was taken out. I have wondered if al-Zarqawi's sudden death that day affected Saddam in any way. We all heard the huge explosion on 7 June 2006 when the U.S. bombed Zarqawi's hiding place and saw the relief on the faces of terps when his death was announced. Al-Zarqawi was turned in by someone on the inside, as was Saddam. I fully expect that the same fate awaits Mr. Bin Laden.

Evil attracts its own demise. It always has, and it always will. Justice is served, whether in or outside of a courtroom. Inside the courtroom is always best, and I am glad that Iraq did not resort to mob rule. I would have understood if they had, but still, their testimony to the rest of the world, under the circumstances, was quite remarkable. I hope it doesn't take a generation for other folks to see it that way, but it would be worth the wait.

We all know that Saddam went to see God on 30 December 2006, a day that is described in detail in the next chapter. I believe that it is a fitting close to this chapter to share portions of his final press release. It is textbook megalomania, a careful attempt on the part of a sociopath to portray himself to the world as a reasonable man, and the fact that Iraq confronted, convicted, and rid themselves of evil such as this gives me hope for the nation. His words are significant as they illustrate both Saddam's denial of his evil and the courage of infant Iraq to punish that evil.

To the great nation, to the people of our country, and humanity: Many of you have known the writer of this letter to be faithful, honest, CARING FOR OTHERS, wise, of sound judgment, just, decisive, CAREFUL WITH THE WEALTH OF THE PEOPLE AND THE STATE . . . and that his heart is big enough to embrace all without discrimination. . . .

HIS HEART ACHES FOR THE POOR, AND HE DOES NOT REST UNTIL HE HELPS IN IMPROVING THEIR CONDITION AND ATTENDS TO THEIR NEEDS.

His heart contains all his people and all his nation, and he craves to be honest and faithful without differentiating between his people except on the basis of their efforts, efficiency, and patriotism.

. . . You should know that among the aggressors, there are people who support your struggle among the invaders, and some of them volunteered for the legal defence of prisoners, including Saddam Hussein. . . . Some of these people wept profusely when they said goodbye to me. . . .

. . . Long live Iraq, long live Iraq . . . Long live Palestine . . . Long live jihad and the mujahideen.

Saddam Hussein

President and Commander in Chief of the Iraqi Mujahid Armed Forces[49]

[emphasis added]

I wept profusely too when we were finally able say goodbye to him, but it was for different reasons. I wept out of relief, out of sadness that his life had been such a blight from which there was no redemption, and out of gratitude to all those who made sure that people like Saddam Hussein could never hurt anyone again. Ever.

CHAPTER 30

Strangely Saddam-less

O n the morning Saddam was executed, I wanted to make sure that I recorded my conflicting feelings about the incident on the same day that it occurred. I wrote the following to friends back home, and I heard later that my letter contrasting Saddam to Lou Lembo was read at Lou's funeral.

30 DECEMBER 2006

This morning, approximately fifteen minutes before Saddam Hussein was hanged, my coworkers and I were picked up to be taken to work. Sean, who worked nights at the Camp Stryker Rec Center, pulled up to drive us there and mentioned that Saddam's execution would take place before 0600. What a strange feeling it was to arrive at work a few minutes later and know that in a moment, a few miles away from me, one of the most brutal men who ever lived was going to meet his Maker.

It was bitter, dark, and blustery outside, as the sun had not yet risen. Winters in Iraq are surprisingly cold, and though this was my third one, I never got used to the polarity in temperature.

The fact that this man who made millions quake was now, himself, going to the gallows created a sense of surreality that cannot be described. When it was announced that he was dead, I cried momentarily, not out of joy, but perhaps due to some sense of relief. Iraqis danced, and I don't blame them. Iraqis wailed, and that I don't get at all.

Later we were told that while he was without his usual swagger as he approached the noose, almost his last words spoken to a human were "straight to hell." That pretty much sums up his view of his fellow man, I think. I have talked to many Iraqis whose lives were at the least made miserable and others who lost family members or friends at the behest of the Butcher of Baghdad. I have heard his victims describe in horrific detail what it was like to be tortured by his goons. I have worked in a building where a woman bled out from being tied up and having her nipples cut off. This building was across the street on an angle from the alligator pits where people suspended over the pit were snacked on by its inhabitants and photographed by the Republican Guard. Those pictures were posted in the building directly across the street from me. Another building where I worked was just a few hundred feet away from the lions' dens where Uday fed his sexual victims to the cats and watched as they were devoured. A man who narrowly escaped the gassing at Halabja has told me of the horrific sight of murdered thousands with eyes bulging and staring up at him when he crept back into town later that same day of the attack.

Retired General Wesley Clark recently described Saddam as being "unpleasant." If Saddam was unpleasant, then should we say that Hitler was "misguided" or perhaps "acting out"? I don't think so.

Saddam's wasted life and inevitable death touched on something else which was recently rubbed raw in my soul—the Holocaust. I am just back from a two-week R and R in Germany. It was one of the most wonderful vacations I have ever had, but it was also incredibly difficult. I went to Dachau, the infamous German concentration camp where at least 188,000 were tortured, experimented upon, hanged, gassed, and tossed in ovens. What made being there even eerier is that my visit was on the first day of Hanukkah, and it was the same week that Mahmoud the Rude (Ahmedinejad) was holding a global conference on the Holocaust in Tehran, of all places, partly to determine if the Holocaust had ever, in fact, occurred. The fact that it was attended by David Duke, former head of the Ku Klux Klan, should raise at least one global eyebrow, I would think.

As a side note, I feel that General Dwight D. Eisenhower had amazing foresight when he insisted that the atrocities of the Nazi camps be filmed and photographed immediately after liberation. He also invited politicians as well as members of the press to come view it for themselves. Who knows how many decades sooner those who deny the Holocaust would have gained enough clout to have its proof of having occurred removed from public school textbooks because they find it offensive!

Beginning at the age of twelve, I passionately studied what went down in Nazi Germany. I have read biographical and autobiographical accounts and seen movies, source document footage, and interviews. Nothing—absolutely nothing—could have prepared me for actually being there, even as sanitized as it now is. To stand in front of the ovens and inside the gas chamber was utterly shocking.

While I don't think there is anything new or different that I could contribute more than sixty years after Dachau was liberated by the 45th and 157th infantry units of the 7th Army, I noticed an undeniable similarity between Dachau and what the Butcher of Baghdad did to his fellow Iraqis. It was the same maniacal hatred, the same megalomania. There is a picture at Dachau at which I stared for a long time. It is a black and white aerial shot of the prisoners as the Allied soldiers are taking the camp. The photo of one man in particular stood out at me—his arms are stretched up and out as both a child and a victor, his eyes veritably dancing, his grin infectious. There are graphic, detailed sketches of the positions used to torture the residents of Dachau; they are exactly the same ones Saddam used on his victims. I suppose there are only so many things that can be done to a human body, and I think it's safe to say that Hitler and Saddam plumbed the depths of their collective curiosity.

Hitler felt Jews were vermin, and they were not the only people group targeted by his darkness. Saddam said that there were "three things which should not be allowed to exist: flies, Jews, and Persians." Saddam was phobic about germs, so I imagine the environs of his seventy-eight palaces were scrupulously kept free of flies. We know what he did to Persians, whom in the present day we refer to as Kurds. What is little known is that he was poised to strike Israel as well as Saudi Arabia with two types of deadly sarin gas and a nerve agent. The only reason why he was not successful is that the Coalition struck first in Desert Storm and the planes slated for the mission were destroyed. Would that the Allies had made a preemptive strike on Hitler! Who knows how many millions might have been saved? Instead, attempts were made to appease the partly Jewish wallpaper hanger, and the results of meeting with Der Fuhrer were hailed as having garnered "Peace in Our Time" by British Prime Minister Neville Chamberlain. I firmly believe that creatures such as these two would never be satisfied with being "contained."

When the Allied soldiers took Dachau, they touched nothing. Instead, they went and rounded up the townspeople, made them come and look, and then made them clean up the aftermath of what they had allowed by turning a blind eye, by pretending they didn't notice. From a psychological operations standpoint, it was a brilliant move on the part of the infantry. Today someone would probably complain that the townspeople were being abused by being held accountable in a practical way. In the Dachau gas chamber, there is a picture of a couple being forced to look at the pile of bodies in the next room. The woman has her hand over her mouth, either from the smell or the horror; the man's face shows no expression. It is sad to me that relatively few of Saddam's henchmen will ever be made to clean up the mass graves or the gore that covered Abu Ghraib. Our guys had that grisly task.

So when and why did I actually weep on the day of Saddam's death? It was when I opened up an e-mail picture of a soldier who helped to liberate Buchenwald, another notorious Nazi death camp. His name was Lou Lembo, and he was the father of friends with whom I attended theological school and with whom I sang for several years. I didn't know Lou well, but he was always kind to me and was adored by his kids and grandkids. He succumbed to cancer and all its accompanying torture, but as a warrior he defied the odds and amazed his docs by living two years longer than expected.

Lou's daughter-in-law says he was a gentleman to the last, and of that I have no doubt. Even after sixty years, she says, Lou would tell with tears in his eyes of the conditions of the prisoners he helped to liberate and restore. I can only imagine how deeply the freshly liberated of Buchenwald appreciated his kindness. I was already aware of Lou's death; what caused my dam of tears to break was that while the picture of Lou was recent, he was dressed in his WWII uniform. What I saw looking out at me was the reminder of what strength it took years ago to stop evil, coupled with the shining eyes and smile of a man who had chosen early on to be a true gentleman. Lou personified what has now come to be called the Greatest Generation.

People in the U.S. may decry the young nation of Iraq's fragile state, but to me, these "weak" Iraqis accomplished what should have happened at Nuremburg. It was the Allies, not the Germans, who tried the likes of Goebbels and Himmler. However, it was the Iraqis who once again defied the threat of death as they had in their elections, and saw to it that the Butcher was held terminally accountable. I, for one, am proud of them. The Coalition was there for them, but they did it; they saw it through despite the threats and the bloodshed. Edmund Burke said that all it takes for evil to triumph is for good men to do nothing. The good men and women of Iraq insisted that justice be served, and they are to be commended. It is my profound honor to be here observing Iraq's dogged journey toward stability, and I bless every one of their efforts that are consistent with the rule of law.

Thank God for men like Lou. Thank God for the men and women whom I encounter every day who are like him. Thank God for those who are willing to hunt down cowards like Saddam Hussein and Nazi war criminals and bring them to justice.

Saddam was finally captured on 13 December 2003. My husband's cousin took the blackout bag off Saddam's head after they caught him and brought him in to check his teeth. The static electricity caused Saddam's hair to be even wilder than it would have been after hiding for five months in a spider hole. That now-famous footage of his teeth being checked for the poison like that which some of the guilty at Nuremburg used to escape justice is playing several times an hour on today's news, as is the footage of his execution. He refused to have the bag put on his head this time, and it seems apparent, from the unedited clip of the unrestrained taunt-fest that burst out at the gallows, that he wanted to look at someone one last time and say, "Straight to hell!" He is gone, and, quite frankly, I don't think he and Lou ended up in the same place.

CHAPTER 31

Barney Fife, Aunt Bea, and the WMDs

J am inquisitive by nature and love to do research. In Iraq I had a life-changing opportunity to listen to the intel people who have the training, the experience, the intuition, and the necessary thinking skills to help me understand all the hoopla about the WMDs. I was able to ask the questions that I think were on the minds of most Americans, and essentially I got another education free.

Once I got in big trouble for asking about the WMDs (Weapons of Mass Destruction) and was even hauled into the Tactical Operations Center and questioned because some intel folks were afraid I was actually working for the media back home. As embarrassing as that was, being chosen to go learn, work, and play for a while in the Great Sandbox during one of the most amazing periods of history-within-History was a privilege I don't deserve.

One of the most puzzling and frustrating things during the time when the WMD issue was hot was how the media and politicians made it look like our (and everyone else's) intel had been left in the care of Barney Fife and Aunt Bea. With respect to Saddam Hussein and the mystical, "mythical" WMDs, you would think that intel as well as all of Mayberry R.F.D. had been irresponsibly turned over by Sheriff Andy Taylor to the care of the two perpetual bumblers.

It is as though you can see the skinny, frenetic, and then truly frantic Deputy Sheriff Fife saying, "Well shucky darn, where *did* dem WMDs go?" The kindly, dull-by-design Aunt Bea would then dutifully wring her hands, cluck and moan a bit, and then suggest that they call Sheriff Andy. Neither one, of course wanted to, because they didn't want to look like something got past 'em on their watch.

I have talked with people who have seen the WMDs in Iraq, touched them, and analyzed them, so from time to time it was natural for me to ask soldiers, "What do *you* think happened to the WMDs?" Once everyone on Capitol Hill started to roll over and say, "Oops, I guess we were wrong on that one," lots of folks were confused. More on that later, so stick with me.

First, though, there is a book that to me is the must-read on the issue, and I would be remiss if I didn't tell you about it: *Saddam's Secrets* by General Georges Sada. "General Georges," as he is affectionately known, was the second in command in the Iraqi Air Force and was legendary in his day as a fighter pilot. He completed his flight training in 1959 and flew until 1986, when Saddam grounded and imprisoned him briefly. He trained all over the world, including in the United States; speaks several languages; and in the early days of the new Iraq served as an advisor to Prime Minister Allawi. In addition, he is one of the few people who withstood Saddam to his face and actually lived.

He also experienced the challenge of being a lifelong Christian in a Muslim world and a non-Baathist in the Iraqi military hierarchy. He was told that the reason he would never be promoted to Supreme Commander of the Iraqi Air Force was that he refused to join the Baathist party. He settled for the lower spot on the podium and more than likely saved countless lives by doing so. He was known, even by the American captives he interrogated during the Gulf War, to be a man of decency.

In *Saddam's Secrets* he discusses two hotly contested and controversial issues as only a man who was actually there can: first, that Saddam was, without question, passionately and proactively set to attack Israel as well as Arab neighbor Saudi Arabia with WMDs; and second, how Saddam got them out of Iraq into Syria right under the noses of the UN inspectors. Here's a summary of what happened.

Just before the Coalition attacked in the Gulf War, Saddam had plans to attack Israel and Saudi Arabia with Sarin I and Sarin II gas and Tabun, a highly dangerous nerve agent that was discovered in Nazi Germany. He called a meeting wherein he expected everyone to rubber-stamp his plan. The planes were loaded and ready to go. Thankfully, General Georges launched into a nearly two-hour improv presentation about why this would be a disaster. He explained that between the excellence of the Israeli Air Force and the estimated ninety-six Iraqi planes that would be lost even if they *did* manage to penetrate Israel's and Saudi Arabia's air space, it was by all accounts not a good plan. It didn't matter to Saddam that at least ninety-six pilots would be lost, which would seriously compromise Iraq's ability to defend itself. Saddam was Saddam, and he was not to be swayed by something like logic when it came to his hatred for Israel. In that respect he reminds me of Mahmoud the Rude (Ahmedinejad), who is arguably as dangerous as Osama bin Laden.

Apparently after General Georges was finished you could have heard a pin drop, and everyone expected Saddam to take out his legendary .45 and whack him on the spot, as was often the custom of Baghdad's Butcher. Instead, Saddam was mad at everyone else and asked, "Why is it that Georges is the only one who will tell me the truth?" The planes stayed loaded but never took off and thankfully were destroyed in the first salvo of Desert Storm.

The covert WMD removal and relocation was truly shrewd,[50] and, like many other things, does not speak well of the UN sanctions nor its inspectors. On 4 June 2002, before OIF began, a dam broke in Syria. Saddam, that man of compassion, saw his opportunity to do something for his suffering Syrian neighbors to the North. General Sada says that at Saddam's behest, commercial airliners were gutted down nearly to the fuselage. These planes, including a group of Boeing 727s and one

Boeing 747, flew fifty-six sorties right past the UN inspectors into Syria under the guise of bringing humanitarian aid to the flood victims. What in fact the planes transported were the WMDs, probably the more fragile components. General Sada knows the pilots involved in the operation. Some of the liquid chemicals were put in tankers and buried at the Syrian border, according to an anonymous eyewitness who was a medic at the last camp where I worked. I was also told by intel officers that our soldiers on more than one occasion were treated for exposure to Sarin within the borders of Iraq, but thankfully there were no fatalities.

There has been a huge amount of furor over Saddam's nuclear ambitions and controversy over whether he intended to develop and use nuclear weapons. General Sada explains in great detail how Saddam attempted to accomplish such a task, and he states that the Chinese were tapped for the job.[51] Incidentally the Chinese were not the only ones whose palms were crossed with silver when it came to procuring the components necessary to make nuclear weapons.

One November night in 2004 I spent a long time listening to the tales of a young and brilliant American soldier named Joe who had to handle some NBCs (Nuclear, Biological, and Chemical weapons). I was working in Uday's former hunting lodge, and we chatted in the same room where David Letterman had visited, entertained, and interviewed the troops in December of 2003. This young man apparently managed to stun the usually unflappable Mr. L. by his story. In the early fall of 2003, just prior to his first tour, Joe married his high school sweetheart. They had been married about a month when he found his wife collapsed in the shower. He carried her out to the car himself and took her to the hospital, where she was diagnosed with meningitis. She died a few days later, and a month after her tragic death Joe was called up to serve in OIF. I think this was the only leg of Joe's journey that Mr. Letterman heard, and "the rest of the story" occurred later.

Joe's father was an American soldier, and little Joey had been raised as an Army brat, largely in Germany. They are descendants of General Francis Marion, also known as the Swamp Fox, the character portrayed by Mel Gibson in the film *The Patriot*. In the Fallujah campaign of 2004, American soldiers came across a weapons cache. It fell upon Joe to translate the German labeling on the sides of the crates, which contained phosgene, a nasty choking agent. As if that weren't enough, because Joe had learned how to analyze nuclear material while he was at West Point, he was also called upon to determine the level of degradation of the uranium they found in Fallujah. It turned out that the uranium had been sold to Saddam by the French, who along with the Germans were so violently opposed to the invasion. Hmmm, I wonder why? Could it be they didn't want anyone to know how they had violated the sanctions and had made a huge financial killing in the process?

So, either General Sada, the anonymous medic, and Joe the Swamp Fox Jr. are all lying about the existence of WMDs, or something else is going on. Over meals or at night in the MWR facility, soldiers, including intel officers, and people in communications as well as counterterrorism would take different theories out for a spin, and I would ponder which one was true. I cannot prove anything, but I can tell you what has ended up making the most sense to me. First of all, virtually nothing gets by Israeli intel. If you are surrounded by people who continually threaten to wipe you off the map because you are the Lesser Satan (just a warm-up for going after the Great Satan, i.e., the United States), you are going to be forced to know what's in your neighbor's cookie jar and under his mattress on a level that some may find real rude. So, for my money, if Israel says there are WMDs or nukes, you can take it to the bank.

I wonder if the so-called "bad intel" mantra so predictably and loudly chanted in the mainstream media beginning in 2004 was actually an intentional strategy to create a diversion so that Israel could get into Syria to assess the situation and then act upon it. Is it possible that everyone from President Bush on down was made (some perhaps willingly and knowingly) to look utterly doofus à la Barney Fife for a greater purpose? While politicians who had initially been in strong support of OIF were vilifying President Bush and the intelligence community for "bad intel" and claiming they had been "duped," someone found out what was really going on in Syria and prepared to do something about it. The waters of Newsland were frothy with frenzied feeding activity over the supposed latest version of "Bush-lied-people-died," while down river the Israeli nets were being cast in order catch the first of some truly big fish in Syria. Hopefully this is not the end of their "catch."

Do I know what I am suggesting to be a fact? Nope. I am only awkwardly connecting the dots. One day in the winter of 2007 not long after Saddam's execution, I overheard a young soldier and an older one discussing the WMDs, and the older one said, "Son, you don't have to worry about the WMDs that are in Syria. The Israelis will take care of them." In light of that statement, it's interesting to me that on 6 September 2007, Israeli fighter jets silently screamed past a pricey Russian antiaircraft detection system, got in and out of Syria, and took out a North Korean-built nuclear facility without a scratch or the smell of smoke.

Syria has been oddly quiet about the whole affair, having been caught with their pants not merely down, but bunched around their ankles. Israel is understandably not saying much, and it wouldn't at all surprise me if they take out the Syrian-stored WMDs next—if they didn't get some already. The Israelis' actions on 6 September are consistent with what General Sada has claimed all along: that Syria currently is the home of some very dangerous weapons. To me they do not conflict at all with the assertions of an Arabic-speaking FBI agent named George Piro who was interviewed in January 2008 by *Sixty Minutes*. Agent Piro befriended and interrogated Saddam after he was captured in December 2003. Saddam told Piro that he used the existence of the WMDs to bluff Iran and protect Iraq from Iranian attack and that the WMDs had been destroyed. Like many statements of Saddam's, I believe this is a partial truth: that some of the WMDS were destroyed, but not all. I believe Saddam withheld the full story from Agent Piro in order keep up the bigger bluff.

I think the most plausible resolution to the controversy is that some of the WMDs were destroyed by the UN inspectors, some were taken to Syria, and some are still buried in the vast Iraqi desert. Even more sobering is General Georges's statement that Saddam told his scientists to memorize all the formulas for the WMDs.[52] It would have only been a matter of time until production would have started up again, and no one would have been safe from the "Crasher," as Saddam's name means in Arabic, if the Coalition hadn't invaded.

Is it therefore reasonable to conclude that millions of lives were secretly spared by Israel's "antics" and more lives will be saved by Israel in the future? It wouldn't be the first time in history that the truest heroes have gone unsung. To me what happened in September of 2007 is as amazing as the Six-Day War, but without the flashy spread in *Life* magazine I remember from forty years ago. I am on tiptoe to see what happens next. I wonder if Sheriff Andy is fixin' to pull up to the station in his squad car to see if he can get to the bottom of this conundrum. I wonder even further if, because people like Georges Sada and George Bush were willing to look the Embodiment of Evil in the face and say "No," it just may be that for now, at least, it's safe for Opie to go fishin'.

CHAPTER 32

Crawling Out
of the Sandbox

The time came when Steve and I knew that it was time for me to crawl out of the Sandbox and "take my toys and go home." I don't suppose there will ever be a way to describe how hard it was to leave and simultaneously be bustin' to get back in my honey's arms again. I know the soldiers understand, as we talked about it often. How can you actually grieve about leaving someplace that was hellaciously hot, dusty, cold, windy, flooded, barren, and dangerous; in places had biting sand flies, camel spiders, and scorpions; and had coworkers who spent their energy lying, gossiping, backbiting, and making themselves and everyone around them miserable, as well as people who thought you were Satan's seed reserved for hell?

We grieved because there was laughter; affection; a purpose and a mission; documented but willfully unacknowledged progress and success; wonderful

273

craziness; remarkable creativity and ingenuity; people who publicly thanked us for invading their country; friendship; camaraderie; unscripted multicultural diversity at its finest; new family; coworkers who spent their energy helping, blessing, loving, and making the life of everyone around them a joy; and children and adults who adored us. And all of *them* hated to see us go.

I heard variations on this theme several times before I departed.

"No, Ali, you *can't* go home; you just got here!"

"Dude, I have a wonderful husband and family at home that I love, and I don't want to be in the Sandbox when I become a grandma. I *have* been here for three years, ya know."

"You *can't* leave us! What will we do without you? We'll miss you."

"I'll miss you too, bud."

I knew I would miss them, but I had no idea just how much. I had no idea how the sound of a Filipino or Indian voice would make my heart leap or how the sight of a soldier dressed in camos would generate a genuine misty moment. Recently I was with Rita at a bridal fair, dreaming with her about her daughter Jana's upcoming wedding. There were about three hundred people in the room, and there was a standing-room-only crowd for the bridal fashion show.

Suddenly I spotted a young kid in ACUs, the digitized all-terrain camo uniform currently worn by our soldiers. He was the lone soldier in the room and had just gotten his "mosquito wings," the chevron sign of having been promoted to Private First Class. I could only assume that he was also there to dream with his bride or possibly wonder what kind of tux would be picked out for him as a groomsman in a buddy's wedding.

I didn't say a word to Rita or the kid; I just knew that I had a chance to get what Steve would lovingly call "my soldier fix," and I was going to take it. (It takes a very special man to understand his wife's need to go up to men in uniform she has never met and treat them like old friends.) I simply slipped up next to the soldier-groom and stood there, wanting to tell him how much I appreciated him, holding my tongue so he could dream about his wedding, and letting myself ache for Iraq.

As I was packing to come home, I was horrified to discover how much stuff I had accumulated in my three years there, and I gave away a lot of it. I had gone for books rather than bling-bling, and I kept most of them, even though I couldn't imagine where we were going to put them. My boss Bennie warned me to ship my stuff out of there as early as possible, as when units are rotating out and shipping their belongings home, you can end up essentially living at the Post Office; he wasn't kidding.

Everything that you have packed has to be unpacked, inspected for contraband, repacked, weighed, labeled, mummified in packing tape, and schlepped over to the cashier. I had five trunks and a bunch of cardboard boxes. You can imagine how thrilled I was at having my packed underwear examined in a room mostly full of guys who were young enough to be my sons. I realized that the folks in the Post Office saw that and worse all the time, just like doctors and nurses don't think twice about seeing folks in their birthday suits, but I was really glad when the whole ordeal was over.

Getting to R and Z was tricky, as they were now on different camps than I was. Z was often out on patrol, and more often now R was working inside the wire. I got permission to visit her in her tent, where we just sat on her bed and cried and prayed. She told me that a fellow terp was suspicious that she now loved God and was asking a lot of questions. Her U.S. Naval captain fiancé had rotated out, and she was waiting for her chance to meet him in Turkey. The paperwork was slow, and she was understandably edgy and lonely.

How do you leave behind someone who has so quickly become one of your own cubs? Thinking back on it as I write this is hard, even though I know she is safely living the life of a newlywed with her husband in the States.

Leaving Z was tougher. My heart told me he would be alright, but I know my heart can be wrong sometimes. We were both upset. "I love you, my mother. I will never forget you," he said. "I thank God for bringing you into my life." Then this tough, young, darling, smart, arrogant, hot-headed, damaged, brave, big-hearted, precious, dear "boy-man" started to cry and said, *"Why do Americans always have to leave?"* He gave me the Arabic kiss of honor that sons give their mothers. They kiss your hand, pick up your hand, and place it on your forehead. And then I lost it completely. I hugged him tight and told him that I would always love him, that I was praying that God would keep him safe, and that we would be able to see each other again.

As I write, I am losing it completely all over again, because I have no idea how he is inside. I knew he needed to get a break, and the chances of getting one were slim. He does get to go home to Baghdad on weekends sometimes, but that is not exactly a break for someone on the muj's Most Wanted List. He has seen the horrors of war on a level that I cannot imagine, and it doesn't take a rocket scientist to tell that he needs rest. R recently heard from "people who know people" that he is OK, and in late April of 2008 I was able to "talk" with him via Instant Messaging. He is recently married and seems happy. I pray that the way will open up for him to come to the States with his bride and rest. I know that R would love to see her "twin brother," even though they fight like cats and dogs, and I would like to see my "son," even though he is (if such a thing is possible) more strong-willed than my darling, fiery, red-headed Gabriel, my firstborn.

I did my best to say my remaining goodbyes face to face and sent e-mails to the few that I missed. The day finally came when I worked my last shift and had to say goodbye to my staff. Two of the men from India teared up. Jerito, who was from the Philippines, wrapped her arms around me and said, "Good bye, mahm. God bless you."

The morning finally came when it was time to get to the airport. Mark, my camp manager at Victory, was in the Stryker camp office, and we started to reminisce about when I had first arrived and had wanted to go with the female soldiers to take stuff to the women's shelter in Baghdad. We were both laughing as he said, "You know, Marshall asked me not too long ago about that. He wanted to know what I had said to you when you came to me for permission." (Marshall was my Stryker camp manager who always went to bat for me, even when I was in trouble.)

"What did you tell him?" I asked.

"I told him that I listened and then said no."

We started laughing again, and I said, "You knew I had to ask, don't you?"

He replied in his slow Texas drawl, "I would have expected nothing less of you."

"Mark," I said, "If we end up in the Sudan, do you think you could handle me working for you again?"

"Of course," he said.

"You know that I am going to want to start a clinic for women who have been subjected to female circumcision, don't you?"

"I would expect nothing less of you," he said, smiling.

"OK, then," I said. "See you in the Sudan."

He gave me a hug. I said bye to the rest of the office crew and ran to the car. A coworker whom I nicknamed Stumpy because he loved to stump people with brain teasers took me to the transit center. A few hours later I was wheels up for the last time.

Paris was waiting, Steve was waiting, and unbeknownst to me I was headed for a reentry adventure that would prove to be both remarkable and rough.

CHAPTER 33

Reentry à la Renoir, Road Trip, and Beyond

A pril in Paris. Germany blooming. Amsterdam emerging from winter. Florence throwing its arms open wide in welcome. I had the best possible run-up to reentry that a girl could ever dream of.

I had wanted to go to Europe since I was a little girl and heard my mother tell about her first jaunt over the pond. Her Aunt Betty and grandmother took her on a trip for her graduation in summer 1937, a year early because they could see the Nazi storm clouds gathering. I remember her telling of the shudder of watching the Hitler Youth march, the fun of sitting on the throne in England, and the wonder of the artwork everywhere. Plus, she went by ship, so that was an adventure in itself.

When I decided to return from Iraq via Europe, I invited my friend Rita Kaye to join me. Rita is from a completely different background than I am. She was born and raised in the South, didn't go to an integrated school until her senior year in

279

high school, married her college sweetheart, got her degree in art, taught school, had kids, homeschooled them, and by outward appearances was and is living the American dream in a charming little historic town in Alabama. However, she has an insatiable desire to live life to the depths, and the comfort of the American dream as she has experienced it leaves her hungry. She and her family have ministered in India, have seen miracles, traveled, given generously to many in need—both in the States and abroad, and are ever spreading their wings both to cover and to fly. I could not ask for a better friend.

Rita is a talented artist and photographer, but she had never been to Europe. I wanted her to be immersed in what would draw her forth into what she really was: a consummate artist. I thought that being face to face with paintings, sculptures, gardens, and buildings she had only seen in books or films and really taking them in would set her on fire. I was right.

We arrived in Paris in late March, ready to tackle the beauty and art world of Europe. Through all our adventures in France, Italy, Holland, and Germany, I felt the healing power of spring in a way I don't think I ever had. It wasn't just the flowers; it was the art. It wasn't just the art; it was the food. It wasn't just the food; it was the friendly people who waited on us. Seeing beauty that thrilled our senses and challenged us to pull our creative talents out of our personal supply of buried fear turned us both on our heads. It was utter renewal—body, soul, mind, and spirit. We dusted the cobwebs out of our beings and laughed and cried till we were spent.

We also encountered some sobering things, proof of the shadow that had once cast itself across Europe through an artist named Adolf, as well as proof that his ilk were trying to make a comeback. In Amsterdam we went to Corrie ten Boom's house, which is now a museum. A cut-away in the wall reveals the secret compartment made to hide the Jews in her family's care.

The bit of stair molding behind which they hid the ration books that got them arrested is still loose. Even though the Nazis couldn't find the Jews, the ration books were proof that more people were being fed than their family. It makes me wonder if we could ever see a similar thing happen in our own country.

I found it interesting, after agonizing through the research for chapter 20 on Terri Schiavo, to remember that Corrie and her sister Betsie also had a ministry to disabled children. Corrie's Nazi interrogator mocked her for this, calling her stupid to care for people he thought were less than human because they were less than whole. I wonder if he would have used the word "houseplant" to describe them. In the Netherlands today, the elderly are afraid to go to hospitals because they may be euthanized by their attending physicians.

Underneath Europe's charm, ill winds are beginning to blow. Outside the Louvre I saw a brass plaque on a pillar indicating that on that very spot in 1944, four leaders of the French Resistance were arrested by the Gestapo during the Nazi occupation of France. They had been betrayed by one of their own. I was chilled by what I saw, thinking of my mother.

I joined Rita in the little shop where she was looking for gifts for her family. When I came out, I happened to look up and see something that made me go from chilled to chattering on the inside. It was a full-length Nazi flag, the kind shown in *The Sound of Music* or a 1930s Leni Riefenstahl propaganda film, showing the Swastika-bedraped Reichstag on the silver screen for der Fuhrer's pleasure. More than likely it was an overpriced souvenir, but I think that post-WWII France would have felt it to be completely inappropriate to hang the flag of those who wanted to take over the world and destroy Jews and anyone else who got in their way.

Call me alarmist, but before you do, read Bruce Bawer's seminal work, *While Europe Slept: How Radical Islam Is Destroying the West from Within.* It abundantly proves my point that terrorism is terrorism, whether it is Nazi, jihadist, or any other bully group. Paris is more vulnerable to jihad than we in the West want to think. So is the rest of Europe. I am just glad I got to see it before someone thinks they are doing God a service by burning the museums. I hope that in the midst of a magical April in Paris, I was not seeing the same kinds of things that unnerved my mother seventy years earlier, but I fear that Europe is in for some tough times. I think we all are.

When my trip ended and I got off the plane in Huntsville, Alabama, there was a soldier walking near me. Of course I couldn't pass him by. I told the soldier what I had done, where I had been, and that I was home for good. He told me he was home on leave and then would go back to Iraq in two weeks. Then he hugged me, looked me in the eye, and said, "Welcome home. Thank you for your service." I lost it, like I always do now whenever they do that. "It truly was my honor, sir," I said. He was my brass band, my welcome home banners, my homecoming ceremony. But Steve, the one who along with my Redeemer would quench the thirst of my soul, was waiting just outside the security area, and I couldn't wait to get to him.

When I saw Steve, I dropped all my stuff and flew into his arms. I don't know how long I silently shook with sobs into his t-shirt while my nose snarfed all over it or how long he held me. I was home! I was home!! I was home!!! My Welcoming Committee soldier told Steve, "She's going to need lots of this," smiled, and went on. He was right. I was going to need "lots of this," yea, more than I ever would have thought.

We honeymooned at home for a few days, and I began to make the apartment that Steve had rented while I was gone into a proper nest. I saw a few friends and made several phone calls. While I was so glad to see people, in a lot of ways I didn't know what to say to them. Imagine *me* not wanting to talk! This discomfort was temporarily put on hold when after about a week the next phase of reentry began. Steve had to get back on the road to make deliveries, and I went with him. The road trip began, and at times it was rocky.

To capture the emotions of reentry accurately, I have used some of my post-Iraq journal entries to tell the rest of the story.

29 April 2007

Tomorrow I will have been home for two weeks, and I am struggling on a number of fronts. Steve and I are on the truck for a three-week delivery/reconnect/ honeymoon trip, and I am once again overwhelmed with gratitude for the husband with whom I have been blessed. I truly cannot imagine what it is like for soldiers and contractors who return to hostile homefronts after having been in a hostile battle zone; my heart aches for them.

I am also thankful past my ability to express for the blessing of being an American. Being in a place where it is considered normal to separate someone's head from their shoulders should they believe differently than you, then coming home to where people can and do display their willful ignorance with relish and seemingly without repercussion is heady stuff.

Last night we were in the truck bunk, which was definitely designed for only one person, and in which cuddling is not optional. Thankfully we are not big folks, and lots of cuddling is our style. We had finished watching a DVD installment of *24*, a popular TV program that centers around a man whom I describe as "saving the world in twenty-minute increments." It deals with fighting terrorism, how politics interfere with that endeavor, having to make impossible snap decisions that no one agrees with, and living with the aftermath, both good and bad.

As I lay on Steve's chest, tears began to leak out while I tried to describe how much I don't feel like talking to people about the three most life-changing and remarkable years of my life. I don't feel like talking at all, quite frankly. For anyone who knows me, a statement like that is serious. "Ali, not wanting to talk? It'll be a cold day in a very hot place before *that* ever happens!" I love my family. I want to be a "normal" wife and mother, whatever that is. I want to get on with my life, as the buzzphrase goes. The problem is that what is going on in Iraq is so huge, so important, that I feel utterly at a loss over even knowing where to begin, and I am wondering how to tap into the strength to even start at all.

In addition, I feel somewhat silly reacting to things that in the course of everyday life are completely normal but in a combat zone could indicate the need to take cover. What makes it even more awkward is that sometimes I feel like I don't really deserve to react, as I was rarely outside the wire. As I have said many times, "I heard the war; I just didn't see much of it." It is just one of those things that goes with being part of the Second Army. The soldiers deserve every bit of support that it takes to successfully reenter and "get back after it," go on with life. I would never want to take anything away from them, but at the same time, I wonder if there will be contractors who end up standing under the bridges and frontage roads of our freeways with signs that say "Will Work For Food" simply because no one took their reentry challenges seriously.

A couple of days ago, our rig was parked at the Iowa 80 Truck Stop, a favorite place of over-the-road truckers. It has tricked-out trucks for sale, a store with everything a trucker could ever want, several shops and restaurants, and a large movie theater with free flicks. A movie called *Tears of the Sun* was on that I had seen several times in Iraq, and it had never caused me any difficulty. The story line had to do with rescuing a missionary doctor and her charges from invading rebels in Africa.

All of a sudden a certain frequency coming from the rapid small-arms fire in the film made me duck right there in the theater. How do you explain something like that? It would be one thing if I had never seen the film before, but I had, and had even seen it in a combat zone where I could also hear the real deal at the same time. Was I just now reacting to a firefight that I had actually heard while I was there? Didn't I know that one of the things they do now to treat soldiers with Post Traumatic Stress Disorder is show them virtual firefights over and over, until the scenes don't register as being life-threatening? I spoke with a friend who had been all over the world with the Drug Enforcement Agency, and, quite frankly, the fact that he still deals with certain sound triggers and cues some twenty-five years later is an odd comfort. If I have to deal with occasionally thinking that incoming is on its way yet again, it is a small price to pay for all that I have gained. I am not going to whine about the fact that at times it is embarrassing and impossible to explain. "You had to be there" has never rung truer.

Because I could talk with Steve from Baghdad almost every day, he more than anyone had a running commentary and understanding of my life there. Even so, trying to communicate to him the heavy burden I feel over where the Hill is going with its portended policy changes that threaten to defeat the people I have so come to love is virtually impossible. What is worse is that I know I face rough times with trying to convey how important it is that we don't bail on Iraq to Americans who are dependent upon what they are told every night on the Tube. I am convinced that the very future of our country hangs upon our victory there, and I know that victory is indeed possible.

Harry Reid says that "the war is lost,"[53] and I am fighting with every bit of faith I possess to love him, even if I have to do it as an enemy. How dare he? How dare he say words that affect the morale of "my kidz," the ones who are literally in the trenches and who know the value of their sweat-soaked endeavors? How dare Speaker of the House Pelosi claim that our Congressmen don't have time for General Petraeus to address them? Surely the Grand Poobahs could find a way to pencil him in, but I think they are afraid to hear what this man has to say. He might present so much evidence of the benefit of our being there that it might expose some less-than-honorable motives for bailing on the part of our policy-makers. While in Baghdad, I heard more than once how frustrating it is for the military to have policy decided by politicians, and boy, do I get it.

Corporal Tyler Rock wrote an e-mail in response to Reid's nonsense, and it was read on a radio broadcast we heard while bouncing down the road. It says it all, and while I won't repeat the expletives, I understand the frustration that would cause their liberal use. He said, "They need us. THEY _____ NEED US, Harry!!!" It seems to me that while Al-Qaeda won't get us, our politicians might.

Back to our hero who saves the world once a week. I wonder how comfortable his team would feel with the idea of telling terrorists that we are going to pull out starting 1 October. "Here's the plan, Mr. Bin Laden, handed to you by our politicians. Just hang in there, buddy; all you have to do is wait. Our representatives will do a whole ton of your work for you by cutting the funding and forcing money and willful ignorance to triumph over your hateful ideology."

I was touched to hear that a group of students from one of the universities in Baghdad made a corporate statement regarding their passionate repulsion to the one-man terrorist event that took the lives of thirty-two people at Virginia Tech on 17 April 2007. They said categorically that they are opposed to terrorism. Opposed to terrorism—think of it! They live with it every day, and because they are getting a chance to get an education where freedom of thought is allowed, the values of decency are actually being expressed. *They* are the proof of what we have accomplished, and they are the future of Iraq. May we not betray them by our lack of spine.

MEMORIAL DAY WEEKEND 2007

My friend Paige and I are going trail riding for the weekend with some friends of hers that I have never met. Paige was utterly, wonderfully discerning of my sensitive state when I first got home, for which I am thankful. I felt like I had just come from Mars, and American humans were so strange. I just didn't want to see anyone, and it wasn't anyone's fault. Paige and I have each been through some tough stuff, some of it at the same time, and I am so grateful that she didn't take the fact that I didn't want to talk much when I first got home as rejection.

Horseback riding has always been therapeutic for me. I found years ago after my divorce in 1990 that the presence of a horse that I owned as part of a homeschool co-op was like having an equine shrink to literally carry me through it. After some Laurel and Hardy-esque capers while getting the horse trailer attached to the truck and getting Molly into the trailer, Paige and I headed out. We had not driven far when I saw two soda cans in the road. I inhaled sharply and rolled into a ball as we drove over them, all the while telling myself that these were just soda cans, not IEDs. Paige just looked over at me and shook her head, saying "Man!" But she is a woman of prayer, and I know she is *for* me. After a while we laughed, as there is nothing else to do, and I was glad that she saw I wasn't faking being momentarily freaked out.

Being back on a horse after a few years' hiatus was indeed restorative, but I find I have absolutely no patience for Americans who grumble. We packed up and left early, as Paige sensed that the constant, garden-variety complaining of the people around me was starting to drain away the refreshment I had experienced by being back in the forest and hearing the squeak of leather saddles. I don't typically do a lot of yelling, but I was getting close to hollering, "All of you, just shut up! There are soldiers who are guaranteeing the fact that you can complain about anything from the president on down to the weather and still live to yip another day, so show them some respect and knock it off!" I didn't, and I'm glad I didn't. I am fully aware that it is unrealistic to expect that people be grateful that they still possess their fingers, toes, hearing, and sanity. I just hope I can find a way to encourage them without laying a big guilt trip on them or losing my temper. God help me, and "that right early."

5 July 2007

Last night we went to our town's annual fireworks display, and I am pleased to say I got through it. It actually went much better than the one I went to at my stepson's home the summer of 2005. That one was sheer misery, and I basically did my labor breathing through all of it. At the time I knew it was pointless to try to communicate how much energy it had taken not to look for something that could function as a bunker and to stop myself from looking for my Kevlar.

However, last night's display was way easier to get through, and I found myself actually enjoying it, until a certain explosion would go off after the glittery ones. BOOOOM!! The sound of that bad boy was a dead ringer for mortar. I just squeezed Steve's strong hands, and he gave me an understanding smile. By now he has gotten used to my oddness. Oh, do I love that man!

Labor Day 2007

I am now in a different combat zone at the Oasis of Hope, an alternative cancer hospital in Tijuana, Mexico. My friends John and Leonel White are in the fight of their lives, John having been diagnosed with terminal colon cancer. John is a Viet Nam vet, a former heliocopter pilot who has had a passionate love for Hueys ever since. He, Leonel, and I could not have come from more diverse backgrounds. They were born and raised in Alabama, and I came from the Left Coast. I got to know them when we first came back from Mexico and Steve was so sick. We went to the same home-based church fellowship, and I helped them homeschool their daughter, Brittany. John adopted me as his "li'l Sis," and I am honored to be with him in this battle. Just as I couldn't have anticipated how much I would be changed by going to Iraq, I am in the middle of yet another experience that has turned me upside down.

Imagine a hospital where the docs, kitchen staff, nurses, maids, and other patients hug you; this is it. There's chapel every morning, and I watch in amazement as the same bonds that occur in combat are developing all around me. This is a very different fight, but the fact is that everyone here is staring down the Grim Reaper, and I am privileged to be in their midst. Most importantly, I see deep things going on in my friends, and I know that regardless of the physical outcome, they are going to go home in better shape than when they came. I know I am.

As if it is not enough to be meeting courageous people, eating wonderful natural food, and making friends that I know I'll love forever, tomorrow I am going to be able to see my dear R, whose remarkable story appears in chapter 25. She married Nathan, and they are stationed in San Diego. Just the idea of being able to see her and know that she is safe and free is thrilling.

4 SEPTEMBER 2007

I got to spend a good part of the day with R. Nathan drove down from San Diego to Oasis and took me back up there. What a reunion! We just sat on the couch and cried, cuddling. The only thing that would have made it better for me would have been if Z were here. I am hoping that he'll be able to enter the naturalization program the State Department has for interpreters who have served in combat. I know he could use the rest, as he has seen things for the past five years that can scar a man for life. I pray that he is able to come to the States, and I hope that when that day comes, he won't be thrown by the downside of American culture. As R says so shyly, "America is not perfect," yet she is at the same time so glad to be here.

11 SEPTEMBER 2007

I am flying back home to Alabama from Mexico, and while this day always sobers me, I know it is now one of the safest days of the year to fly. I am actually looking forward to the flight. I think fondly of the Fighting 69th, the New York National Guard soldiers who started protecting us in America at Ground Zero the day we were attacked and who became some of my favorite soldiers in Iraq. I am so glad I got to experience a bit of New York City fun and craziness while in Iraq. Those guys—what a hoot!!

17 October 2007

Staff Sgt. Michael Helmen, who had been our praise and worship team leader at Victory Chapel, had been in Georgia for six months doing special training with fancy computer stuff. He was on his way home to Ft. Hood in Texas, and I had the honor of opening our home to him for a quick home-cooked meal on his way through. There is a framed picture of R being baptized on the bookcase in my living room, and it leans against the brick from Saddam's alligator pit. "There's our girl," I said after I hugged him. I could tell her picture was the first thing he noticed when he stepped inside the door. "There's our girl," he echoed.

To have the honor of cooking supper for one of our finest warriors whom I love like a son is indescribable. I hope my own boys never have to go to war, but I believe I tasted of the joy a mom experiences when her son comes home safely. We ate with our fingers as the Ugandans had taught us, as well as in special honor of our dear friend Kenneth Katangole. I did my best imitation of Kenneth's raspy voice, and then said, "Michael, I miss Iraq." He replied, "I miss Iraq, too." This is not the only time I have heard this since I have been home, from soldiers as well as contractors. "Are we crazy for missing it so much?" Michael just smiled.

The hours flew by as we talked and prayed, and then he had to hit the road. Somehow I know that Michael is going to be family for the rest of my life, and every moment with him and his family is a treasure to my heart. Sometimes I wish I could just leap up on some table somewhere and say, "Look, folks, it's people like Michael Helmen who are willing to die for you!" There are others I could name who in their own way are as remarkable. I get frustrated because I feel so limited in my ability to express my thanks. God willing, I'll do my best for the rest of my life to see that they get the thanks they deserve.

1 NOVEMBER 2007

Today was my birthday, and it was one of the hardest I have ever had. My friend and adopted brother John White, a true warrior in every regard, fought his last battle with cancer today and went home. While it looks like cancer won, I watched that man stand firm while enduring indescribable pain. I sang him some of his favorite songs that we sang at Oasis, and a few hours later he was gone, having cried out to Jesus to take him. As I stared at his body, the shell that used to house him, I thought, "A warrior to the last."

4 NOVEMBER 2007

We buried John today. It was a flawless fall day, the trees bright with color. I was able to play his guitar and sing two songs he loved at the funeral. While the funeral was a fitting tribute to his life, full of hope and celebration, for me it paled in comparison to the graveside service done by the military. With precision and compassion, they retired the colors that had been draped on his casket and gave them to Leonel. Three spent shell cases had been tucked inside the folded flag, representing Duty, Honor, and Country. Touching in a completely different way was the "twenty-one dove salute." I don't know if it's because people feel the sound of rifle fire is too jarring or what; I must admit I wish we could have had both.

However, the release of the doves was something I'll never forget. Twenty were released, and then Leonel and Brittany released the last one. It took off to join the others, and those birds did an air show, dove style, that rivaled the Blue Angels. Afterward I spoke to the soldier who played Taps at the ceremony and found out he had been across town in Baghdad at the same time I had been at BIAP. Somehow having someone who had been in Iraq present to say farewell to John made the whole situation easier. However, when *he* thanked *me* for *my* service, the tears flowed afresh. All I could say is, "You're welcome; it truly was my honor."

Not long before John died, he bought a Miata, and we went out for a spin in it. He even let me drive. It was sweet and smooth, and I realized it is a good thing I don't have a car that can move so fast. I think I'd be in a heap of trouble. The car sported a license plate that is the privilege of only Viet Nam vets to display: "Ours was a just cause."

The other day as I was taking supper to Leonel and her family, I stopped and looked at that license plate on my way into the house. I thought of the fact that there was a time when emotionally I would have spat on such a thing and at the very least scoffed at it. How glad I am, from having been with these guys in different kinds of battles, that I can say, "Yep, more than just."

My grief over losing my friend and watching his family suffer is sharp, but strangely, I realize that I am over the hump of reentry. I can't really explain why. I just know it's true, and I am thankful. How odd that a man I once would have labeled a "baby killer" became the brother I never got to have and that we ended up in a very real foxhole together. Oh, Grace, how you amaze me!

Afterword

MAY 2008

I HAVE BEEN OUT OF THE SANDBOX for a little over a year, and *Ballad* is finally finished. Its gestation period was about nine months, the same as is generally the case for humans. It was indeed an intense labor of love. Just as I experienced the protective care and affection of complete strangers when I was carrying my physical children, the anticipation and support of people I have never met who are hungry to hear "the real story" was a source of tremendous strength. Furthermore, just as I had dreams for my children before they popped out and have deeper dreams now for both them and my stepkids, I have dreams about *Ballad's* song in our culture and what I would like to see it accomplish.

My dream is to get a copy of my book into the hands of each soldier who has spent some time slugging it out in the Great Sandbox, either in Iraq or Afghanistan. In

293

addition, I want to get a copy into the hands of a spouse or other family member at home, weary with deployments or getting through their first one. If my "thank you" can be a small cup of cold water in an indescribably hot desert, whether physically, emotionally, spiritually, or otherwise, it will have been worth every dollar spent and every tear shed to birth *A Ballad for Baghdad*. Our soldiers and their families deserve all the thanks the rest of our country can give them, I think now more than ever. If you want to help me with that dream, please go to www.BalladForBaghdad.com, and perhaps we can partner together to say "thank you."

As for the song "A Ballad for Baghdad," my dream for it is the same as for the book. If it can be sung in a foxhole, on the way to work, or at the kitchen sink as a way of reminding folks to hang on and push through when everyone and everything says it's stupid to try, I would unashamedly say, "Mission accomplished." I don't care about a hit song; I just want to put the hurt on whining and victimization and to help people to not just count their blessings, but to actively thank all those who have made our indescribable blessings possible, starting with God.

My personal goal of not "having fruit and cheese with that whine"—living a life filled with passion, purpose, *gratitude,* and guts—is more intense than ever, especially in the particularly frustrating craziness of this presidential election cycle. And yes, in answer to a question I am often asked, I still miss Iraq, the Iraqis, and the soldiers, and I would go back tomorrow.

Dr. Laura Schlessinger recently published a book entitled *Stop Whining, Start Living*. One of the chapters is called "The Earth Is Not the Center of the Universe—and You and I Aren't Either." How fitting, irrespective of one's politics, religion, or the lack of either. I am convinced that if our nation and culture are going to survive, we are going to have to jump out of the back of our ungrateful, wailing, self-absorbed "waaaaaambulance" and run hard in the other direction, not stopping to rest or catch our breath until the shrieking siren has faded from our hearing.

This morning, my youngest daughter Jessalyn gave me the perfect way to finish *Ballad* on just the right note. She was telling me over the phone about her recent marvelous trip to Ireland, a short-term missions trip taken with her husband Barry and a group from their church. She has been going on trips like these since she was a little girl and has always come home deeply touched by the struggles of others and grateful for the opportunity to travel, to help, and to change. "Mom," she said, "I just don't want to lose what I experienced and come back and live life like everyone else." Me neither, Jessa girl, me neither, and God willing, we won't.

Chronology

20 March 2003	U.S. and Coalition forces invade Iraq.
9 April 2003	Baghdad falls.
14 December 2003	Saddam Hussein is captured in a "spider hole" in northern Iraq.
23 May 2004	Ali arrives in Houston for Contractor Camp.
13 June 2004	Ali leaves for Iraq via London and Dubai.
17 June 2004	Ali arrives in Iraq.
28 June 2004	Iraq is secretly turned back over to Iraqis; Paul Bremer returns to the U.S.
1 July 2004	Saddam Hussein is arraigned and charged with murder.
October 2004	Ali's trip to Memphis, Tennessee, via Dubai.
2 November 2004	George Bush is reelected as President of the United States.
22 December 2004	Suicide bomber in Mosul Dfac kills 22, wounds 66.

30 January 2005	Voting Day #1 in Iraq, creating 275-member legislature.
February 2005	Ali's trip to Mozambique.
31 March 2005	Terri Schiavo dies after being court-ordered to starve/dehydrate to death.
June-July 2005	Ali's trip to Seattle (rerouted through Kuwait and Canada).
15 October 2005	Voting Day #2 in Iraq—constitution is ratified.
19 October 2005	Saddam's trial begins.
November 2005	Ali's trip to Hawaii.
15 December 2005	Voting Day #3 in Iraq—parliamentary election.
22 February 2006	Al-Qaeda bombs Samarra mosque with the purpose of starting a civil war.
March 2006	Ali's trip home to Alabama and road trip to Phoenix.
7 June 2006	Abu al-Zarqawi is killed in a U.S. air assault.
June 2006	Ali's trip to Jordan.
21 August 2006	Second and separate murder trial of Saddam Hussein begins.
5 November 2006	Saddam is found guilty and sentenced to hang.
December 2006	Ali's trip to Germany, including tour of Dachau.
30 December 2006	Saddam is executed.
23 March 2007	Ali leaves Iraq for home via Europe.
13 April 2007	Ali arrives in Huntsville, Alabama. Home at last!

Glossary

ABUs – Airman's Battle Uniform

ACUs – Army Combat Uniform

AFN – Armed Forces Network (radio and TV)

Baathist Party – the socialist political party of Saddam Hussein; also active in Syria

BIAP – Baghdad International Airport; the airport as well as several surrounding camps

de-mob – quit or finish one's contract and head back home

Dfac – Dining Facility, also known as Mess Hall or Chow Hall

ECP – Entry Check Point

FOB – Forward Operating Base; essentially a military establishment, large or small, in a hostile zone

hooch – living quarters while in country

IAF – Iraqi Air Force

IBA – Individual Body Armor

IED – Improvised Explosive Device

JAG – Judge Advocate General, a military lawyer

mil air – military transport planes such as C-17s and others

MP – Military Police

MRE – Meal, Ready to Eat; the Army's version of a TV dinner—no refrigeration required

MWR – Morale, Welfare, and Recreation; Department of Defense agency which supports the troops

NBC – Nuclear, Biological, and Chemical weapons

NCIS – Naval Criminal Investigative Service

NCO – noncommissioned officer

OIF – Operation Iraqi Freedom, the official name for the war in Iraq

OpSec – Operational Security; the practice of exercising caution while communicating

PAO – Public Affairs Office; the Army's PR office

psy-ops – Psychological Operations

PTs – Physical Training uniform, military issue

PTSD – Post Traumatic Stress Disorder; formerly known as Combat Stress

PX – Post Exchange; military variety store

RPG – Rocket-Propelled Grenade

SCWs – Sub-Contract Workers; support staff from non-U.S. countries

SEALs – Sea, Air and Land; special forces of the U.S. Navy

Shia, Shi'ite – the majority branch of Islam throughout the Middle East

Sunni – the minority branch of Islam professed by Saddam Hussein

TCNs – Third Country Nationals; see SCWs

terp – interpreter

TIP – Trafficking in Persons; illegal use and transport of workers, often for sexual slavery

VBIED – Vehicle Borne Improvised Explosive Device; car bomb

WMDs – Weapons of Mass Destruction

Recommended Reading

Ali, Ayaan Hirsi. *Infidel.* New York: Free Press, 2007.

Bawer, Bruce. *While Europe Slept: How Radical Islam Is Destroying the West from Within.* New York: Broadway Books, 2006.

Bellavia, David. *House to House.* New York: Free Press, 2007.

Benard, Cheryl. *Veiled Courage: Inside the Afghan Women's Resistance.* New York: Broadway Books, 2002.

Burnham, Gracia. *In the Presence of My Enemies.* Wheaton, Ill.: Tyndale House, 2003.

Corsi, Dr. Jerome R. *Atomic Iran.* Nashville, Tenn.: WND Books, 2005.

Flynn, Captain Sean Michael. *The Fighting 69th: One Remarkable National Guard Unit's Journey from Ground Zero to Baghdad.* New York: Penguin Books, 2007.

Fuhrman, Mark. *Silent Witness: The Untold Story of Terri Schiavo's Death*. New York: HarperCollins, 2005.

Gibbs III, David, with Bob DeMoss. *Fighting for Dear Life: The Untold Story of Terri Schiavo and What It Means for All of Us*. Bloomington, Minn.: Bethany House Publishers, 2006.

Goldberg, Bernard. *Bias: A CBS Insider Exposes How the Media Distort the News*. Washington, D.C.: Regnery Publishing, 2002.

Hannity, Sean. *Deliver Us from Evil: Defeating Terrorism, Despotism, and Liberalism*. New York: HarperCollins, 2004.

Herzog, Chaim. *The Arab-Israeli Wars: War and Peace in the Middle East*. New York: Vintage Books, 2005.

The Koran. New York: Bantam/Dell, 2004.

North, Oliver. *American Heroes: In the Fight against Radical Islam*. Nashville, Tenn.: B&H Publishing Group, 2008.

——. *War Stories: Operation Iraqi Freedom*. Washington, D.C.: Regnery Publishing, 2003.

Patterson, Col. Buzz. *War Crimes: The Left's Campaign to Destroy Our Military and Lose the War on Terror*. New York: Crown Forum, 2007.

Pearsall, Dr. Paul. *Super Joy: In Love with Living*. New York: Doubleday, 1988.

Sada, General Georges. *Saddam's Secrets*. Nashville, Tenn.: Thomas Nelson, 2006.

Sasson, Jean. *Mayada: Daughter of Iraq: One Woman's Survival under Saddam Hussein*. New York: Dutton, 2003.

Schlessinger, Dr. Laura. *Stop Whining, Start Living*. New York: HarperCollins, 2008.

Sharansky, Natan. *The Case for Democracy: The Power of Freedom to Overcome Tyranny and Terror*. New York: Public Affairs/Perseus Books, 2004.

Spencer, Robert. *The Politically Incorrect Guide to Islam and the Crusades*. Washington D.C.: Regnery Publishing, 2003.

Steyn, Mark. *America Alone: The End of the World as We Know It*. Washington, D.C.: Regnery Publishing, 2006.

FICTION

Rosenberg, Joel. *Dead Heat*. Wheaton, Ill.: Tyndale Publishing, 2008.

——. *The Ezekiel Option*. Wheaton, Ill.: Tyndale Publishing, 2005.

——. *The Last Days*. Wheaton, Ill.: Tyndale Publishing, 2003.

——. *The Last Jihad*. Wheaton, Ill.: Tyndale Publishing, 2002.

"A Ballad for Baghdad"

BY ALI ELIZABETH TURNER

© 2007

Thrown down in the sand,
Can't hardly breathe, till a hand
Of kindness reaches down to you
And gently lifts you to your feet,
Brushing all the sand away,
Looking into your face to say
To those who hope and pray
For your defeat

Chorus

Oh, we will not forget you, Baghdad,
Tired jewel of beleaguered Iraq.
To the remnant who longs for justice
We say, "You've come too far to turn back.
You've come too far to ever turn back."

As we watched your dream be born,
You wept and danced for joy
On a winter's morn.
Three times you looked death in the face
And said, "We choose to be free."
Your purple fingers were the loveliest sight
A tired soul could ever hope to be blessed to see.

Chorus

Don't give up on your blood-stained dream.
Don't give an ear to those who deem
Your freedom to be pointless
Or your struggle not worth the strain.
There's a highway building and it's coming your way,
And Deliverance is that highway's name.

Chorus

Oh, we will not forget you, Baghdad,
Tired jewel of brave Iraq.

To the remnant who longs for justice,

To the remnant who works for justice,

To the remnant who fights for justice,

We say, "You've come too far to go back.

You've come too far to turn and go back.

You've come too far; don't turn and go back."

𝒩otes

CHAPTER 7 – JOURNALISTIC JIHAD?

1. Ayman al-Zawahiri, letter to Abu Musab al-Zarqawi, 9 July 2005; quoted in Buzz Patterson, *War Crimes: The Left's Campaign to Destroy Our Military and Lose the War on Terror* (New York: Crown Forum, 2007), 81.

2. "'Quagmire' Analogy Gets Much Use," FOX News, 28 June 2005, http://www.foxnews.com/story/0,2933,160854,00.html (accessed 2 April 2008).

3. Lt. Col. Tim Ryan, "Aiding and Abetting the Enemy: The Media in Iraq," Blackfive, http://www.blackfive.net/main/2005/01/aiding_and_abbe.html (accessed 31 March 2008).

4. Stephen Hayes, "Saddam's Cash," *Weekly Standard*, 5 May 2003, http://www.weeklystandard.com/Content/Public/Articles/000/000/002/605fgcob.asp (accessed 3 April 2008).

5. "Saddam's Cash."

6. Allan Wolper, "John Burns on Covering Iraq: Then and Now," *Editor and Publisher*, 15 September 2003, http://www.editorandpublisher.com/eandp/news/article_display.jsp?vnu_content_id=2053105 (accessed 3 April 2008).

7. John Burns, "There Is Corruption in Our Business," *Editor and Publisher*, 5 September 2003, http://www.editorandpublisher.com/eandp/article_brief/eandp/1/1979014 (accessed 3 April 2008).

8. www.IraqTheModel.com, 24 June 2005 post (accessed 31 March 2008).

9. You can read a transcript of the ads here: http://www.theotheriraq.com/images/Advert1.pdf

Chapter 11 – Don't Mess with the Babysitter

10. "Kennedy: Military Fuels Insurgency," CBS News, 27 January 2005, http://www.cbsnews.com/stories/2005/01/27/iraq/main669915.shtml (accessed 24 May 2008).

Chapter 12 – A Tale of Two Hostages

11. Richard Galpin, "Iraqis Voice Revulsion over Killing," BBC News, 17 November 2004, http://news.bbc.co.uk/2/hi/uk_news/4020159.stm (accessed 26 May 2008).

12. "Margaret Hassan: Your Reaction," BBC News, 23 November 2004, http://news.bbc.co.uk/2/hi/talking_point/4017529.stm (accessed 23 May 2008).

13. "Margaret Hassan: Your Reaction."

14. Mussab al-Khairalla, "Iraqis Distraught at Hassan's Murder," Iraqi Solidarity News (Al-Thawra), 17 November 2004, http://iraqsolidaritycampaign.blogspot.com/2004/11/iraqis-distraught-at-hassans-murder-by.html#links (accessed 26 May 2008).

15. "Iraqis Angry with 'Savage Beast' Muslims Who Killed Aid Worker," Google Group soc.culture.iranian, 17 November 2004, http://groups.google.com/group/soc.culture.iranian/browse_thread/thread/cf1285f730494382849894e451d30ec1%23849894e451d30ec1 (accessed 26 May 2008).

16. Mark Dooley, "It's Time that We Decided Who Is the Real Enemy in Iraq," Independent.ie, 21 November 2004, http://www.independent.ie/opinion/ analysis/its-time-that-we-decided-who-is-the-real-enemy-in-iraq-486242.html (accessed 24 May 2008).

Chapter 13 – Stellar Soldiers

17. Memo from Peace and Justice Commission, City of Berkeley, 29 January 2008, http://www.ci.berkeley.ca.us/uploadedFiles/Clerk/2008-01-29_Item_12_ Marine_Recruiting_Office_in_Berkeley.pdf (accessed 24 May 2008). A video of the city council meeting is available here: http://berkeley.granicus.com/ MediaPlayer.php?publish_id=444 (accessed 24 May 2008).

18. Zanne Joi, "Real Angels Don't Drop Bombs—in Progress," Code Pink Road Journals, 7 October 2006, http://codepinkjournals.blogspot.com/2006/10/real-angels-dont-drop-bombs-in.html (accessed 24 May 2008).

Chapter 15 – The Unholy Ghraib

19. "Does the U.S. Support Torturing Terror Suspects?" partial transcript from *The O'Reilly Factor* 12 September 2006, 13 September 2006, http://www.foxnews.com:80/story/0,2933,213629,00.html (accessed 24 May 2008).

Chapter 17 – A Hoot of a Hostage Incident

20. "G.I. Don't Know . . . ," Snopes.com, http://www.snopes.com/media/goofs/ gijoe.asp (accessed 24 May 2008).

21. "Message Board Member Admits to Hoax of US Soldier's Capture," SITE Institute, 4 February 2005, http://web.archive.org/web/20050305140741/ www.siteinstitute.org/bin/articles.cgi?ID=publications18505&Category=publi cations&Subcategory=0 (accessed 24 May 2008).

Chapter 20 – Stetsons for Terri Schiavo

22. A timeline of key events is available on the website for the University of Miami Ethics Programs here: http://www6.miami.edu/ethics/schiavo/timeline.htm (accessed 24 May 2008).

23. Mary Schindler and Robert Schindler, with Suzanne Schindler Vitadamo and Bobby Schindler, *A Life that Matters: The Legacy of Terri Schiavo—A Lesson for Us All.* (New York: Warner Books, 2006), 52.

24. An audio recording of this broadcast is available at "Terri's Case Documented," Theresa Schiavo Blog, 31 October 2005, http://www.theresaschiavoblog. blogspot.com/2005/10/terris-case-documented.html (accessed 5 May 2008).

25. Arthur Weinreb, "Terri's Wishes," Canada Free Press, 29 March 2005, http:// www.canadafreepress.com/2005/weinreb032905.htm (accessed 28 April 2008).

26. Penny Lea, "Sing a Little Louder," Heritage House '76, 2006, http://www. abortionfacts.com/literature/literature_909sl.asp (accessed 28 April 2008).

27. David Gibbs with Bob DeMoss, *Fighting for Dear Life: The Untold Story of Terri Schiavo and What It Means for All of Us* (Bloomington, Minn.: Bethany House Publishers, 2006), 176.

28. "Agonizing Wait for Terri Schiavo's Parents after Filing Late-Night Plea to Supreme Court," transcript of *American Morning*, 24 March 2005, http://transcripts.cnn. com/TRANSCRIPTS/0503/24/ltm.01.html (accessed 15 May 2008).

29. Heidi Law, affidavit filed in Pinellas County, Florida, 1 September 2003, http://www.terrisfight.org/userfiles/File/Affidavit%20H%20Law%20083003. pdf?phpMyAdmin=d87db2d1686da7d3769db95a1ec7ff28 (accessed 9 May 2008); Carolyn Johnson, affidavit filed in Pinellas County, Florida, 28 August 2003, http://www.terrisfight.org/userfiles/File/Affidavit%20C%20Johnson%2 0082803.pdf?phpMyAdmin=d87db2d1686da7d3769db95a1ec7ff28 (accessed 9 May 2008); both affidavits reprinted in Mark Fuhrman, *Silent Witness: The Untold Story of Terri Schiavo* (New York: Harper Collins, 2005).

30. "Friend: Terri Wanted Divorce before Accident," NewsMax.com, 25 March 2005, http://archive.newsmax.com/archives/ic/2005/3/25/102508.shtml (accessed 28 April 2008).

31. Michael Schiavo, deposition in guardianship case, Pinellas County, Florida, 19 November 1993; reprinted in Mark Fuhrman, *Silent Witness*, 120-121.

32. Heidi Law, affidavit filed in Pinellas County, Florida, 1 September 2001.

33. Michael Schiavo, deposition in guardianship case, Pinellas County, Florida, 19 November 1993; reprinted in Mark Fuhrman, *Silent Witness*, 128-129.

34. Quoted in David Gibbs, *Fighting for Dear Life*, 131.

35 Carla Iyer, affidavit filed in Pinellas County, Florida, 29 August 2003, http://www.terrisfight.org/userfiles/File/Affidavit%20C%20Iyer%20082903.pdf (accessed 9 May 2008).

36. David Gibbs, *Fighting for Dear Life*, 133.

37. Gibbs, 134.

38. Gibbs, 135.

39. Sharon Tubbs, "The Spirit and the Law," *St. Petersburg Times*, 25 May 2001, www.sptimes.com/News/052501/Floridian/The_spirit_and_the_la.shtml (accessed 15 May 2008).

40. George Felos, *Litigation as Spiritual Practice* (Nevada City, Calif.: Blue Dolphin Publishing, 2002), 240.

41. NewsMax.com staff, "Felos: Starving Terri Looks 'Beautiful,'" 27 March 2005, www.newsmax.com/archives/ic/2005/3/27/95930.shtml (accessed 15 May 2008).

42. Michael Schiavo, interview on *Larry King Live*, 27 October 2003, http://transcripts.cnn.com/TRANSCRIPTS/0310/27/lkl.00.html (accessed 15 May 2008).

43. E-mail, 1 December 2005.

44. Steven Ertelt, "Barack Obama Would Take Back Vote Helping Terri Schiavo Avoid Euthanasia," LifeNews, 26 February 2008, http://www.lifenews.com/bio2347.html (accessed 15 May 2008).

CHAPTER 25 – R AND Z, OUR SUNNI TWINS

45. "He Reigns," words and music by Peter Furler and Steve Taylor. Copyright 2003. Used by permission.

CHAPTER 26 – SALT AND LIGHT

46. *The Four Feathers*, DVD, directed by Shekhar Kapur (Hollywood, Calif.: Miramax Studios, 2002).

CHAPTER 29 – EVERY DOG HAS HIS DAY

47. Ramsey Clark, "Why I'm Willing to Defend Hussein," *Los Angeles Times*, 24 January 2005, http://www.commondreams.org/views05/0124-26.htm (accessed 24 May 2008).

48. "Saddam Trial Judge Ejects Ramsey Clark," Reuters UK, 5 November 2006, http://uk.reuters.com/article/vreakingNews/idUKL0519205920061105 (accessed 24 May 2008).

49. "Saddam's Final Words," *The Daily Telegraph*, 30 December 2006, http://www.news.com.au:80/dailytelegraph/story/0,22049,20990518-5001021,00.html (accessed 26 May 2008).

CHAPTER 31 – BARNEY FIFE, AUNT BEA, AND THE WMDs

50. For more details than I have included here, see Georges Sada, *Saddam's Secrets* (Nashville, Tenn.: Thomas Nelson, 2006), 249-263.

51. Sada, 255-257.

52. Sada, 255.

CHAPTER 33 – "REENTRY À LA RENOIR AND LA ROAD TRIP

53. "Reid: Someone Tell Bush the War in Iraq Is Lost," FOXNews, 19 April 2007, http://www.foxnews.com/story/0,2933,267181,00.html (accessed 24 May 2008).

About the Author

photo by Rita Campbell

ALI ELIZABETH TURNER is a self-described "recovered feminista/socialista" who grew up in Seattle during the turbulent years of the Civil Rights Movement, the Hippie Movement, and the Women's Liberation Movement. She once tried to shut down Wright-Patterson Air Force Base in Dayton, Ohio, and the Cleveland County, Ohio courthouse to protest the war in Viet Nam. Her life radically changed in the early seventies as a result of the Jesus People Movement, and she began a journey which led her from believing that soldiers were "baby killers" to being an ardent soldier supporter. She lived in Baghdad, Iraq, from 2004 to 2007 on several Coalition military bases, where her job was to help run Morale, Welfare, and Recreation Centers and gyms for the Coalition and Iraqi forces.

Ali previously served in capacities as varied as a private school administrator in America and Mexico, a hotel pianist, banquet server, worship leader, baker, music teacher, and pastoral counselor. She is currently a wellness coach. She and her husband Steve live in Alabama, own a small trucking company, and between them have four grown children.

Bonus

A Ballad for Baghdad is more than a book;
it's a song inspired by Ali's time in Iraq.
As a thank-you for purchasing this book, a copy of the song written, played,
and sung by Ali Elizabeth Turner is your free gift.

Download your unplugged, acoustical studio MP3 version by going to
www.BalladForBaghdad.com

"A Ballad for Baghdad," © 2008, Shirwood Productions

Sing the Ballad!

CPSIA information can be obtained at www.ICGtesting.com
Printed in the USA
LVOW071856190312

273822LV00001B/1/P